Europe after Derrida

Europe after Derrida
Crisis and Potentiality

Edited by
Agnes Czajka and Bora Isyar

EDINBURGH
University Press

Edinburgh University Press is one of the leading university presses in the UK. We publish academic books and journals in our selected subject areas across the humanities and social sciences, combining cutting-edge scholarship with high editorial and production values to produce academic works of lasting importance. For more information visit our website: www.edinburghuniversitypress.com

© editorial matter and organisation Agnes Czajka and Bora Isyar, 2014, 2016
© in the contributions is retained by the authors

Edinburgh University Press Ltd
The Tun – Holyrood Road
12 (2f) Jackson's Entry
Edinburgh EH8 8PJ

Typeset in 10.5/13 Adobe Sabon by
Servis Filmsetting Ltd, Stockport, Cheshire,
and printed and bound in Great Britain by
CPI Group (UK) Ltd, Croydon CR0 4YY

First published in hardback by Edinburgh University Press 2014

A CIP record for this book is available from the British Library

ISBN 978 0 7486 8336 9 (hardback)
ISBN 978 1 4744 1076 2 (paperback)
ISBN 978 0 7486 8337 6 (webready PDF)
ISBN 978 0 7486 8339 0 (epub)

The right of the contributors to be identified as authors of this work has been asserted in accordance with the Copyright, Designs and Patents Act 1988, and the Copyright and Related Rights Regulations 2003 (SI No. 2498).

Contents

Acknowledgements	vii
Notes on the Contributors	ix
Introduction: What Will Become of Europe? *Agnes Czajka and Bora Isyar*	1
1. Mind the 'Cap' *Samuel Weber*	9
2. Derrida's Europe: 'Greek, Christian and Beyond' *Simon Glendinning*	30
3. A Roman Europe of Hope: Reading Derrida with Brague *Bora Isyar*	49
4. Other Shores: Insularity, Materiality and the Making (and Unmaking) of 'Europe' *Stuart McLean*	61
5. Europe's Constitution for the Unborn *Matthias Fritsch*	80
6. The Borders of Contemporary Europe: Territory, Justice and Rights *Tracey Skillington*	95
7. We, the Non-Europeans: Derrida with Said *Engin F. Isin*	108
8. Of Europe: Zionism and the Jewish Other *Sherene Seikaly and Max Ajl*	120
9. The European Ideal in the Face of the Muslim Other *Zeynep Direk*	134
10. Christianity, Secularism and the Crisis of Europe *Ian Anthony Morrison*	149
Index	163

Acknowledgements

The editors would like to thank Nicola Ramsey, Michelle Houston, John Watson, Rebecca Mackenzie, Eddie Clark and all others at Edinburgh University Press who were of immense help over the course of this project.

We would also like to thank Jonathan Wadman for his rigorous reading of and insightful comments on the text.

Finally, we would like to thank Bryan Wall, and our friends and family for their help and support.

Notes on the Contributors

Max Ajl studies development sociology at Cornell University, Ithaca, NY. His research focuses on the political economy of oil and agriculture, Middle East sociology, and the Israel–Palestine conflict. He also studies political ecology and rural development. He is an editor at *Jacobin* and his essays and reviews have been published widely, including in *Middle East Report* and *Historical Materialism*.

Agnes Czajka is a lecturer in politics and international studies at the Open University in the UK. Prior to joining the OU, she taught politics at Sabancı University in Turkey and sociology at the American University in Cairo and University College Cork. Her work has appeared in *Comparative Studies of South Asia, Africa and the Middle East*, *Studies in Political Economy*, *Open Democracy*, *Jadaliyya* and the *Near East Quarterly*.

Zeynep Direk is a professor of philosophy at Galatasaray University. She has co-edited (with Leonard Lawlor) *Derrida: Critical Assessments of Leading Philosophers* (2002) and her articles have appeared in the *Southern Journal of Philosophy* and *Research in Phenomenology*, among other journals. Her research interests include phenomenology, contemporary French philosophy and feminism. Her current research focuses on the history of the term 'value' in ethics and on questioning 'value'-based discourses in contemporary applied ethics and politics.

Matthias Fritsch is an associate professor of philosophy at Concordia University, Montreal. He is the author of *The Promise of Memory: History and Politics in Marx, Benjamin and Derrida* (2005) and co-editor (with Michel Seymour) of *Reason and Emancipation: Essays in Honor of Kai Nielsen* (2007). His articles have appeared in *Constellations*,

Derrida Today, *Philosophy and Social Criticism* and the *European Journal of Political Theory* among other journals. Dr Fritsch's research interests include social and political philosophy (in particular democratic theory and Marxism), and nineteenth- and twentieth-century European philosophy (especially German critical theory and deconstruction). He is currently working on a notion of democracy that addresses the concerns of both Neokantian egalitarian universalism and the deconstructive concept of futurity.

Simon Glendinning is a reader in European philosophy in the European Institute at the London School of Economics and Political Science. His recent publications include *Derrida: A Very Short Introduction* (2011), *In the Name of Phenomenology* (2007) and *The Idea of Continental Philosophy* (Edinburgh University Press, 2006). He is also the editor of *Arguing with Derrida* (Blackwell, 2001) and co-editor (with Robert Eaglestone) of *Derrida's Legacies: Literature and Philosophy* (2008). Dr Glendinning's research focuses on investigating European identities.

Engin F. Isin is a professor of politics in Politics and International Studies (POLIS) at the Open University. He is the author of *Citizens without Frontiers* (2012), *Being Political: Genealogies of Citizenship* (2002), and *Cities without Citizens* (1992). Professor Isin has also co-edited *Acts of Citizenship* with Greg Nielsen (2008) and *Enacting European Citizenship* with Michael Saward (2013), and he is currently the co-chief editor of *Citizenship Studies*.

Bora Isyar's articles have appeared in *Nations and Nationalism*, *Journal of Common Market Studies*, *Open Democracy*, *Near East Quarterly* and various edited volumes. His research interests include continental philosophy, political theory, and theories of democracy.

Stuart McLean is an assistant professor of anthropology at the University of Minnesota. He is the author of *The Event and its Terrors: Ireland, Famine, Modernity* (2004). His articles have appeared in *Cultural Anthropology*, the *Irish Journal of Anthropology* and *Social Analysis* among other journals. Dr McLean's interests include anthropology of modernity, social and cultural theory, and the European Union. He is currently working on a monograph titled 'A Poetics of Emergence: Imagining Creativity Beyond "Nature" and "Culture"'.

Ian Anthony Morrison is an assistant professor of sociology at the American University in Cairo. His articles have appeared in the *Review of European and Russian Affairs*, the *Canadian Journal of Career Development* and various edited volumes. Dr Morrison's research interests include social and political philosophy, citizenship studies, politics of secularism, sociology of religion and psychoanalytic theory.

Sherene Seikaly is an assistant professor of history and Middle East studies at the American University in Cairo. Her articles have appeared in *Mediterraneans* and various edited volumes. She is the co-editor of the *Arab Studies Journal* and the co-founder of the *Jadaliyya* e-zine. Dr Seikaly's interests include colonialism, economic thought and cultural production. She is currently working on a monograph titled 'Meatless Days: Consumption and Capitalism in Wartime Palestine'.

Tracey Skillington is a lecturer in sociology at University College Cork. She is the author of *Climate Justice and Human Rights* (forthcoming) and her articles have appeared in the *British Journal of Sociology* and the *Irish Journal of Sociology* among others. She is also a general editor of the *Irish Journal of Sociology* and senior editor of the book series New Visions of the Cosmopolitan. Dr Skillington's research interests include critical theory, cosmopolitanism, European identity, human rights and models of democracy.

Samuel Weber is Avalon Foundation Professor of Humanities at Northwestern University, Evanston, IL and co-director of its Paris Program in Critical Theory. Professor Weber studied with Paul de Man and Theodor Adorno, whose book *Prisms* he co-translated into English. He has also published books on Balzac, Lacan and Freud. Among his recent publications are *Benjamin's -abilities* (2010), *Targets of Opportunity: On the Militarization of Thinking* (2005) and *Theatricality as Medium* (2004). Professor Weber's current research projects include 'Toward a Politics of Singularity' and 'The Uncanny'.

Introduction:
What Will Become of Europe?

Agnes Czajka and Bora Isyar

Since 2008, and for reasons dating back to at least the turn of the millennium, sizeable sections of the globe have been repeatedly hit by the aftershocks of a polytypic crisis. Christened 'the great recession' by economic analysts (Rampell 2009), 'the lesser depression' by Nobel laureate Paul Krugman (Krugman 2011), and 'the long recession' by financial institutions led by the International Monetary Fund, the longevity of the crisis has defied expectations. In Europe, the crisis presented as the sovereign debt crisis (also referred to as the eurozone crisis), which made it difficult, if not impossible, for certain eurozone member states to repay or refinance their government debt. With concerns over a financial meltdown intensifying, steps were taken to implement a series of financial support measures – including the European Financial Stability Facility (EFSF) and the European Stability Mechanism (ESM) – and bailout packages were 'offered' to the most vulnerable governments. Despite these and a plethora of other measures, the details of which cannot be adequately engaged with here, it would require unprecedented levels of optimism to claim that the crisis has been managed, let alone overcome.

There are three reasons, we think, for the persistence of the crisis in Europe. The first, and perhaps most obvious, is the nature of the measures devised to tackle it. Yet it is not the aim of this volume, nor is it within its scope, to engage in a critique of these measures. Suffice it to say the said measures seem to have exacerbated the crisis, contributed to the escalation of debt and initiated a vicious cycle that pushes indebted states further into precariousness (Lapavitsas 2012).

The second and perhaps equally obvious reason is the effect the aforesaid measures have had on the citizens (and other residents) of vulnerable or indebted states. As is evidenced by the increasing popularity and intensity of anti-austerity protests across Europe, a significant number of Europeans have been displaced with, and indeed angry at, the macro- and micro-economic measures devised to tackle the crisis. Among the most common concerns expressed by these Europeans is that the crisis has been reduced to an economic (or in fact a financial) crisis. The millions that have taken part in the protests have rejected the characterisation of the crisis as an exclusively financial one, and have argued that the social implications of the crisis as well as the austerity measures implemented to tackle it must be addressed, as it is the people – and not 'impersonal states' – who have suffered the consequences of both.

Increased unemployment, decreased incomes, the depletion of social services, mass emigration and the dissolution of communities are some of the consequences of both the crisis and the resultant austerity measures that those who have taken to the streets of Athens and Madrid feel have not been addressed by European institutions. The perceived indifference (even inhumanity) of such institutions has generated mistrust both in these institutions (Hughes 2012), and in the European project as such (European Trade Union Institute 2013). This, in turn, has made the proverbially volatile markets even more vulnerable, thus further exacerbating the crisis. And so, the measures that have been taken to manage the crisis have succeeded only in deepening it and making it appear even more intractable.

The persistence of today's crisis can certainly, albeit only partially, be explained by the inadequacy of the measures devised to tackle it and their adverse effects on already vulnerable populations. Yet there is a third, more fundamental, reason for its intractability and obstinacy: today's crisis is a manifestation of the unresolved (and unresolvable) crisis of yesterday, a crisis of identity centred on the questions of 'What is called Europe?' and 'How should Europe be?' As such, today's crisis is a crisis of a former today; it is an old crisis, a crisis to which Europe has been unable to respond.

Numerous measures were implemented to resolve the crisis of identity that was, and should have been, the crisis of yesterday. A common currency was created; institutions such as the European Parliament, the European Court of Justice and the European Commission were formed; spatial, cultural, even ethnic identities were invented to foster integration and ground European unity; and an exterior, an outside against which Europe would be defined and secured through selectively penetrable boundaries, was articulated. Yet the questions – 'What is called Europe?' and 'How should Europe be?' – and the crisis which they expressed remained inadequately answered. Almost a quarter of a century later, the crisis has re-emerged, in another guise.

Just over two decades ago, Jacques Derrida diagnosed a manifestation of the crisis in *The Other Heading: Reflections on Today's Europe* (1992). There, in response to the crisis of identity that plagued his Europe, Derrida proposed that we understand European identity as structured through an interminable encounter with its absolute other, the perpetuity of which produces an inherently unfixed and volatile identity for Europe. The coexistence and co-constitution through which this unfixable identity is produced and reproduced is not dialectical; Europe's identity is not to be constituted through a synthesis of antithetical elements into a unified whole. Rather, it is irreconcilable difference that lies at the origins, and comprises the essence of Europe.

For Derrida, Europe and its others do not exist as separate objects interacting with one another. Instead, Europe exists only through 'the non-identity to itself, or if you prefer, only in the difference with itself' (Derrida 1992: 9). Thus, like all 'identity', Derrida's Europe exists through its identification with a culture of itself as a culture of the other, 'a culture of the double genitive' and of difference to itself (Derrida 1992: 10). Derrida's Europe, then, forms a precarious singularity based not on identity as homogeneity, but on a singular and yet differential unity. Its unity is a unity that is always deferred through the becoming (something other than it is) of Europe as a non-identity and through the cultivation of difference-to-itself (with itself) as the constitutive element of this non-identity.

Mindful of this interpretation of Europe, we suggest that the measures devised to tackle the crisis of today (and yesterday) have disappointed because they have consisted of technologies designed with the homogenisation, unification and self-identification of Europe in mind. They are measures through which the irreducible and unfixable differences that constitute Derrida's Europe are negated. Yet it is precisely Derrida's Europe – as an answer to the questions of 'What is called Europe?' and 'How should Europe be?' – that is necessary if we are to understand the essence of today's crisis. The obstinacy of the crisis, the recent twentieth anniversary of Derrida's diagnosis of the crisis of Europe today and the approaching tenth anniversary of his death demand, we think, a critical re-engagement with Derrida's thought on Europe, and with Europe *after* Derrida.

In addition to demanding a resuscitation of Derrida's Europe, today's crisis can also occasion a rethinking of debt through Derrida's interpretation of gift and debt. Derrida's conceptualisation of debt can be of use in thinking through the manner in which Europe today (haunted by the increasing debt among its constituents) is being defined and enacted. What kinds of subjectivities are being constructed through the production of debt? If, as Derrida argues, creditors and debtors are self-identical subjects (be they individuals or communities), what implications does this have for European identity? It is, after all, Europe itself (through institutions such as the Rescue Fund and the Central Bank) that credits those who comprise Europe in the name of Europe. Interrogating the potential relationships between gift, debt and Europe can open up spaces for critical interpretations of how Europe *is* and what it can *become*, as well as for interpretations of the manner in which relationships of power are reconfigured through gift-giving and debt-making.

One could ask, for instance – bringing together Derrida's work on debt and Friedrich Nietzsche's conceptualisation of debt and guilt – what possible effects would the power inherent in relations of debt have on *being* European? If, as Nietzsche asserts, a relation of debt cannot be thought apart from a relationship of guilt, what implications does this have for the manner in which 'European creditors' are constituting themselves vis-à-vis 'European debtors' and Europeanness itself? We have already seen the potential threat that the crystallisation of this relationship of debt can pose to democracy when the so-called 'Merkozy' directorate conceptualised a Europe influenced more by de Gaulle than Monnet, where creditor states make crucial decisions at the expense of debtors (O'Brennan 2013). That the countries that are most *indebted* – Portugal, Italy, Greece and Spain – were together called PIGS, not merely as one would expect, by far-right organisations but also by academics, newspapers, and bond analysts is revealing.[1] It discloses, at the very least, the manner in which the relationship of debt has led to the emergence of a normalisation of insult and offence against those countries (and their citizens) that are indebted to the creditors.

What, then, are the implications of this state of affairs for 'European responsibility' and Europe's responsibility towards itself (a concept Derrida explored at length)? For Derrida, responsibility cannot be reduced to duty (the duty to pay your debt or pay the consequences) but is, on the contrary, incalculable, unknowable and always already related to the call of the unknown, of the to-come (Derrida 1995). If that is the case, can we talk of a European responsibility (and responsibility as such) under circumstances dominated by an economy of debt?

The crisis, finally, can prompt us to think through the concept of crisis itself, as well as the relationship between Europe and crisis. Some of the questions that follow from this (all of which are addressed by the chapters that comprise this volume) are: Does the emphasis on *today*'s crisis imply that it is radically (or perhaps absolutely) different from the many other crises – such as the ones addressed by Paul Valéry, Edmund Husserl and Derrida himself – that belonged to their respective todays? Or, despite their irreducibility to one another, is there an intrinsic link between these crises, established, among others, by the relationship between what is called Europe and the idea of crisis itself?

If we answer the latter in the affirmative, it is then imperative also to rethink what crisis means, what it implies and what it brings to light. It is the contention of a number of authors in this volume that an engagement with the relationship between Europe (and, although beyond the scope of this work, all communities) and crisis (not merely a particular form of crisis, but a crisis of being, an existential crisis) is called for. What such an engagement can disclose is the potentiality of crisis, grounded in its aporetic structure of threat and chance.

A Nietzschean affirmation of a crisis of being would recognise the inherent threat implied by this crisis (the threat of non-existence stemming from the absence of ipseity, a threat grounded in the recognition of the lack of a sovereign, self-same identity) but would interpret this threat simultaneously as a chance: a chance to open up to the unforeseeable other, to the unforeseeable future, to the to-come, to democracy to come. True to the nature of Derrida's thought (which cannot be reduced to and yet can be said to be exemplified by deconstruction), the chapters in this volume address such aporias, which are constitutive of Europe.

In the 'Mind the "Cap"', Samuel Weber asserts that the manner in which Europe responds to the aporia (and the conflict) between individuality and singularity will be the legacy of Europe. Weber sees Europe as inherently captured by this aporetic relationship between singularity and individuality (revealed, for instance, in the Reformation, which perceived human existence as irreducibly singular, and the Counter-Reformation, which constructed it as individual, and as such, as part of a continuum rooted in the self-identity of a divine creator). Europe, for Weber, bears the name of a potentiality to affirm an openness to that which is never entirely predictable in its heterogeneity and singularity. The question that remains is whether, after this ongoing crisis, Europe will be able to fulfil its potential by keeping itself open to the other (and to the future).

The absence of a self-same identity and the corresponding lack of clarity regarding what Europe is is also attended to by Simon Glendinning. Like Weber, Glendinning does not perceive this lack of clarity to be a shortcoming in need of remedy, but rather, a condition to be embraced and affirmed. Focusing on the work of Rodolphe Gasché and Emmanuel Levinas – which, Glendinning argues, forms the necessary background to reading Derrida on Europe – he explores the possibility of imagining European responsibility without beginning or end. Without ipseity, or self-identical and ostensibly glorious origins, can we still imagine a European responsibility?

Bora Isyar likewise asserts the need to read Derrida's work on Europe against the background formed by another thinker: Rémi Brague. Offering a critical encounter between the two, Isyar asks whether Brague's work can help us understand Derrida's insistence on retaining Europe as a political, social, cultural and ethical idea despite Europe's colonial past and xenophobic present. Isyar suggests that Brague's conceptualisation of Europe as Roman – as always already appropriating that which is foreign to itself – can support Derrida's interpretation of Europe as an identity and a culture that are always already different to themselves. It is the Roman character of Europe that constitutes its hope – the hope of an absolute opening to the other in all of its unpredictability, and as such, of always becoming something other than itself.

Stuart McLean suggests that Europe's non-coincidence with itself is manifest not only, as is often argued, in the Mediterranean – which is open to the globe, which refrains from imposing itself on others, and which, as Derrida asserts, is not and never will be Europe – but also in the offshore islands that 'belong' to Europe. Reading Gilles Deleuze's conceptualisation of desert islands alongside Derrida's assertion that Europe is at once old and young, McLean argues that Europe's offshore islands reveal that Europe always exceeds all possible versions of itself. Through its islands, Europe becomes external to itself, encountering difference instead of dwelling within self-sufficient parochialisms and universalist histories.

The question of the other of Europe is also attended to by Matthias Fritsch, albeit in a very different manner. Working his way through the aporia of constitution and constitutional relations, Fritsch asserts that the question of Europe cannot be addressed without referring to its temporal others alongside its geographical or cultural others. Noting that the ill-fated European Constitution would have safeguarded the freedom of future peoples while limiting and binding them simultaneously, Fritsch argues that thinking with Derrida can help us interpret Europe in its generational, discontinuous connectedness. Due to its temporal non-coincidence, its foundations (like all constitutional foundations) must appeal from the inside to the outside, to the other, whose countersignature they depend on.

Tracey Skillington explores the manner in which Europe's geographical and cultural others are constituted within EU institutions and

European policy discourses. Skillington's analysis reveals two conflicting logics that haunt today's Europe: that of openness, expressed by the language of cosmopolitan solidarities and rights, and that of closure, characterised by strict communitarianism, traditional conceptualisations of sovereignty and limited rights for others. Without resolving this aporetic condition of Europe, Skillington suggests that a Derridean ethics of cosmopolitanism and hospitality can help us negotiate these two logics with greater awareness.

Engin Isin also detects a lack of openness in Europe's comportment towards the non-European other. Reading Derrida with Edward Said, he problematises Europe's inability to come to terms with its debt to the non-European. As Isin aptly argues, Europe's problematic comportment towards the non-European also characterises relations within today's crisis-ridden Europe. Isin suggests that imagining Europe as a 'vanishing mediator', in the manner articulated by Étienne Balibar, offers an alternative. As a vanishing mediator Europe is constituted (like Brague's Europe) through the translation of languages and cultures, which annuls its claim to being the 'original' or 'more authentic and civilised' culture.

The question of the oriental other is also addressed by Sherene Seikaly and Max Ajl. Seikaly and Ajl explore the historical position of European Jews as the oriental within Europe. The uneasy space occupied by the figure of the Jew, they show, is an exemplar not only of Europe's problematic relationship to its others, but also of its inherent non-ipseity. Seikaly and Ajl proceed to explore the consequences of Zionism's appropriations of these self-same technologies of othering for Jews and Palestinians alike. As a project of the becoming European of Jews, they argue, Zionism replicated the violence of Europe's historical encounters with its external others and the other within itself.

The last two chapters of the book engage with one of the most prominent of Europe's others: the Muslim other. Focusing on the relationship between Europe and Turkey, but attending also to Europe's Muslim minority, Zeynep Direk calls for the deconstruction of European secularism and a critical engagement with Europe's theological politics. Direk argues that Europe continues to be governed by a theological politics alongside its technocratic governance, resulting in a lack of democracy manifested most clearly in the manner in which Muslims are excluded from European culture, identity and institutions. For Direk, Turkey's accession to the EU would constitute hope for Europe, revealing its ability to embrace a new cosmopolitan universalism grounded in religious and cultural pluralism.

In the concluding chapter, Ian Anthony Morrison attends to the seeming contradiction in the constitution of Europe that grounds some of the material realities discussed by Direk. As Morrison aptly argues, Europe is secular in relation to Muslim migrants and Christian in the face of Muslim Turkey. Europe, as this contradictory constitution reveals, and as is the case for all communities haunted by autoimmunity, cannot sustain itself as an ipseic entity and identity. Rather, it is haunted by the presence of multiple identities within itself. It is only by coming to terms with the manner in which these identities constitute one another, and by recognising the role of the other in the constitution of the European self, that Europe can establish itself as the open, as the name of democracy to come, which Derrida imagined two decades ago.

Note

1. Just like the crisis, this acronym has a number of variations. After 2008, some commentators referred to the 'PIIGS' to include Ireland and during the 2008 UK bank rescue package period, some analysts amended it to 'PIIGGS' to include Great Britain.

References

Derrida, Jacques (1992), *The Other Heading: Reflections on Today's Europe*, Bloomington: Indiana University Press.
Derrida, Jacques (1995), *The Gift of Death*, Chicago: Chicago University Press.
European Trade Union Institute (2013), *Benchmarking Working Europe 2013*, Brussels: ETUI.
Hughes, Kirsty (2012), 'EU democracy in crisis: mired in a perfect storm or rebounding?', Open Democracy website, 16 January, http://www.opendemocracy.net/kirsty-hughes/eu-democracy-in-crisis-mired-in-perfect-storm-or-rebounding (last accessed 18 June 2013).
Krugman, Paul (2011), 'The lesser depression', *New York Times*, 21 July, http://www.nytimes.com/2011/07/22/opinion/22krugman.html?_r=0 (last accessed 18 June 2013).
Lapavitsas, Costas (2012), *Crisis in the Eurozone*, London: Verso.
O'Brennan, John (2013), 'The European Union in a Time of Crisis: Multiple and Inter-locking Vectors of "Democratic Deficit" and Why Legitimation Matters', unpublished paper presented at Dreams of Freedom? Conversations on Aesthetics, Ethics and European Democracies, 9 March, Crawford Art Gallery, Cork, Ireland.
Rampell, Catherine (2009), '"Great Recession": A Brief Etymology', *New York Times*, 11 March, http://economix.blogs.nytimes.com/2009/03/11/great-recession-a-brief-etymology (last accessed 18 June 2013).

Chapter 1
Mind the 'Cap'

Samuel Weber

Prefatory Note: This chapter started out as an interview, a discussion with the editors of this volume. But after receiving the editors' initial questions and trying to respond to them, it soon became clear that to address them, as well as the more general question of 'Europe after Derrida', it would first be necessary to discuss just what 'Europe' was for Derrida. This in turn required unpacking, in some detail, the major essay he devoted to Europe, namely *The Other Heading (L'Autre cap)*. Although on the surface relatively straightforward, that essay turns out to be extremely intricate in the tissue of its arguments. The result was the monological essay below, which itself is split between reading Derrida's text and relating its implications to the ongoing European 'crisis'. However one understands it, it seems clear that this current crisis involves far more than just a crisis of currency, the euro, and this in turn requires discussion both of intra- and extra-European forces and factors. However, to respect requirements of length, the latter aspect had to be severely reduced in this version of the essay. Given the complexity of the issues involved, interdisciplinary discussion is probably the only form in which an effective understanding of the crisis as well as alternatives to them can ever be articulated.

Derrida's major text on Europe, known in English as *The Other Heading*, was written and originally published (in French) in October 1990, which is to say, at a critical juncture in the development both of Europe and of the World. The Berlin Wall had been torn down, and German reunification took place in the same month that the essay appeared. The following year the Soviet Union was formally dissolved. Thirteen years later, in January 2002, twelve of the then fifteen member states of the European Union adopted the euro as their common currency. I mention these dates to indicate just how different the situation of Europe was at the time

Derrida was writing this text from today. But this difference was already anticipated by Derrida, not of course in its positive details – despite extraordinary foresight he was no prophet nor did he ever pretend to be one – but in its general possibility and indeed inevitability. It was, and is, a difference inherent in the word and notion of 'today', which was one of the major motifs of Derrida's essay. It recalls Hegel's famous '*diesda*', 'this-there', at the beginning of the *Phenomenology of Spirit*, which to the 'natural consciousness' seems the most immediate and self-evident of things and yet turns out to be the most abstract and most mediate. Except that Derrida's 'today' is already 'mediated', since it is borrowed from another text, written some sixty years earlier, by Paul Valéry, 'Greatness and Decadence of Europe' (1927), which inscribes the word in a very different context from that of Hegel's 'this-there': not as the putative object of a constative gesture pointing towards something held to be 'there', differentiated and situated as a 'this' prior to its encounter with anything or anyone else. Valéry's 'TODAY', written in capital letters, defines a moment that is anything but fixed and stable, for it situates a question that is also a call to action: 'What are you going to do TODAY?' he enquires of his readers in a brief thought experiment, after asking them to accept the hypothesis that they have been granted full powers to do whatever they think best, in an optimal situation free of all doubt and hindrance. The question no doubt haunted Derrida while he was writing his essay, not formulated in the conditional ('What would you do if . . .' à la Nietzsche in 'The Greatest Weight' (Nietzsche 1974: 273–4) but in the present indicative ('What are you going to do TODAY?') as though formulated within the scope of a single 'today', limited in its actuality, but no less urgent.

It is this sense of urgency, tied to an interpellation that singles out its addressee in a way not entirely unlike that which Martin Heidegger, in *Being and Time*, associates with the 'call of conscience' (Heidegger 1962: 317–25), that marks not only this essay of Derrida's, but his writing as a whole. However, this particular essay is unusual for a number of reasons. First, because it allows Derrida to address an issue with which he had always been intimately involved, although he had rarely thematised it directly and as such: 'Europe'. Derrida had of course written extensively on and about the unity and disunities of 'Western' thought, on French, German and Anglo-American literature and philosophy. But the specific question of 'Europe' had, I believe, never formed the major topic of investigation prior to his being invited to contribute to a 1990 conference on European cultural identity. Coming at a time when Europe was clearly at a turning point in its history, at least in its post-Second World War history, this was an invitation that he could hardly refuse. For 'Europe' had always been a problem for him, whether acknowledged or not, through the more or less simple fact of being born and raised in French-ruled Algeria, which is to say outside Europe geographically, and yet still very much under its sway through the French administration, schooling, culture and language that defined and determined his early years. His expulsion from French public school during the years when the Vichy government controlled Algeria only emphasised his ambiguous situation in regard to a continental culture and politics that were always ready to remind him of the precariousness of his position. It is also no doubt one of the reasons why he could never simply be comfortable with a task defined as addressing 'European cultural identity', as though that identity could somehow be taken for a given and needed primarily only to be defined and discussed, never called into question as such. However, that is precisely one of the main points Derrida insisted on making early in this essay, and it is a reminder that will prove useful in any consideration of the European situation 'today'. He offered this remark as the second of two so-called 'axioms', whose history we will recall in a moment. But here is the 'axiom' itself:

> What is proper to a culture is never to be identical to itself. Not to not have any identity, but to be able to identify itself, to say 'me' or 'we' only in the non-identity to itself or, if you prefer, only in the difference with itself. There is no culture or cultural identity without this difference with itself . . . What differs and diverges from itself would also be a difference from and with itself, a difference both internal and irreducible to being at home (*chez soi*). (Derrida 1991: 16; 1992: 9–10)[1]

And in these days of 'homeland security', the consequences Derrida elicits from this 'axiom' resonate powerfully: '[This difference] gathers and divides the hearth of the home irremediably. In truth it only gathers it, bringing it back to itself, to the extent that it opens it to this divergence.' (Derrida 1991: 16; 1992: 10). Since, as a result, a culture can 'never have a single origin' and since it must always be to some extent and essentially a 'culture of the other', what remains to be discussed and determined is the specific set of heterogeneities that preside over the formation and transformation of a culture, if that notion can be applied to 'Europe'. One of the major arguments this essay seeks to explore is just what this intricate interplay of heterogeneities, producing something like a coherent although constantly evolving identity, might consist of, with respect to that entity called 'Europe', if it is an entity at all. (But if not, what is it?)

Before I continue to follow Derrida in this exploration, I want to backtrack a moment to look at the curious way in which what Derrida calls his 'axioms' emerge in this text. It is curious, because they result from a 'feeling', in French a '*sentiment*', that is, from something rarely associated with axioms. Actually, the 'axiom' seems to respond not just to a feeling, but to a situation in which feelings seem inseparable from uncertain knowledge:

> Something unique is on the move in Europe, in what is still called Europe, even if one no longer knows for certain what this word names. Indeed, to what concept . . . to what real individual, to what singular entity should this name be assigned today? Who will draw its borders?' (Derrida 1991: 12; 1992: 5)

It is this singular situation that evokes the feelings that will lead to the 'axiom' quoted. The dominant feeling is that of anxiety: 'an anguished experience of imminence' (Derrida 1991: 12; 1992: 5) in which 'hope, fear and trembling take the measure of the signs that arrive today from everywhere in Europe where precisely in the name of identity, cultural or not, the worst violences . . . are being unleashed' while at the same time, 'and there is nothing accidental in that', there is also 'the breath, the breathing, the "spirit" of the promise' (Derrida 1991: 12–13; 1992: 6).

Having thus defined his apprehension of a situation where peril is mixed with promise, Derrida, still at the outset of his remarks, feels compelled to utter something like a confession:

> I will confide in you a feeling . . . that of an old European feeling somewhat exhausted. More precisely of someone who without being entirely European by birth, since I come from the southern shore of the Mediterranean, considers himself, increasingly with the years, a kind of European mixed blood,

combining something of Europe's age with the youth 'of the other shore'. It is this 'feeling' that produces the first of the two 'axioms' of 'this little talk': 'I will say "we" instead of "I", another manner to pass surreptitiously from feeling to axiom' (Derrida 1991: 14; 1992: 7).

Before commenting on this passage, allow me to recall a memory I have from 'Old Berlin', during or maybe even before the Wall. In the eastern sector, in the subway stations, one was often confronted with huge posters proclaiming '*Von Ich zum Wir*': 'From I to We', the response of East Germany to the burgeoning individualism of the West. But this call to the collective was surely one of the reasons why Theodor Adorno, at about the same time, was demonstrably allergic to the use of 'we' in his writing and speaking.

Derrida's entire essay on Europe is framed by a passage from 'I' to 'we' that, precisely in being remarked and made explicit, prepares the way for a return of the 'I' as a marker of singularity: the 'I' will disappear for a while as feelings withdraw before 'axioms', but it will return at the end of the essay to emphasise that in fact it has never really been absent. For the perspective of singularity will remain throughout as one of the key markers and questions that accompany the discussion of 'Europe'. What makes this strange inscription of the 'I' and of its 'feelings', or later, in respect to Valéry, of its 'impressions', is that it is never simply personal but rather marks an unresolved question: what is the place of the singular and the individual, which as I will argue are by no means identical, with respect to that collective thing we call 'Europe' without knowing exactly what this name means or implies?

Whatever the answer to this question, if there is one, it is clearly significant that the first person singular is explicitly inscribed, withdrawn, and then reinscribed in Derrida's remarks on Europe. It is as if this move were to underscore a certain irreducible singularity of experience as the self-receding condition of the discourse on a Europe to come. This emphasis on the singularity of the writer, as well as on its singular occasion – a conference on European cultural identity – serve as traits that distinguish Derrida's text and style from that of many others writing on political and cultural questions. The singular occasion and encounter remain an indelible condition of that discourse. With them a distinct perspective is introduced into the discussion. It is one that will be concerned not just with 'objective' traditions and issues, but with their relation to a certain singularity, that of the finite living being, one feeling his age, and indeed this produces a tone that characterises Derrida's approach to this question.

All of this comes together in the problem of 'exemplarity', which has been well studied by both Michael Naas, in his introduction to the excellent English translation of this text, and Marc Redfield.[2] Europe, Derrida argues, has always presented itself as 'exemplary' in the double, ambiguous and indeed ambivalent sense of this word. For what is exemplary claims not only to be representative of a larger category than itself (the singular representing the general or the universal as its example), but also to be a privileged exemplum of the genre. And where this genre defines itself in universal terms as 'spirit' or 'mankind', this claim of exemplarity becomes extremely problematic, indeed dangerous. For every determinate entity is, qua determinate, finite, limited, partial; never the whole. When therefore a determinate entity claims to be exemplary, it inevitably privileges the traits and characteristics that it attributes to itself, thereby establishing a hierarchy that is inevitably exclusionary, and often if not always hegemonic.

In Derrida's text, however, the passage from 'I' to 'we', from first person singular to first person plural, does not take place in a neutral setting. The admission of this 'I' that he is feeling 'somewhat exhausted' (*accablé*: also 'overwhelmed', 'overburdened', 'weighed down') acknowledges the singular perspective and experience to which the discourse that follows will bear witness, to be that of a finite, mortal, living being. Finitude and mortality are thus the traits that will recede temporarily, when the speaker-writer moves from first person singular to the plural, although they will never entirely disappear. For any treatment of the question of 'Europe' that does not take into account this singularity – not singularity in general, but that of the living being in particular, with all of its consequences – will never be able to do justice to the problems that word raises: the problem of its today, which is also and inextricably bound up with those that are past as well as those to come.

It is curious how ready most of us are, most of the time at least, to take for granted the word 'today': that it is one and the same, that what it designates is a unity. How ready we are to overlook its literality and its etymology. For the word, in English as in French (not, however, in German), consists not just of a noun but also of a preposition, even if we hardly notice it as such. The preposition 'to', in French *au*, introduces a certain distance into what we take to be a monolithic unity: it says literally: 'to-the-day' rather than just 'the day'.[3] Today is not just any old day; it is a particular, singular day, and as such one 'towards' which we are directed. This determination of 'the day' as a singular to-day curiously removes it from itself, depriving it of anything like a monolithic self-identity. The German poet Friedrich Hölderlin, in a poem commented on early in his life by Walter Benjamin, 'Blödigkeit' ('Timidity'), wrote of 'the thinking day' (*der denkende Tag*) that is 'granted to poor and rich alike' and that is associated with the 'turn of time' (Hölderlin 1992: 444) as the medium of mortality. Derrida's fascinated emphasis on the time of the 'today' as in itself both limited and riven sets the scene as it were for his effort to reflect upon the situation not just of European cultural identity, but of 'Europe today', 'today' being not just the today of the conference for which he first wrote the essay, in the year 1989, but also the TODAY when Valéry called upon his readers to think about what they, you, were going to do. And it is also, mutatis mutandis, our today as well, a today that is changing constantly, from the time when I first began to write these words to the time you first read them, and beyond: a to-day that is never simply over and done with but also ever to-come and that therefore prevents any 'we' or 'I', not to mention 'Europe', from coming full circle.

This consequences of this quasi-Heraclitean, Derridean sense of 'today', of time as a process of unremitting limitation, alteration and evanescence, go further than is usually perceived. For it is not so much Heraclitus that is the model here, but his pupil, Cratylus, who, in an anecdote recounted by Aristotle in his *Metaphysics* (Aristotle 1941: IV, 5, 1010a) outdid his teacher.[4] Being confronted with the Master's famous dictum that one cannot step into the same stream twice, Cratylus is said to have added, 'Not even once.' Or, as the German expression goes that Benjamin used as the title of a short essay: '*Einmal ist Keinmal*' ('Once is Nonce') (Benjamin 1972, 1999).

This does not suggest that the 'once' is simply an illusion, but rather that it is the constitutively divided and never directly accessible aftermath of a repetition that Derrida will reformulate as 'iterability'. In this sense the singular is relational but never fully identifiable. This is not just a deficiency, since its non-definability keeps the singular open to the future. It is why 'today' in its uniqueness and singularity is both urgent and yet always to come. We can perhaps sense it, feel it, be affected by it, acknowledge it, but never simply recognise it as something self-identical. Feeling can perhaps best be understood as a response to an encounter with a singular alterity that cannot be reduced to the self-identical object of a concept or to a subset of the self. If this is so, the political implications of such feelings have yet to be explored, and this is in part what Derrida's essay attempts to do and what it thereby challenges us, as readers, to continue doing.

But all of this is, to be sure, in no way exclusive to 'Europe'. Wherein then does the distinctive singularity of 'Europe today' reside? Without addressing this question, which means without forgetting the more general law that divides every 'today' from itself, nothing pertinent can be said about what is called 'Europe' today. Could it be that 'Europe today' exemplifies a certain fracturing of the today – and that this is what defines its distinctive specificity? We will return to this question shortly.

But first let us see how Derrida approaches it; and in this essay he indeed mainly approaches it, challenging those who come afterwards, listeners, readers of another day, to pursue and develop his approach. One way of doing this is to consider the literality of his French text, which has been rendered into English superbly by Michael Naas and Pascale-Anne Brault. I entirely agree with their decision to try to bring Derrida's French as close to idiomatic English as possible: in general I am convinced that this is the best strategy to follow when translating, even if it means forsaking the literality of the original. Derrida's writing in particular often plays on and with a variety of connotations of colloquial, non-technical French that would be entirely lost in English were one to attempt to retain what seems to be the primary semantic 'content' of the terms he uses. This is particularly so of the title, which in English reads 'The Other Heading,' and in French 'L'Autre cap'. 'Heading' surely captures many of the connotations of *cap*, while in no way being a simple reproduction of the word. Derrida chose the word *cap*, as he puts it at the outset, in part at least because of its 'navigational' associations (Derrida 1991: 19; 1992: 13), and 'heading' picks up the sense of directed movement, as well as the bodily 'head', that every *cap* as the orientation point of a voyage implies.[5] Thus, Valéry's question, 'What are you going to do TODAY?', can be read as implying 'Where are you *heading* today?' The Heraclitean-Cratylian metaphor of a river or stream, as a flux, is thus implicit in Derrida's choice of the word *cap*. But the French word also connotes something that inevitably gets lost in the English translation: its topographical connotation. *Cap* in this sense is not unlike the English 'cape', not as an outer garment (although this is by no means entirely irrelevant), but as a promontory, where the land sticks out or advances into the ebb and flow of the ocean, providing a point that can be used to 'orient' or coordinate a movement; providing as it were something to hold onto. For the navigators of the seventeenth century, in which European countries began to explore and conquer the world beyond the oceans, capes exercised this function. Even today, in ordinary, colloquial French, the expression *tenir le cap*, 'keep the course', returns again and again in the speeches of the current French president, François Hollande, as he seeks to convince his countrymen and women that he will indeed fulfil his electoral promises, and that above all, he is holding fast (*tenir le cap*) to a defined political course despite the many obstacles with which France is confronted. This expression in turn recalls the age-old formula that re-emerged in China during the rule of Mao Zedong, who was designated as the 'Great Helmsman', a figure going back at least to Plato, for whom the captain of a ship served as model for a just constitution and polity (Plato 1999: 297a).

Holding true to one's course, to a *cap*, can thus appear as a way of responding to an uncertain future, one that seeks to maintain the familiar and impose the same. To use this word to describe the situation and traditions of 'Europe', however, is to imply at least two further aspects. First, the acknowledgement of possible change, even if this is experienced through anxiety and apprehension as a menace or risk. And second, the effort to dominate that change and place it in the service of the existing order. Change is not denied but recognised as that which must be harnessed, channelled, controlled.

The 'cape' then implies an encounter with alterity, with the possibility of alteration and transformation, but a response that seeks to absorb those changes – one could even say 'cover' them, as does a cape – by integrating them into its perceived identity. In this sense, Europe indeed can be described as a 'continent', even if geographically it by no means coincides with one, not only because it fails to occupy a clearly definable land mass, like Australia or North America, but because it is constantly tending to go beyond itself, which is to say, beyond its given borders. It is a continent always on the verge of becoming incontinent: of exceeding its limits, whether through colonial expeditions, interventions, annexations, external or internal wars, or through political, social and cultural changes that would leave it unrecognisable.

Derrida sums up this tendency in the following alternative, which also makes explicit the ambiguity contained in the title of his essay: it is the ambiguity of 'the other cape'. This phrase can be read in at least two radically different ways. First, there is the sense of simply 'another cape', to be reached, rounded and left behind. A change, but only as more of the same. But second, there is an alternative to the one just described, one that also belongs to European history and its traditions, namely the tendency to move without the guidance of a cape, guided by something other than a cape, in French, *l'autre* du *cap*.

What would it mean for Europe to move towards something other than a cape? To answer this, we must clarify what it means to move towards a cape in the first place: towards this one or another one, always another. This takes us to two other words formed from this root word, *cape*: except that in English, these two words merge into the same word, with two quite distinct if not unrelated meanings. Those words, in French, are *la capitale* and *le capital*, which in English can be differentiated only by the use of the definite article: respectively 'the capital' (as in seat of government) and 'capital', designating a certain economic and financial entity, one which appears, magically or not, to have the quasi-theological, quasi-biological power of reproducing itself in ever greater amounts.

These two words, or word meanings, are, to be sure, historically not unrelated: the development of capital had much to do with the development of capital cities, although in very different senses: Venice and the Hanseatic cities were (and remain) very different from London and Paris. Nevertheless, a certain urban concentration seems inseparable from the development of European capitalism; precisely because of the mobility of 'capital', involving the movement of goods and money, geographically fixed 'capitals' have been all the more necessary to coordinate trade and commerce. In the United States, the founders of the federal system of government deliberately separated the capital cities of individual states from their economic and cultural 'capitals', in sharp contrast with Europe. In general, one can argue, although Derrida does not do so explicitly, that European development was marked by an ever tighter link between capital and capitals, the most pronounced expression of which today is the designation of the heart of British finance in London as 'the City', the 'Capital of Capital'.[6] In this sense, Britain, which in many ways has always prided itself on being outside 'the continent' of Europe, is both on its periphery and at its centre and intends to remain there, as can be seen from its situation as member of the European Union but not of the eurozone, a willing member of its 'common market' while keeping its distance from any fiduciary union.

What of course makes this paradoxical relationship, peripheral and yet central, all the more significant is the special relationship the UK has not just to Europe, but to the United States. Derrida does not address this in his essay, but the limitations of his essay challenge its readers to do what it does not. In this case, this means extending the arguments to address the relationship between Europe and America. Unfortunately there is no space to do this topic justice here: I can only indicate a few elements of a discussion I hope to undertake elsewhere. First of all, the convergence of the two 'capitals', capital city and financial capital, does not take place in the same way in the United States as it has in Europe. New York, finance capital of the United States, is by no means the political capital of the country, nor is it its uncontested cultural capital. Second, the separation of the two capitals is politically sustainable because of the greater cultural unity of the country with respect to Europe. Indeed, for reasons of ideology, the convergence of economics and politics is kept as concealed and separate as possible in the United States. Europe on the other hand has always been a battleground on which opposing religions, cultures and countries wage internecine struggles. It is in part in response to the more recent of these, the First and Second World Wars, that the current effort at European unification has been undertaken. Such a response has never been quite as urgent for the United States, which ever since the Civil War has been able to take for granted a certain cultural and political homogeneity, one that has not depended wholly on institutional forces to be maintained. We see some of the more questionable results of that attitude in the recent willingness of the Republican Party to block basic functions of government, such as the federal budget, something that is (still?) unthinkable today in Europe, in part precisely because of a historical awareness of the disastrous effects of such parliamentary inefficacy, an awareness that at least in France has produced a presidential system much stronger than any the United States (or Germany for that matter) would countenance.

And so, at least with respect to the United States, the European emphasis on the importance of 'capitals' does seem to be a distinctive feature of its tradition and culture. In this context, however, Derrida insists on a point that has become all the more urgent since he wrote, namely that 'centralizing drives do not always pass via States (for it can even happen, and one can cautiously hope for this, that in certain cases old state structures help combat private and transnational empires)' (Derrida 1991: 39–40; 1992: 37). Derrida refers here to the media as an example of a non-topographical 'centralisation' that 'capital' can impose above and beyond the authority of centralised nation states. Nothing could be more relevant to any political discussion today, and one of the distinctive aspects of 'Europe' with respect for example to the United States can be seen in the manner in which the state relates to the media, imposing a level of regulation in the public interest that is virtually absent from the United States. Unfortunately I cannot pursue this point here, but presumably its implications and enormous consequences will be fairly clear to anyone familiar with the situation of the media in Europe and in the United States.[7]

Derrida's brief, indeed parenthetical, remark serves as a reminder that the two senses of the word 'capital' are closely allied but hardly identical. Financial capital can establish its hegemony at the expense of centralised state structures: the whole economic, social and political problem of globalisation and, more particularly, the 'delocalisation' it makes possible is thereby touched on, however briefly. But what can we, today, learn from Derrida's very brief discussion of that other meaning of 'capital', this time not topographic but economic? Without going into a technical discussion of the various implications of this term, I will simply underscore one aspect that Derrida takes from Valéry's portrayal of Europe as defined by, and in danger of losing, its 'spiritual capital'. This is the notion of 'maximisation': spirit, like capital, involves what Derrida calls 'the maxim of maximality' (Derrida 1991: 68; 1992: 68–9). Spiritually, it is, says Valéry, through the maximisation of its finitude that Europe lays claim to a certain 'universality'. Capital, like spirit, would be defined by a certain capacity to maximise, i.e. to reproduce ever greater amounts of what essentially remains identical to itself.[8] Capital, like spirit, would thus involve what in political economy is called 'expanded reproduction', namely more of the same. This would be the dynamic and temporal correlative of the 'cape' as the most advanced point of the mainland: the point at which it surpasses itself while remaining itself: its outermost but also its own-most frontier.[9] Nevertheless, as a point, a cape also suggests not just a continuum of land but its separation. And this takes us to one of the key differences between spirit and capital. Let me quote here a passage from Valéry that Derrida also cites and comments:

> 'Culture, civilization, these names are extremely vague and one can amuse oneself in trying to differentiate them, oppose or conjugate them. I won't dwell on this. For me, as I've told you, what is involved is a capital that forms itself, puts itself to use, preserves itself, grows itself, which vacillates like all imaginable capitals, of which the best known is surely what we call our body ...' (quoted in Derrida 1991: 65; 1992: 65–6)

Commenting on this passage Derrida insists first on the linking of capital to imagination, and second on the connection Valéry establishes between capital and the body. This in turn suggests something that can take us back once again, if briefly, to the consummate interpreter of capital, Karl Marx. Since one of the things Derrida calls for, in this essay as elsewhere, is a rereading of Marx's *Capital* that could militate against the dogmatism his work has often evoked (Derrida 1991: 56; 1992: 56), allow me to return to the very first page of that book, to a footnote, in which Marx, in the process of defining capitalism as commodity production, quotes one of his predecessors, the English economist Nicholas Barbon. Barbon says: 'Desire implies want, it is the appetite of the mind, and is as natural as hunger to the body ... The greatest number of things have their value from supplying the wants of the mind' (quoted in Marx [1867] 1995: 1). In short, already for Marx, from a purely economic point of view, no distinction radically separates 'the wants of the mind' from those of the body. Commodity production, the basis of capital, takes place within a framework of 'want' in which mind and body are inseparably involved. Contrary to a tendency in Marxist or post-Marxist thinking, exchange-value is meaningless without use-value, which in turn addresses 'wants' involving the body no less than the mind, but also desire and the imagination no less than purely material needs. Capital, in short, involves 'spirit' but also 'body', as Valéry points out and Derrida repeats. And in so far as it involves bodies, it is linked not simply to material existence, but to the existence of singular living beings, beings who, qua singular, are also finite and mortal. For the body does not merely 'materialise' existence, it singularises it.

If the tendency of capital therefore is to maximise itself, to proliferate and multiply, this takes place against a background of the finitude of singular forms of life. But as is well known, if capital can be defined as the effort to maximise a certain selfhood, that self, while related to life, is by no means identical to it. Surplus value, at least in the Marxian–Ricardian perspective, is generated by the difference in the reproductive cost of living labour with respect to the value of the commodities it produces. In order to increase surplus value, labour costs must be reduced. The tendency then is to find the cheapest possible living labour (today often through delocalisation and its effects) and/or to replace living labour by 'dead' labour in the form of machines and other inanimate devices (automated production facilities, for instance).

What is decisive, in the passage from Valéry quoted, is his use of the reflexive form, which I have endeavoured to retain in English: capital is a movement of self-reproduction, of reproduction of a self which, however, is not necessarily a living self, much less a living individual. And yet, it remains bound up with what Valéry calls 'our body'. And this body is not simply one and the same: it is, as Derrida adds, 'sexualised' and as such divided and different from itself. Bodily existence is not simply singular: it is also and at the same time singularly divided, and in this sense it is 'singularly plural', to use a term of Jean-Luc Nancy's: irreducibly heterogeneous and conflictual.

From this perspective, Derrida argues that 'Europe' must be understood as the palaeonymic designation of a paradox in progress: the paradox of a certain exemplarity that inscribes the universal in the singular, but without simply absorbing and subsuming its singularity. If a major part of European history over the past six or seven centuries has to be seen in the context of the development and ultimate globalisation of capital as the dominant mode of social reproduction, its continuance 'today' cannot but involve the prolongation of this structural conflict between singularity and its claim to universality.

But there are at least two ways this conflict can be negotiated. The one that has been and remains historically dominant is marked by the history of European colonialism and expansionism, in which the mainland seeks to dominate its colonies, a history continued and often radicalised through the development of those colonies themselves. Symptoms of this include the hegemony of the United States following the Second World War, or, on a more local scale, the development of 'postcolonial' autocracies, imposed by the former colonial powers, often exploiting ethnic and religious differences in accordance with the logic of private appropriation of wealth. This globalises the notion of progress as the substitution of one cape for another, obscuring the ways in which the very notion of 'cape' itself implies the maintenance or expansion of the same.

But there is an alternative movement also at work in this process of capitalist maximisation, since in seeking to perpetuate the same, it inevitably also maintains in various forms the heterogeneity that is at its core, albeit in submerged and concealed forms. If exemplarity involves the effort to inscribe 'the universal in the body proper of a singularity' (Derrida 1991: 71; 1992: 72), then this bodily singularity will never simply be transformable into a spiritual infinitude of endless surplus value by virtue of the finitude that is the 'proper' of the 'body proper'. Mortality is surely capitalisable, as wars demonstrate, but not easily transcendable, except where a certain religious perspective is fused with capitalism as 'guilt', a process Walter Benjamin retraces in his fragment 'Capitalism as Religion'. And the sanctification of capitalism goes together with what he designated as the 'aestheticizing of politics', for which the celebratory representation of the destruction of living beings in war or other forms of organised killing provides the paradigm (Benjamin 1996, 2003).

Such sacralising of capital and aestheticising of politics, which allow one cape to replace the other indefinitely, go hand in hand with a discourse that relies upon the first person plural to constitute a perspective that speciously pretends to transcend the limitations of singularity. The alternative to this is a style of writing that practices a certain form of 'responsibility', one that always involves responsiveness to, and in, the singular. This is why, towards the end of his essay, Derrida reintroduces the first person singular into a discourse from which it has never really been absent:

> I have, the unique 'I' has the responsibility of bearing witness for universality. Each time the exemplarity of the example is unique. This is why it can place itself in series and allow itself to be formalised in a law. (Derrida 1991: 72; 1992: 73)

This is why a certain discourse in the first person singular frames Derrida's essay on 'the other cape'. For this use of a never entirely personal, but never entirely impersonal first person singular is there to remind us that even, and perhaps especially, regarding 'Europe', a collective entity can never be separated from the history of the singularities of which it is composed. If this is a general rule, it seems to have a particular, 'exemplary', value in regard to Europe, its history and its traditions. Aspiring to universalise what cannot be positively universalised, Europe's effort to advance and unify itself has always encountered the resistance of that which will not disappear into unity. In seeking to reproduce itself, it inevitably encounters its others, not simply as external forces and factors but as its most intimate and internal constitution.

This is also why towards the end of this essay 'feelings' and 'impressions' re-emerge to take a prominent place in a discussion that would seemingly transcend both. In the final passage quoted from Valéry, the poet-critic 'concludes' by giving his 'personal impression' not just of Europe but of France: 'Our particularity (and sometimes our ridiculous but most beautiful title) is to believe ourselves, to feel ourselves to be universal . . . men of the universe. Note this paradox: to have as specialization the sense of the universal' (Derrida 1991: 73; 1992: 74). Derrida notes that this 'belief' and this 'feeling' are surely not exclusive to Europeans, although he does not deny that they may have a distinctive relation to European history and culture. What should be emphasised, at the end of his essay, is the way this 'feeling' bears witness to the splitting of the 'cape' and its possible replacement by something other than a cape, something other than a 'heading'. And Derrida concludes by asserting that responding to this paradox, to this cleavage, to this other opportunity, means not just apprehending or recognising it, but 'affirming' it. Instead of heading towards a cape, and towards another one after it – in short, instead of what today is called 'moving forward' – the history of Europe enjoins one to endure an experience of the antinomy, of what Derrida later will call 'aporia', affirming one's openness to what is never entirely predictable, to the 'event', in its irreducible heterogeneity and singularity.

But what Derrida does not emphasise, here at least, and what I would therefore want to insist on, is that such singularity in turn always presupposes that from which it diverges, namely the expectation of another cape. The event is never self-contained in its singularity but always relational: it presupposes a certain teleology and intentionality, precisely in order then to dislocate the particular form in which they are expected. The singular therefore is not simply a logical category: it is always a historical one: it is that which doesn't 'fit in', but which as such presupposes as framework something 'fitting'. In this sense, Derrida is quite right to write of it as something 'other than a cape', retaining thereby the reference to a cape, a goal or orientation point, as that from which the singular diverges.

However, all of this, being so generally true and applicable, still does not suffice to distinguish what might be truly singular, truly distinctive, to Europe. I want therefore in conclusion to introduce one further element that is not explicit in Derrida's essay, although he does touch on it in various other writings. I want to suggest that the particular way in which Europe becomes an exemplary site for the antinomies or aporias of exemplarity, of the inscription of the universal in a singular body, can be retraced to a particular period (I hesitate to say 'event') in European history. I believe this is something that Benjamin was profoundly aware of, when he wrote *The Origins of the German Mourning Play*.[10] For what captivated Benjamin's interest was not the Reformation as such but the responses it evoked, which he grouped together under the title 'Counter-Reformation', a notion that he insisted should not be restricted to any one religious group (i.e. Catholicism). If the Reformation in his view was concentrated in Martin Luther's attack on 'good works' in the name of 'faith alone' as the sole path towards salvation, then the challenge this posed required all institutions to review and revive their attitude towards the radical singularity of the mortal living being. For Luther's subordination of 'good works' to 'faith' as something situated in the singular living being called into question the redemptive value of all human endeavours, whether individual or collective. This uncertainty, in sharp contradiction with the violent assertiveness of Luther's own writings, comes to haunt all of European modernity, whether in the devastating wars of religion that began a series of self-destructive conflicts that reached well into the twentieth century or in the attempt at retrieving a measure of certainty and stability through philosophical or scientific endeavours.

What plays itself out in this struggle between Reformation and Counter-Reformation could be described as the struggle, uniquely European perhaps, between a sense of human existence as irreducibly *singular*, and therefore cut off not simply from others but from itself as well, and a sense of human existence as *individual*, in which the singular, bodily existence of mortal human beings is seen as part of a continuum that is rooted in the self-identity of a unique and divine creator. If the Christian Good News is that there is a path back to this original unity and eternal life, the history of Europe is marked by the divisions and uncertainties concerning just how that path is to be travelled and negotiated. The notion of resurrection seeks to bridge the gap between the singular and the individual, in so far as it marks the rise of the mortal, singular body, purged of its sinful fleshly existence, and thus spiritualised in communion with a divine and universal creator. The singular resurrected spiritualised body thus attempts to fulfil the promise of the 'individual' as that living being that is supposed to be originally and ultimately indivisible, inseparable from its self, secular avatar of the immortal 'soul'.

This struggle between two inextricable notions of the living, qua singular and qua individual, may indeed constitute the form in which Europe has developed its identity historically: a form that in its conflictual character may be distinctly European. What would then turn out to be a specifically European legacy and resource would be the capacity to sustain this conflict in what Derrida calls the 'test of the antinomy', the 'ordeal' of the aporia. The inability to sustain that 'ordeal' would then take the historically decisive form of a yearning to transcend the tension and resolve the conflict. What is today called 'neo-liberalism' appeals to this yearning, while threatening to upset the fragile balance that has been established over years of European history between the singular and the individual, between the public and the private.[11]

It is symptomatic of this delicate balance that immediately following the Second World War an economic ideology was developed in Germany that continues to dominate European political life today. It was the ideology of the 'social market economy'. The term was introduced in 1946 by the German economist Alfred Müller-Arnack and it became the dominant economic and political ideology of postwar Germany, from Adenauer and Erhard to Gerhard Schroeder.

Müller-Arnack displayed a significant historical awareness when he designated 'the social market economy' as an 'irenic formula', designed to reconcile the private interests of the 'market' with the public interest of society, capital with labour. The word 'irenic', from the Greek *eirene*, meaning 'peace', goes back to a text published in 1593 by the Protestant theologian Franz Junius the Elder under the title *Eirenicum*, which sought to promote a reconciliation of Catholic and Protestant warring factions after the devastating wars of religion, a devastation that halved the civilian population in the German-speaking areas where most of the conflicts took place. The fact that the leitmotif of postwar German socio-economic ideology presented itself as a compromise between the two major factions of western Christianity seems particularly significant given that the idea of a 'social market economy' has not only become the shibboleth of a reunified Germany but has also found its way into the Lisbon Treaty, which became effective on 1 December 2009.[12]

The Christian notion of redemption thus permeates the economic thinking of the social market economy, which, in order to be 'highly competitive' as the Lisbon Treaty explicitly demands, must be able to remain creditworthy. To be creditworthy, debts must be redeemable in full, which in the given system means repaying debts incurred together with the specified interest in the specified time frame. The contemporary German insistence on austerity as a path to economic, political and national salvation reflects a mode of thinking that is ultimately theological: man is indebted to his creator; his debts, like his sins, are self-incurred and must be redeemed with interest. The debt 'matures', but unlike the life cycle of singular beings, it does not diminish and disappear but rather augments in 'value'.

Thus, the heterogeneity of the singular is interpreted as the debt that the individual, whether private citizen or sovereign state, must under all circumstances pay back, with interest, to other individuals. The singularity of the self is thus 'economised', rendered measurable, quantifiable, maximisable (through interest) and in this sense 'redeemable'. The notion of an irreducible heterogeneity, in which the relation of self to other cannot be quantified because it is never measurable, is thereby excluded from the sphere of social, political and economic reality.

This economic-theological – and above all 'redemptive' – 'logic' thus subordinates the 'other of the cape' to the injunction to 'move forward', from one cape to the next. And thereby a very old story seems to repeat itself. Europe today subordinates what is to come to what has been. And if the United States is understood to name the system that is seeking most powerfully to perpetuate this theological and redemptive economy by imposing it on a globalised world, it can be considered to be the eminent practitioner of the logic of the 'other cape'. It seems as if the observation made by Valéry almost a century ago still holds true, at least in part: Europe, he wrote, 'aspires to be governed by an American Commission' (Valéry 1960: 930).

If this aspiration is true of only a part of Europe (transcending national borders), it may be helpful to recall that the most celebrated of all capes, the Cape of Good Hope, is not known by the name initially given to it by its Portuguese discoverer, Bartolomeu Dias. Originally he called it the *Cabo das Tormentas*. Europe seems destined today to make the perilous journey towards this cape. How it will navigate that journey is the question posed today (and surely tomorrow) for 'Europe after Derrida'.

Notes

1. On occasion I have slightly modified the English translation.
2. See Naas (1992) and Redfield (2007).
3. I thank Jonathan Wadman for the following observation: 'According to the *Oxford English Dictionary*, the "to" element in "today" actually means "on" or "at", a throwback to a meaning which is largely obsolete in other contexts. This of course is also another meaning of the French word *au* as in *aujourd'hui*. Incidentally, the German word for "today", *heute*, comes from the Latin *hodie*, which in turn is a concatenation of *ho+die* "on this day".' The need to which this

etymological note bears witness – the need of emphasising this particular, singular day – can perhaps be seen as a response to the tension between the generality implied by the word – 'today' is always and ever the same, 'everyday' – and the singularity of each and every day, irrevocably different from every other one. It is a tension articulated and exploited by the French writer Pascal Quignard and the French filmmaker Alain Corneau, in the book and the film *Tous les matins du monde* ('All Mornings in the World') – followed by the phrase 'never return'.

4. Given that Derrida acknowledges at the outset 'hope, fear and trembling', it can be noted that this anecdote is relayed at the very end of Søren Kierkegaard's *Fear and Trembling* ([1843] 1983: 123). To be sure, Kierkegaard's narrator, Johannes de Silentio, misses an excellent chance to keep silent, something attributed by Aristotle to Cratylus, when he interprets the remark as a denial of movement altogether and as a return to Eleatism. In our context, however, it can also be read as heralding the introduction of a movement different from what we usually take to be such, namely what Heidegger would call 'locomotion' (*Bewegung*) in contrast to 'being-moved' (*Bewegtheit*) (see Heidegger [1927] 1962: 439–44, where *Bewegtheit* is translated as 'movement' to distinguish it from *Bewegung*, 'motion'; for reasons I take to be obvious, I prefer 'being-moved' to 'movement' as an English rendition of *Bewegtheit*).

5. 'Heading' also retains the textual allusion of *cap* to the top of a page or the title of a chapter.

6. Exactly one year to the day before I wrote this, the 7 January 2012 issue of *The Economist* ran a leading article with the headline 'Save the City'. The leader explained: 'Britain is the home of the world's capital of capital but no longer prizes it. That is a mistake.'

7. Obviously there are enormous differences in the situation of the media in different European countries: the history of Berlusconi in Italy for instance, or the predominance of private commercial interests in the German media, contrasts somewhat with the situation in France and the UK. But I would still argue that the tradition of regarding the media as belonging at least in part to the public domain has long been one of the decisive differences between Europe and America.

8. Compare here Karl Marx's famous characterisation of the capitalist as amasser of wealth (*Schatzbildner*) in *Capital*: 'His experience is that of the world-conqueror: each new country is only a new frontier' (Marx [1887] 1995: 71). A page earlier Marx indicates the context in which this frenzy develops: 'Modern society, which, soon after its birth, pulled Plutus by the hair of his head from the bowels of the earth, greets gold as its Holy Grail, as the glittering incarnation of the very principle of its own life' (Marx [1887] 1995: 70). This connection between religion and economics, between gold as the 'glittering incarnation of the very principle of its own life', can hardly be taken too seriously and too literally today, when the leaders of finance and speculation, Bernard Madoff, Lloyd Blankfein and others, all claim for themselves a quasi-divine status: 'doing God's work' in Blankfein's immortal words (quoted in Phillips 2009).

9. This is also what lies behind the new buzzword in academic management and policy: 'excellence'. To 'excel' is to be better than the others, but not fundamentally different.

10. It is significant that this title omits the historical reference to the 'baroque', which occurs throughout the book itself. I would see in that a sign of the larger implications of Benjamin's study, which although focused on a particular historical period presents what can be seen as a paradigm of European modernity itself.

11. Paradoxically perhaps I associate here the singular with the public, the individual with the private. The German word for 'public', *Öffentlichkeit*, stresses

the openness of the public sphere, which is also a defining trait of the singular as I have been discussing it here.
12. Article 2 of the Treaty of Lisbon states:
    (i) The Union's aim is to promote peace, its values and the wellbeing of its peoples.
    (ii) The Union shall offer its citizens an area of freedom, security and justice without internal frontiers, in which the free movement of persons is ensured in conjunction with appropriate measures with respect to external border controls, asylum, immigration and the prevention and combating of crime.
    (iii) The Union shall establish an internal market. It shall work for the sustainable development of Europe based on balanced economic growth and price stability, a highly competitive social market economy, aiming at full employment and social progress . . . (Treaty of Lisbon 2007).

References

Aristotle (1941), *Metaphysics*, in *The Basic Works of Aristotle*, ed. Richard McKeon, New York: Random House.
Benjamin, Walter (1972), 'Kurze Schatten', in *Gesammelte Schriften, Band IV: Kleine Prosa/Baudelaire Übertragungen*, Frankfurt am Main: Suhrkamp, p. 369.
Benjamin, Walter (1996), 'Capitalism as Religion', in *Selected Writings, Vol. I: 1913–1926*, ed. Marcus Bullock and Michael W. Jennings, Cambridge, MA: Belknap Press, pp. 288–91.
Benjamin, Walter (1999), 'Short Shadows', in *Selected Writings, Vol. II: 1927–1934*, Cambridge, ed. Michael W. Jennings, Howard Eiland and Gary Smith, MA: Belknap Press, pp. 739–40.
Benjamin, Walter (2003), 'The Work of Art in the Age of its Technical Reproducibility', in *Selected Writings, Vol. IV: 1938–1940*, ed. Howard Eiland and Michael W. Jennings, Cambridge, MA: Belknap Press, pp. 269–70.
Derrida, Jacques (1991), *L'Autre cap*, Paris: Minuit.
Derrida, Jacques (1992), *The Other Heading: Reflections on Today's Europe*, Bloomington: Indiana University Press.
Heidegger, Martin [1927] (1962), *Being and Time*, New York: Harper.
Hölderlin, Friedrich (1992), 'Blödigkeit', in *Sämtliche Werke und Briefe, Band I*, ed. Michael Knaupp, Munich: Carl Hanser.
Kierkegaard, Søren (1983), *Fear and Trembling/Repetition*, Princeton, NJ: Princeton University Press.
Marx, Karl [1867] (1995), *Capital, Vol. I*, Moscow: Progress.
Naas, Michael (1992), 'Introduction: For Example', in Jacques Derrida, *The Other Heading: Reflections on Today's Europe*, Bloomington: Indiana University Press, pp. vii–lix.
Nietzsche, Friedrich [1887] (1974), *The Gay Science: With a Prelude in Rhymes and an Appendix of Songs*, New York: Vintage.
Phillips, Matt (2009), 'Goldman Sachs' Blankfein on Banking: "Doing God's Work"', *Wall Street Journal*, 9 November, http://blogs.wsj.com/marketbeat/2009/11/09/goldman-sachs-blankfein-on-banking-doing-gods-work (last accessed 19 June 2013).
Plato (1999), *The Statesman*, Indianapolis: Hackett.
Redfield, Mark (2007), 'Derrida, Europe, Today', *South Atlantic Quarterly* 106(2), 373–92.

Treaty of Lisbon (2007), http://www.consilium.europa.eu/uedocs/cmsUpload/cg00014.en07.pdf (last accessed 19 June 2013).

Valéry, Paul (1960), *Oeuvres, vol. II*, Paris: Pléiade.

Chapter 2
Derrida's Europe: 'Greek, Christian and Beyond'

Simon Glendinning

Greece

How, if at all, should we conceive the cultural identity of the cultural region that we call 'Europe'? An observation that is frequently made about Europe's cultural identity is that it is the bearer of more than one heritage: *from the start everything European is hybrid*. This originary 'heritage of more than one heritage' has been variously conceived, but more often than not it has been framed in terms of the idea that, as the Lithuanian-born naturalised French philosopher and Talmudic scholar Emmanuel Levinas puts it, 'Europe is the Bible and the Greeks' (Levinas 2001: 182). In the 1860s the British poet Matthew Arnold, thinker of the corrosion of European faith, made essentially the same basic point: 'Hebraism and Hellenism – between these two points of influence moves our world' (Arnold 1869: 143). In the 1960s the Algerian-born naturalised French philosopher Jacques Derrida cited Arnold's formulation as the epigraph of his early essay on Levinas, 'Violence and Metaphysics', in which Levinas's distinctively un-Greek 'work of art' *Totality and Infinity* – a text which Derrida said proceeded not through descriptive elucidations or deductive arguments but formulaic repetitions that returned with 'the infinite insistence of waves on a beach' (Derrida 1978: 103) – was juxtaposed with the classically treatise-like texts of two giant 'Greeks', Edmund Husserl and Martin Heidegger (Derrida 1978: 103).

Derrida's citation of Arnold gives us to understand that the interplay of these influences is not just one lively 'culture kampf' in our world among others but is originary for our world. In alternating currents – the Bible and the Greeks, Hebraism and Hellenism, Athens and Jerusalem, Philosophy and the Church, the love of wisdom and the wisdom of love – these two great heritages are always at work, 'always already' struggling in and thereby opening up the 'there' of everything European, as the elemental forces at the heart of every configuration of Europe's cultural identity or, let's say, of Europe's spirit. Arnold continues: 'At one time it feels more powerfully the attraction of one of them, at another time of the other; and it ought to be, though it never is, evenly and happily balanced between them' (Arnold 1869: 143).

In his formidable study of Europe as 'a philosophical concept', Rodolphe Gasché occupies this space in a relentlessly 'Greek' mode. Through a scholarly commentary on selected works by (in turn) Husserl, Heidegger, Patočka and Derrida, Gasché explores and defends various ways of construing a distinctively Greek beginning to Europe's (supposedly) distinctive cultural identity. The last part of the book then turns to Derrida, who had, of course, himself taken up Husserl, Heidegger and Patočka in the context of his own brief and difficult writings on Europe, most directly in *The Other Heading* and *The Gift of Death*. And yet Gasché's reading of Derrida seems strangely unprepared for the resistance Derrida's thought offers to a particularly philosophical tendency in the texts it takes up. For Gasché it is always to Greek thought and a Greek origin that, finally, 'Europe owes its distinctness' (Gasché 2009: 265). But, when all is said and done, I am not convinced that the insistence on Europe's Greek origin that one finds in Husserl, Heidegger and Patočka is, even 'in a certain way', maintained by Derrida. Indeed, I think Derrida is closer to Arnold on this theme than he is to these great Greek philosophers – although without Arnold's conviction that 'an even and happy balance' between Athens and Jerusalem 'ought to be' possible. That, as Arnold puts it, 'it never is' is something I think Derrida conceives as a 'wound' to be endured – and perhaps, in its endlessness, also enjoyed or affirmed.

Gasché does, in fact, get very close to this thought of an internal or constitutive Graeco-Biblical wound in Europe's identity, although he always resists it in final favour of Greece. In the course of a discussion of the genealogy of 'Europe-responsibility', he rightly highlights that Derrida conceives European responsibility as inseparable from the duty 'to take responsibility for that heritage of discourse on what Europe is' (Gasché 2009: 265). The question is, however, whether taking responsibility here requires that one simply follow the philosophical (and especially phenomenological) tradition of thinking Europe's heritage as having a fundamentally Greek 'beginning' (Gasché 2009: 277). On this, as I say, Gasché is not for turning. Indeed, while he notes that Derrida emphasises a certain Biblical and especially 'Christian' input as 'also part' of the story, and more or less underlines that 'Derrida stresses the need to remain faithful to *both* aspects of European memory'

(Gasché 2009: 282, my emphasis), his viewpoint remains stubbornly Greek.

As I hope to show in this chapter, this has implications for one's sense of what might be possible in undertaking a European duty to take responsibility for Europe. For while the Greek ideal entails a demand for 'full thematisation' of one's theme (Gasché 2009: 282), its Christian alternative will claim that every effort at thematisation *a priori* fails to achieve a cognitive finality. Here the 'Platonic and Christian' heritages cannot be brought into a final form of ideally adequate balance as Arnold had hoped for, but are defined as always entailing an endless aporia: 'it requires', as Gasché himself acknowledges at one point, 'that both traditions be simultaneously honoured without mitigation of the radicality of their demands' (Gasché 2009: 284). It is an aporetics of responsibility for Europe without end – and, I would suggest, without a certain beginning either.

Gasché's appreciation of the duty to honour 'both traditions' is, in my view, inseparable from Derrida's thinking on European cultural identity, which is also a duty to conceive that identity as not only Greek but also, and more paradoxically, as not only Graeco-Christian. Honouring 'both traditions' demands that one's thinking of Europe be, as Gasché rightly puts it, 'hospitable to other historically and culturally decisive intra-European differences (such as Judaism and Islam, not in the abstract, however, but with all their shades and forms)' (Gasché 2009: 285).

Gasché praises Derrida for a 'distinguished accomplishment' that consists in both acknowledging and complicating 'the continuity between Greece and Europe' (Gasché 2009: 292). Nevertheless, Gasché remains wedded to Greece, and he goes so far as to claim, with Friedrich Nietzsche, that since the Greek beginning was precisely the one that 'allowed alterity to circulate within the logos', the European heritage, in all its later growing diversity, also grows 'more Greek by the day' (Gasché 2009: 298). In other words, for Gasché it is because Europe is primordially Greek that it can become empirically more than Greek, and hence remain structurally more than ever Greek. It can become all of this for Gasché because the more Greek it has been 'from the beginning' the more 'more than Greek' it can subsequently become.

One can always detect traces of precedents in apparently unprecedented events. However, I want to take the (more than merely) Graeco-Christian hybridity of Europe as more than a structure of possibility that emerges from an original Greek source. Following Derrida (himself invoking Nietzsche) I think it will always be 'more prudent' to suppose, when thinking the 'place' called Europe, that what is at issue is 'Greek,

Christian and beyond' (Derrida 1997b: 103). However, the logic Gasché ascribes to the Greek source still holds: the 'beyond' here does not only indicate an empirical non-exhaustiveness of the Graeco-Christian heritage in the formation of European culture (to include 'Judaism and Islam, at the very least', says Derrida too), but also an openness within the (let's say) *predominantly* Graeco-Christian body of Europe to a beyond which is not only its own (sense of) beyond: a tradition of more than one tradition that 'tends of itself to break with itself' (Derrida 1997b: 103), and hence remains faithful to itself in that very movement. I will return to this openness to a beyond that is beyond the horizon of any anticipated beyond later in this chapter.

Poco

Gasché has always wanted to champion an approach that would be a model of, as he puts it, '"serious", that is, philosophical discussion' (Gasché 1988: 1). However, scholarly though it is, sober though it is, it would be a mistake to think that it was passionless or disinterested. Gasché's 'serious' discussion takes its bearings from an intensely critical perception of what passes for scholarship and theoretical judgement in the vicinity of his chosen topos. In his early work it was certain 'literary critics' who felt the full force of his rebuke. As he got underway his writing became suddenly and explosively charged with disdain and contempt. The gloves came off, and Gasché launched against the 'feeble' work of those he regarded as both naïve and simplistic (Gasché 1988: 1).

And so it is too with his 'study of the evolution of the notion of "Europe" in phenomenological thought' (Gasché 2009: 5). What he calls the 'astute' reader, 'the philosophically, and especially the phenomenologically, schooled reader', will understand that such a study is irreducibly concerned with philosophy itself, and with some of its most central issues: 'universality, rationality, apodicticity, responsibility and world' (Gasché 2009: 4). However, these issues, bearing as they do on everything 'shaped by the demand to transcend whatever is particular', connect equally irreducibly with what Gasché perceives as the utterly inadequate work on Europe that stands in 'opposition' to his own inquiry: work that can only conceive these 'values' ('universality, rationality, apodicticity, responsibility and world') as 'Eurocentric', and which always insists that 'European rationalism', far from transcending its situation, 'is situated, and hence relative . . . and particular' (Gasché 2009: 8). Here again, the impetus for Gasché's discussions seems to be a sense of the profound failure of a currently dominant discourse to do justice to the complexity of issues, in this case concerning 'the thought of Europe' (Gasché 2009: 9). The academic reflex of our time on this theme, with its lazy historicism (it's all a matter of context) and pan-politicism (philosophy is disguised ideology), calls for a counter-discourse that is philosophically and especially phenomenologically informed. Europe is not to be construed simply in terms of 'the continent and its history', not simply, then as 'a geographical and political entity' (Gasché 2009: 16). On the contrary, for Gasché it is absolutely crucial that we acknowledge, in a rigorous engagement with what we understand by 'Europe', 'something else as well'. And then, perhaps surprisingly, he immediately admits: 'One does not exactly know what this is' (Gasché 2009: 16).

I will return to this quasi-anonymous confession of 'non-knowing' towards the end of this chapter, where it will join up with considerations concerning the 'beyond'. At this point, however, I want simply to note that Gasché's wanting to construe the question of Europe as calling for a distinctively philosophical and especially phenomenological study could, perhaps, have retained a studied indifference to what it understands as its 'opposition'. And, in fact, for the most part that is exactly what Gasché does. However, as I have just indicated, the horizon of his inquiries also includes that opposition and a desire to confront it. Indeed, at the very moment where his text declares the necessity to restate the question of what is understood by 'Europe', Gasché identifies a stubbornly dogmatic discourse that stands squarely in the way of such inquiry. This is one of the most extraordinary moments in his extraordinary book:

> Undoubtedly, there are many who confidently pretend to know exactly what Europe has stood for, and continues to stand for – namely a hegemonic phantasm and moribund worldview. By depicting Europe and the West as a homogeneous power of domination over the rest of the world, postcolonial criticism of European imperialism, and its construction of non-European cultures, knows perfectly what Europe is. Indeed it knows it so well that it indulges in the same lack of differentiation of which it accuses the West in its relation to its others. It thus turns Europe into the blind spot of its own discourse. (Gasché 2009: 16)

There is no evidence in his book that Gasché has attended closely to everything that goes on in 'postcolonial criticism' today; no more, indeed, than he did with regard to 'literary criticism' in the 1980s. So the charge of presenting as homogeneous something rather differentiated and complex might be turned against him. However, just as his earlier critique of literary criticism hit a nerve, so his rounding on postcolonial criticism today seems to me a timely if somewhat hazardous intervention.

Gasché does not labour the issue. The postcolonial certainty regarding Europe's identity is not returned to until the closing pages of the book, where again it is identified in a context of an understanding of Europe that is limited to an assessment of the 'factual power' of a certain geographical entity, 'a particular part of the world' (Gasché 2009: 341). On that understanding, Europe's identity has shifted from one of colonial arrogance – marked by an idea of 'universality' which embellished its 'historical pretensions with respect to the non-European world' – to becoming, rather rapidly, a 'so-called postcolonial' provincialised backwater. From first to last Gasché thinks that this kind of reductively 'factual' conception of Europe's identity will not do, and that a philosophical investigation of the concept, indeed an investigation of Europe as a philosophical concept, is needed too. On the other hand, however, one may well be disappointed to find that his work retains a stubborn (if frank) 'lack of clarity regarding the relation of the philosophical concept of Europe to Europe as a particular part of the world' (Gasché 2009: 341). Indeed, I cannot help think that the 'Greek' and hence fundamentally philosophical counter-understanding of Europe that Gasché winds up with is far less interesting than the enigmatic gesture of not-knowing that he begins with. Against postcolonial orthodoxies, Gasché insists, '"Europe" is not understood as a geographical entity but, in Husserl's words, as a spiritual figure, in short as a philosophical concept' (Gasché 2009: 341). OK, yes, but unless a route is found by which to engage this philosophical counter-understanding with discussions (everywhere!) about Europe as a particular part of the world, one can only wonder what it is all for.

It is not as if Gasché is content to see Husserl's words (or anyone else's) deliver final clarity on the question of Europe's identity. But what seems to slip away from the scene of Gasché's renditions of philosophical reflections on Europe is something the original gesture of not-knowing seemed to hold impressively, if quietly, in view: their bearing on questions of clarity itself, on what it means for our understanding to 'lack clarity', and on the sources of ongoing inadequacy in the philosophical understandings we possess – and which we possess regarding, precisely, ourselves and the 'we' that 'we ourselves' are.

And I couldn't agree more with Gasché that these rather conventional questions about philosophical questions are not independent of questions about Europe's identity. But it is dispiriting to find, at the far end, that there is still 'a lack of clarity regarding the relation of the philosophical concept of Europe to Europe as a particular part of the world'. What is the point of it all if, with regard to the conception of Europe found in philosophy and especially phenomenology, 'it is hard to see what such a conception might have to do with Europe' (Gasché 2009: 340), with Europe TODAY?

In what follows, I want to suggest that the Levinasian schema 'Europe is the Bible and the Greeks' (I am using the Kantian term 'schema' deliberately, to invoke the idea of something that will mediate between the conceptual and the empirical) can assist the effort to make steps in the philosophy of Europe towards, as I think we can put it, *Europe today*. However, before I can plot any of those steps, I think it will be helpful first to get a sharper sense of how the Levinasian schema also opens a reading of philosophical texts that can otherwise seem hardly or barely written in the name of Europe at all, still less Europe today. Consider, for example, the opening chapter of *Being and Time*, where Heidegger broaches a historical interpretation of the way 'we ... in our time' have become disoriented: 'What stands in the way of the basic question of our Being (or leads it off the track) is', he suggests, 'an orientation thoroughly coloured by the anthropology of the ancient [Greek] world [the conception of man as the *zoon logon echon* (animal rationale)] and Christianity [the conception of man as made in God's image]' (Heidegger 1962: 48).[1] Or again, consider Derrida's claim in *Of Grammatology* that there are systematic and irreducible links between, on the one hand, the conception of the sign, through which, still today, 'we' generally obtain our understanding of writing, and, on the other hand, 'the epoch of Christian creationism and infinitism when these appropriate the resources of Greek conceptuality' (Derrida 1976: 13). What is at issue here is not simply the history of a specific region of the globe, but the emergence of what Heidegger would call the clearing or lighting (*Lichtung*) of the 'there' (*da*) of a determinate historical *Dasein*: the opening and holding sway of a world marked by a distinctive form of understanding, imagination and feeling – a distinctive localisation of the *cogito*. To put this in terms of the Levinasian schema, Europe is the *phenomenological event*, still not over, of the Graeco-Christian understanding of the world and of the significance of our lives – a heritage of more than one heritage that Heidegger, who wanted to rethink that heritage in a properly radical way, called 'humanistic'. With this heritage above all we are homing in on the basic structural articulations of the clearing, the 'there', the 'somewhere where I am' of European *Dasein*. It is in this dimension, I believe, that we might achieve the *thought of place*, which can hold together the 'philosophical' and 'geopolitical' senses of Europe's identity.

Valéry

The task, then, is to provide some kind of reading of the schematic traces of this old cultivated place. The Husserlian stress on Europe that Gasché stresses in turn, the conception of Europe as 'a configuration of spirit', certainly belongs to such an enterprise. But, as we know especially from Derrida's *Of Spirit*, coming to terms with the attempt to come to terms with ourselves in this way is also something more and other than merely another Husserlian 'infinite task'.

Gasché's slightly heavy-handed shoe-horning of Derrida into the dominant phenomenological understanding of Europe's origins is something I have already touched on. It also tends to sideline a significant presence in the Derridean reading list on Europe: Paul Valéry. To be fair, Valéry is not altogether passed over. Indeed, towards the end of a sixty-page-long rendition of Heidegger's reflections on Friedrich Hölderlin's hymn-work concerning the Greek beginning of Europe, Gasché remarks on Heidegger picking up a question from Valéry 'of whether Europe is to become merely "a small cape of the Asiatic continent" or to remain the brain of the entire terrestrial body' (Gasché 2009: 205). Following the remark on Heidegger's reference to Valéry is a footnote which reflects on the fact that 'well before Derrida, who, in *The Other Heading*, took up Valéry's famous essay ['The Crisis of Spirit'], Heidegger thus had already had recourse to this text in his elaborations of Europe' (Gasché 2009: 205). Nevertheless, despite the unflagging attention to detail, there is no sign that he (Gasché) is aware that Derrida was aware of Heidegger's having already had recourse to Valéry. Gasché may be excused, however, since it seems only obliquely recognised by Derrida himself, in a footnote to the French edition of *De l'esprit* (Derrida 1987: 145, n.1). And as one of the translators of that book admits, rounding on himself, this oblique acknowledgement does 'not appear at all in the English translation: it should be in footnote 3 to page 93 – the translation was done from page proofs, but even so . . .' (Geoffrey Bennington, pers. comm.).

Valéry apart, one can nevertheless helpfully think of Gasché's book as supplying the crucial background reading to reading Derrida on Europe, and 'a close reading of several pages from *The Other Heading*' concludes the chapter of the book that in turn concludes the work of reading the philosophically and phenomenologically informed approaches to Europe's identity. The Derridean contribution, including *The Other Heading*, is not, I should stress, held back for the final pages. There are three chapters devoted to Derrida's attention to Europe. However, the renditions of Husserl, Heidegger and Patočka in the chapters that precede these are, I think, intended at least in part to pave the way for seeing 'Derrida's distinguished accomplishment' among philosophers *of* Europe in what Gasché thinks is the right light. And in that respect, the fact that Valéry is somewhat eclipsed does carry over into the reading of Derrida that Gasché develops. This comes through particularly sharply in an aspect of the opening of *The Other Heading* that might have proved especially useful to Gasché in his thinking about the relation between the philosophical and geopolitical senses of 'Europe', and the powerful contribution that philosophy can, I think, make to concerns with the latter. For we should recall that the essay entitled 'The Other Heading: Memories, Responses and Responsibilities' – an essay that is included as the major part of the book published under the title *The Other Heading: Reflections on Today's Europe*, a book which is prefaced by a short text entitled, simply, 'Today' and includes a short piece on public opinion entitled 'Call it a Day for Democracy'– is in many ways a sustained attempt to engage with the provocation with which Valéry challenges what Derrida calls 'a familiar interlocutor, one at once close and still unknown', a challenge containing a word written in capital letters, 'heightened like the challenge itself': 'Well! What are you going to do? What are you going to do TODAY?' (Derrida 1992: 11–12).

I will come back to Derrida's response to this provocation at the end of this chapter, but I want to note at this point that Gasché's own citation of a pivotal moment of Derrida's response is not part of his close reading of *The Other Heading*, but, from a considerable distance, belongs to a sort of foreword which obliquely introduces that engagement in terms of 'the prime responsibility of the European' – a responsibility construed in terms of accepting and inheriting 'the discourses and counterdiscourses concerning his own identification' (Gasché 2009: 266). In order to highlight this idea, Gasché cites (or rather partly cites, in curtailed fashion) Derrida's engagement with a movement (let's say of deconstruction) that he supposes 'is taking place now' and which belongs to an 'event' which, as a promise, marks 'the today' of Europe *today*. Gasché's curtailed citation is to a 'double injunction of being faithful to [and here Gasché begins citing and interpolating Derrida] 'an idea of Europe, [to] a difference of Europe, but [to] a Europe that consists precisely in not closing itself off in its own identity' (OH, 26)' (Gasché 2009: 266).[2]

In what follows I want to make an effort to read this passage without cutting it off quite so quickly, and in doing so explain how Valéry's challenge to 'a familiar interlocutor, one at once close and still unknown' provides a point of intersection that gathers Gasché's themes of the quest for clarity, the shortcomings of postcolonial theory and the promise of phenomenological approaches to Europe's identity.

Philosophemes

The Levinasian schema offers a short cut that can seem to make the highway to clarity about the matter that concerns Gasché's winding text much straighter than it is. However, by engaging with the re-elaboration of the question of clarity itself in texts in which something we might call the deconstruction of the schemata of the Graeco-Christian heritage is not just underway but explicitly in view, a different understanding of this apparent short cut can be advanced.

Let's go back to Gasché's quasi-anonymous confession of not knowing exactly what this 'something else' is that is evoked by the name 'Europe' beyond the geopolitical sense (Gasché 2009: 16). This confession is not typical of academic writings, and, I think surprisingly, Gasché does not draw attention to it. This is odd given that, while unusual in most contexts, and partly hidden in parentheses in Gasché's text, this is in fact a very classically philosophical, especially phenomenological, gesture. Coming reflectively to terms with phenomena that are both (in some way) known and (in some other way) 'not exactly known' is precisely the form of clarification that phenomenologically inspired philosophy takes. The starting sense of unclarity, the not-exactly-knowing that is at issue here, is one that contrasts sharply with the state of pretheoretical ignorance that comes before making discoveries or building theories in science. For the phenomenological philosopher it is precisely this contrast that brings into view the contour of a distinctively philosophical question.

Something similar holds, Gasché is perhaps implicitly if rather obliquely claiming, with the question of Europe. Here too there is some sort of generally unthematised, prereflective understanding, something in some way already available that can make it possible to get an investigation underway. Yet there is also a kind of opacity and non-knowing, a non-knowing that calls not for new knowledge – whether this would concern (what we think we understand already as) Europe's accomplishments or its failures, or new information concerning (what we think we understand already as) Europe's 'location, culture and history' (Gasché 2009: 16) – but an effort to find one's way about with a concept or idea concerning which it is not 'immediately clear to what content such a concept or idea is assigned' (Gasché 2009: 17). 'Europe', in short, is, as Gasché puts it, 'something like a philosopheme' (Gasché 2009: 17).

We have already seen that Gasché will present the Derridean

understanding of 'the prime responsibility of the European' as one of coming to terms with and inheriting 'the discourses and counterdiscourses concerning his own identification'. And we have also noted that Derrida's text in *The Other Heading* is shaped by the way it responds to Valéry's provocation and challenge to a 'familiar interlocutor' who is 'at once close and still unknown'. We should at least see the outlines here of a work of reading that sees the task of reading the 'old discourse about Europe', an old discourse which, Derrida states, is always 'a traditional discourse of modernity' (Derrida 1992: 28), as an effort consistently to treat the question of Europe philosophically (and especially phenomenologically), and hence as a challenge to get clear about oneself as being the familiar addressee of Valéry's apostrophe.

To achieve this, or in one's own way to come to terms with the challenge, would be to have provided, today, a thought of Europe that would be irreducible to a merely geographical or political entity, irreducible then to the kind of understanding of Europe that would launch postcolonial theory. However, and despite the 400-plus dense and difficult pages he devotes to it, it is not clear that Gasché delivers any kind of serious blow to postcolonial thinking: as I have stressed, the closing chapter of the book, the 'Epilogue', highlights the 'lack of clarity regarding the relation of the philosophical concept of Europe to Europe as a particular part of the world'. Why should we not think, as many postcolonial thinkers could well be inclined to think, that philosophical ruminations about 'universality', 'responsibility' and 'world' are nothing but an ideological cloak intended to justify factual Europe's disgraceful global colonial ambitions?

Of course, the idea that European responsibility might be compatible with the violent colonisation and conquest of supposedly 'inferior' peoples is not a remotely credible position today. On the other hand, the conception of 'Man' that Heidegger identifies as at the problematic heart of *our* inadequate self-understanding, the understanding of ourselves that belongs to *us* qua *Dasein* – the being that is, we can now sense, given the sources of *Dasein*'s self-understanding, nothing other than European Man – the conception that belongs then to a fundamentally humanist heritage, never provided an ideological cloak for that kind of racist colonial project anyway. On the contrary, classic humanism was universally demanding precisely because it was conceived as universally applicable: human beings, from whatever cultural group and from whatever region of the globe, share a common humanity, and as such share a common destiny: namely, to become truly human. 'Eschatology and teleology – that is man' (Derrida 1992: 14).

The politics of this humanism is massively Europe centred, to be sure, since political developments in geographical Europe, 'in our continent', are conceived as likely to give the law 'for all other continents', as Immanuel Kant famously put it (Kant 1991: 52).[3] But this idea of Europe taking a position at the head of the heading for Man is profoundly cosmopolitan in its intention, not disgracefully racist. It is heartening to see Gasché willing to stick his neck out on occasion in order to head off haranguing charges that this Europe-centred tradition is always making demands on non-Europeans and never Europeans themselves:

> Undoubtedly, the demand to transcend all customary beliefs and the exigency of radical self-criticism that goes along with the concept of universality is experienced as a foreign imposition on all particular opinions and entrenched positions that (whatever the particular reasons may be) consider themselves beyond the necessity to explain themselves to others. The demands inscribed in the idea of universality are exacting demands, but they are not demands that would be limited to non-Europeans. (Gasché 2009: 340)

Quite so. And, of course, the discourse of European humanism is not exempted from this demand either. The river-bed of the Graeco-Christian heritage was for a long time stubbornly sedimented with respect to an idea of history as the 'history of Man', almost invariably narrated as a teleo-messianic narrative of the movement of 'Man' from an original 'natural' or 'animal' or 'savage' or 'barbarian' condition towards the final achievement of a distinctively 'cultural' or 'human' or 'advanced' or 'civilised' condition. This kind of grand narrative – a discourse of the history of the world that is at once a discourse of Europe's modernity – is precisely the idea of a transition for 'Man' with respect to which Europe has always placed itself at (and as) the head. However, this traditional discourse is no longer in good shape. Indeed, the classic cosmopolitan desire that ran through it – a desire expressed, profoundly problematically, in terms of a universalisable culture of European civilisation – has been slowly replacing itself by an increasingly democratic cosmopolitan desire. Through processes visible in what is often identified as the 'social modernisation' that Jürgen Habermas takes to have gone 'hand in hand' with European secularisation (Habermas 2006: 2), the cosmopolitan idea of the dignity of every other is both transformed and retained in the principle that *each and every one counts one*. In other words, powerful resources for a political alternative to the forms of racist nationalism that postcolonial theory has tended to identify with Europe as such *also* have their origin in the European, that is to say Graeco-Christian or onto-theological, philosophical tradition. As Derrida noted in a lecture at the University of Sussex in 1997, the cosmopolitan outlook is one

> which comes to us from, on the one hand, Greek thought with the Stoics, who have a concept of the 'citizen of the world', and also, on the other hand, from St. Paul in the Christian tradition, where we find another call for a citizen of the world as, precisely, a brother. St Paul says that we are all brothers, that is, sons of God. So we are not foreigners, we belong to the world as citizens of the world. (Derrida 1997a)

Of course, it would be unwise to think one knew where racist ideas begin or end or what it means to be free of them, and nothing changes overnight on this terrain. Nevertheless, while the classic cosmopolitan desire for a universalisable culture of European civilisation, a desire based on a humanist construal of human differences, was undoubtedly and inherently vulnerable to the worst forms of racial naturalisation, it also freed the space for a movement of egalitarian, democratic cosmopolitan desire to make its way, and hence also for a new 'European' hope: the hope for what one might call a 'universalisable culture of singularities'.[4]

Some might think that Europe, more than anywhere, ought not to try to advance itself as promoting a universalisable culture or hope of anything. However, it is not at all obvious that such a link to a proposed European example can or should be altogether avoided. For example, it has been argued by Louisa Passerini that a new European subjectivity would be acceptable only if it were to abandon 'the illusions of grandeur and hegemonic expectations of the old subject'. On this view, Europe should forgo every gesture of universalisability and learn to live 'within its own limits' and 'to accept its own particularity', 'for example' as 'a cultural region' among others (Passerini 2006: 107). Fine, but even this attempt to get Europe to draw in its horns clearly fails to escape the universalist logic internal to any thought of the example. Not only would such horn-drawing be regarded (presumably) as universally fitting – there is surely no call here for some other 'cultural region' to take up the position of 'the old subject' of Europe and to cultivate hegemonic expectations in Europe's stead – but the very question of what a 'cultural region' is seems utterly inseparable from the European example. Europe as a cultural region among others? Oh yes! A *cultural* region – no doubt about it! *Very* cultural in fact (think of all those *great* works of literature, art and music, theatre, architecture, cuisine, sport, and so on that we call 'European'). Europe, a cultural region? Yes, yes! *Par excellence*, yes! Indeed, isn't the opposition between nature and culture itself one of the basic features of the old European discourse of the (beginning and thence the) 'end of Man'?

As Gasché puts it, those who are happy simply to denounce as 'Eurocentric' certain 'ideas (such as universality, apodicticity, self-responsibility, and so forth)' (Gasché 2009: 8), those who understand Europe primarily as a geographical and political entity or cultural region and who would set themselves in 'opposition' to investigations of Europe as 'something like a philosopheme', are 'defeated' by the fact that their own opposition to Eurocentrism 'is shaped not only by the fundamental demand to transcend whatever is particular but also that which still tinges this idea itself with particularity' (Gasché 2009: 8). In short, the thought of Europe as a regional culture is still the thought of a potential European example. One still advances towards the other when one undertakes to close in upon oneself in an exemplary way.

Beyond

The Levinasian schema may help to fill out somewhat the sense of Europe as having a philosophical and not merely geopolitical significance. However, there is at least one respect in which it threatens to obscure rather than clarify the sense of Europe as a 'philosopheme'. This is related to something that Gasché brings out particularly effectively in the part of his book devoted to the critique developed by Jan Patočka of the cognitivism fundamental to traditional Platonic and orthodox Christian conceptions of value, and hence of our understanding of the world and the significance of our lives: the Platonic/Christian affirmation that a proper grasp of this significance is ultimately, decisively, a matter of our having adjusted our beliefs to how things are.

To call that cognitivism into question, as Patočka does and, as Gasché convincingly suggests, Derrida does too, does not condemn them to thinking that facts about Europe's history – and the role played there by the old discourse about Europe itself – are fictions. They may even be in certain respects objective (in that interestingly complex historical sense of 'objective'). But what they will not back down from is the denial that these facts are decisive. To borrow from David Wiggins's discussion of 'cognitive underdetermination' in judgements of value:

> Such [facts] may be important to us. But they depend for their significance upon a framework that is a free construct, not upon something fashioned in a manner that is answerable to how anything really is . . . [It] is not something that we (as we say) found or discovered. (Wiggins 1998: 124)

So it will always be questionable to treat Europe as the object of a properly and exclusively theoretical rationality. This object is not outside us, 'we Europeans' of today. As those who inhabit the heritage that has brought Europe into being, it is inside, internal to the very 'who' that we are, 'at once close and still unknown'.

And, today, I believe, we, we Europeans, are learning to interpret matters differently than we did yesterday. The metaphysics of European humanism, the anthropology of the rational and theomorphic creature, is not to be regarded as a discovery but as an inventive elaboration – one that is, as Wiggins puts it (problematically but tolerably), 'gradual, unconscious and communal' (Wiggins 1998: 124) – that belongs to the founding mythography of the globalising adventure of European Man, the civilisation that will have wrought itself in terms of the transition of Man from *Homo barbarus* to *Homo humanus* by way of cultivating the *humanitas* of *Homo*. This distinction between civilisation and barbarism has, of course, a history, indeed an objective history. But it is not just a distinction *within* history – it has itself been world-forming, informing the lives of those who have celebrated the golden thread of their heritage and, of course, the lives of those who, in the name of that monogenealogy, lay outside and did not measure up to what the Europeans of the nineteenth century called 'the standard of civilisation'.

It is from this point of view that the Levinasian schema may be dangerous. It belongs to a sending of Europe that is not only narrow and exclusive but still too, as it were, traditionally European. Yet, as I have suggested, perhaps even this conception of a European tradition of more than one tradition can belong to a cultivation of place that is promising, exemplary perhaps, in its capacity for self-interruption. Thus, to go back to the Derridean formulation of the 'beyond', we should recall that his supplement to the Levinasian schema rounds it out in a way that precisely refuses a final turn of the delimiting screw:

> One should more prudently say 'Greek, Christian and beyond', to designate those places towards which we are still timorously advancing: Judaism and Islam, [to be included] at the very least . . . However, above all, and starting from and still in Nietzsche's wake, [to designate] the entire passage beyond whose movement bears his name. That is to say, everywhere where a tradition thus tends of itself to break with itself (Derrida 1997b: 103).

This 'passage beyond' is inside Europe's identity: it does not indicate a break from it, nor does it suggest that what has been adduced so far as inside this identity (the Greek, the Christian) is a preliminary gesture that only needs an 'and so on' tagged onto the end of an otherwise only partially completed list, to be completed later when all the facts are in (although Derrida quite rightly prefers a more judicious acknowledgement of factual influences). Rather, it indicates a kind of fundamental or irreducible readiness to take a risk with itself, an openness for the change in heading, for the displacement of itself beyond itself – but, as I have stressed, remaining faithful to itself in that movement. For this reason, the 'passage beyond' is never a movement that simply rejects or attempts to destroy Europe's heritage or wants to move on to something completely different. It is a movement which, in the name of Europe, for example in the name of 'we good Europeans', aims to propel it in a new direction out of (i.e. both 'from' and 'beyond') its own sources: not to destroy the heritage but to give it a future.

This, finally, may be what lodges a dimension of not-knowing into every understanding of 'the idea of Europe'; it is what makes Europe something like a philosopheme. The apparent lack of a 'completely thematisable identity' is thus not a shortcoming to be 'overcome' by a more rigorous or powerful analysis.[5] On the contrary, it helps us see that with this philosopheme a certain 'beyond' of every thematisable understanding of Europe's identity is also what we need to save: that 'beyond' belongs *inside* its present identity, and beyond-knowledge opens the very space of responsibility.

Is Europe a special case in this regard? Perhaps the example of Europe is not just one example among others. Geoffrey Bennington's reflection on the phenomenologically foregrounded example of time seems to invite countless substitutions. And yet the example of Europe seems especially fitting. Here, exemplarily, the sort of not-knowing that we saw Gasché affirming against postcolonial certainties, far from being a preliminary condition that might be transformed into one of full clarity, should perhaps be read quite differently:

> less as a preliminary gesture, recognising a difficulty that philosophy will then confront and resolve (so that the natural *telos* of any philosophical explanation of time [for example, or of Europe, for example] is to overcome that not-knowing and replace it with clear and explicit knowledge), and more as a positive or affirmative claim: perhaps time [for example, or Europe, for example] is such that my knowledge of it can only *ever* be of the order of non-knowledge, or a 'knowledge' that fades or disappears when questioned or called upon to present itself in the form of a theory or a thesis. (Bennington 2004: 6–7)

The point here is not simply that future experiences or discoveries might lead us to revise any made-up mind we have hitherto achieved. Rather (and to paraphrase Bennington once more), even the very best, most attentive, rigorous and painstaking thought of Europe will not, even in principle, lead us to 'triumphant conceptual clarity'. It will, rather, 'produce a complexity in thought that, *beyond* what understanding we can (and should) nevertheless aspire to, *calls for something*' (Bennington 2004: 5; emphasis added). Calls for what?[6] Nothing one says here will be immune to the very limitation it is trying to come to terms with. However, what seems central is that finding oneself (necessarily) unequal to the task of achieving a yearned-for complete conceptual clarity (knowing *what Europe is*, for example) tends only to accentuate rather than diminish a sense of one's responsibility, *now*, to respond to that task.[7]

'What are you going to do TODAY?' Valéry asks his familiar but unknown interlocutor. Taking up the provocation to think well concerning Europe's cultural identity (and even questioning whether 'cultural identity' is, today, still fitting) some fifty years later, Derrida wagers that 'we *today*' want 'a completely new "today" of Europe' (Derrida 1992: 12); a today in which one no longer finds it remotely adequate to respond to Europe today by indulging in either Eurocentric back-slapping and self-congratulation or anti-Eurocentric avowals of guilt and self-accusation.[8] Beyond these 'exhausted programs', Derrida finds, nevertheless, that the traditional conceptuality of 'all European discourse about Europe' (Derrida 1992: 27) does more than offer an unforgettable resource for our own thinking. Instead, and 'right along with' that inherited conceptual resource, right inside that heritage, he finds that an irrecusable responsibility 'imposes itself on us' – a responsibility to 'make ourselves the guardians of an idea of Europe' (Derrida 1992: 29). Not, he emphasises, the guardians of a specific regional culture, one distinctive human community among others, but – and here is the passage that Gasché had cut short in his run-up to reading *The Other Heading* – 'of a difference of Europe that consists precisely in *not* closing itself off in its own identity *and* in advancing itself in an exemplary way toward what it is not' (Derrida 1992: 29). To be this new advancing guardian, to be this new avant-garde for an idea of Europe, is never an exclusively or exhaustively theoretical or thematisable affair. It means 'to take risks, to stick one's neck out . . . [to take] the lead in taking an initiative and sometimes even to go on the offensive' (Derrida 1992: 49). It means getting caught up with Europe, for example.[9]

Notes

1. As Stephen Mulhall notes, the orthodox Christian anthropology also represents 'us' as 'reaching yearningly beyond our creaturely existence' and this desire for transcendence is retained in Heidegger's 'idea of Dasein as transcendent' (Mulhall 2005: 46–7). If we add that the possession of the *logos* remains in view with Heidegger's conception of the constitution of *Dasein*'s 'there' as characterised primordially by 'discourse' (Heidegger 1962: 172) it becomes clear that his 'fundamental ontology' does not so much 'detach' itself from the tradition or reject it as 'radically rethink' it (Mulhall 2005: 47).
2. For information, I think the citation from *The Other Heading* here should be corrected to OH, 29.
3. I say 'give the law' here rather than 'legislate', which is the standard translation of Kant, but the German text states that the developments 'in our continent' make it the one '*der wahrscheinlicher Weise allen anderen derinst Gesetze geben wird*'.
4. This phrase appears in the expression of a hope still worth having in Derrida (1998: 7). I discuss the transition from classic to democratic cosmopolitanism in more detail in Glendinning (2009).
5. It is in this vein that Stanley Cavell seeks from philosophy 'an acknowledgement of human limitation which does not leave us chafed by our own skins' (Cavell 1976: 61). He does not get caught up in issues concerning, for example, the colour of this skin, however.
6. Bennington suggests that what it calls for is 'something of the order of *enactment* or *confession* or *witnessing*' (Bennington 2005: 5). This is an interestingly disparate order and I have attempted to boil it down somewhat in the main text.
7. This is the logic at work, I think, in the transition Wittgenstein makes in (the notoriously obscure) remark in the *Investigations* from the impossibility of giving philosophy peace to nevertheless 'now' demonstrating a method (Wittgenstein 2009: §133).
8. 'Am I taking advantage of the "we" when I begin saying that . . . we *today* no longer want either Eurocentrism or anti-Eurocentrism?' (Derrida 1992: 13, 26).
9. The second half of this essay takes up and develops some themes about philosophy and postcolonial theory that I explore in a short paper in the LSE online working paper series Europe in Question entitled 'Europe, for Example'.

References

Arnold, Matthew (1869), *Culture and Anarchy: An Essay in Political and Social Criticism*, London: Smith, Elder.
Bennington, Geoffrey (2004), 'Reading Time', in *Other Analyses: Reading Philosophy*, Bennington Books, pp. 1–26.
Cavell, Stanley (1976), 'The Availability of Wittgenstein's Later Philosophy', in *Must We Mean What We Say?*, Cambridge: Cambridge University Press, pp. 44–72.
Derrida, Jacques (1976), *Of Grammatology*, Baltimore: Johns Hopkins University Press.
Derrida, Jacques (1978), 'Violence and Metaphysics: An Essay on the Thought of Emmanuel Levinas', in *Writing and Difference*, London: Routledge & Kegan Paul, pp. 79–153.
Derrida, Jacques (1987), *De l'esprit: Heidegger et la question*, Paris: Galilée.

Derrida, Jacques (1992), *The Other Heading: Reflections on Today's Europe*, Bloomington: Indiana University Press.
Derrida, Jacques (1997a), 'Politics and Friendship: A Discussion with Jacques Derrida', University of Sussex, 1 December, http://www.livingphilosophy.org/Derrida-politics-friendship.htm (last accessed 20 June 2013).
Derrida, Jacques [1994] (1997b), *Politics of Friendship*, London: Verso.
Derrida, Jacques (1998), 'Faith and Knowledge: The Two Sources of "Religion" at the Limits of Reason Alone', in Jacques Derrida and Gianni Vattimo (eds), *Religion*, Cambridge: Polity Press, pp. 1–78.
Gasché, Rodolphe (1988), *The Tain of the Mirror: Derrida and the Philosophy of Reflection*, new ed., Cambridge, MA: Harvard University Press.
Gasché, Rodolphe (2009), *Europe, or the Infinite Task: A Study of a Philosophical Concept*, Stanford, CA: Stanford University Press.
Glendinning, Simon (2009), 'Japheth's World: The Rise of Secularism and the Revival of Religion Today', *European Legacy* 14(4), 409–26.
Habermas, Jürgen (2006), 'Religion in the Public Sphere', *European Journal of Philosophy* 14(1), 1–25.
Heidegger, Martin ([1927] 1962), *Being and Time*, Oxford: Blackwell.
Kant, Immanuel (1991), 'Idea of a Universal History with a Cosmopolitan Purpose', in *Political Writings*, 2nd ed., Cambridge: Cambridge University Press, pp. 41–53.
Levinas, Emmanuel (2001), *Is It Righteous to Be?*, Stanford, CA: Stanford University Press.
Mulhall, Stephen (2005), *Philosophical Myths of the Fall*, Princeton, NJ: Princeton University Press.
Passerini, Louisa (2006), *Memory and Utopia: The Primacy of Intersubjectivity*, Sheffield: Equinox.
Wiggins, David (1998), 'Truth, Invention and the Meaning of Life', in *Needs, Values, Truth*, 3rd ed., Oxford: Oxford University Press, pp. 87–138.
Wittgenstein, Ludwig (2009), *Philosophical Investigations*, 4th ed., Chichester: Wiley Blackwell.

Chapter 3
A Roman Europe of Hope: Reading Derrida with Brague

Bora Isyar

> Something unique is afoot in Europe, in what is still called Europe even if we no longer know very well what or who goes by this name. Indeed, to what concept, to what real individual, to what singular entity should this name be assigned today? (Derrida 1992: 5)
>
> Just what is it that we are talking about when we speak of Europe? (Brague 2002: 1)

These questions, posed by Jacques Derrida and Rémi Brague around the same time (1991 and 1992 respectively), lead the two thinkers to problematise what it means to be European, to belong to Europe, and what the name 'Europe' signifies. Avoiding essentialisation of all sorts, both Derrida and Brague aim to disclose what (if any) hope the name and singular entity that is called Europe carries for being political today. This chapter attempts to selectively read these two thinkers together to precipitate what Alan Milchman and Alan Rosenberg have called an *Auseinandersetzung* – a critical encounter that does not aim at an agreement or a synthesis between thinkers but, by working through differences in their thought, aims to engage with that which is being problematised (Milchman and Rosenberg 2003: 8). It is my contention that through this engagement we will be able to articulate the hope that the name Europe carries even (and perhaps especially) when a crisis fundamentally calls into question the very existence of the entity that name refers to. Specifically, I propose that the manner in which Brague defines Europe – as '*Romanity*' – can help us come to terms with Derrida's insistence on imagining a Europe beyond all Eurocentrism. It can, likewise, help us to endure (instead of just giving up on the idea of 'Europe') in the face of a new (but at the same time very old) crisis.

The chapter begins with an analysis of Derrida's interpretation of Europe as a community and identity that is, like all communities and identities, characterised by autoimmunity. I then discuss how the autoimmune character of Europe, by constituting a threat to the very existence of European identity (as a self-same identity) is actually the hope for a different Europe (whose identity is constituted by being always already different from and non-identical to itself), a Europe-to-come. The chapter concludes by analysing Brague's interpretation of Europe as Romanity, and suggests that this interpretation offers us a glimpse into why Derrida, and all who feel 'European among other things' (Derrida 1992: 83), insist on rethinking and reinterpreting Europe as bearing the potential to offer hope when times of crisis, destruction and war seem to negate all hope.

A New Crisis, Old Threats

When Derrida wrote *The Other Heading*, Europe, as a political entity, was undergoing massive transformation, the effects of which could not yet be foreseen. The fall of the Berlin Wall, the collapse of the Soviet Union and the anticipation of the Maastricht Treaty, which would formally establish the European Union, meant for many, including Derrida, the imminent arrival of times that would be characterised by the simultaneous presence of chance and danger (Derrida 1992: 5). Finding himself face to face with a discordance between a very old European identity (established through various acts of physical, symbolic and economic violence) and a 'virgin body' that 'refused itself to anticipation', Derrida asked, in hope and yet also with fear and trembling, what the face of new Europe would look like, where (if anywhere) it would head, and how it would respond to its responsibility (Derrida 1992: 5).

We could argue that the question that Derrida asked two decades ago presents itself to us today, once again in times of great uncertainty, and once again we do not yet know what is to become of Europe – perhaps, put in a different way, what we will make of Europe. The source of our fear and trembling today, the crisis of Europe, is new and yet old. What is novel about this latest crisis are the unprecedented and unbridled growth of financial markets and the dominance of a very particularly defined economic technology of governance, which attempts to make social, political, and cultural domains entirely dependent on itself. The emergence and taken-for-granted validity of technocratic governments (such as in Italy), which undermine the very fundamentals of democratic regimes; the cruel austerity measures that turn a blind eye to the very people who are most desperate (in Ireland, Greece and elsewhere); and the emergence of national hierarchies within Europe, buttressed by stereotypes of 'lazy and corrupt' southern Europeans and 'hard-working and honest' northern Europeans (Böll and Böcking 2011), themselves grounded in 'petty little nationalisms' (Derrida 1992: 38), are all symptoms of the dominance of the aforementioned technology of governance.

However, there is also something very familiar, very old, and very well known that shows its face through the crisis of today: the intensification of nationalist discourses, the rise in xenophobia and racism, and the increasing popularity of far-right political movements (Walker and Taylor 2011). The 'defence leagues' established all around Europe, the daily acts of violence committed against immigrants in Greece, the infamous case of Anders Breivik and the numerous explicitly racist policies implemented by the Hungarian government are but a few variants of an old and yet persistently present danger that Europe seems unable to rid itself of. The question we need to ask, I argue, is how this particular form of violence can and does persist over time. It is in answering this question that Derrida's thought on Europe becomes pertinent.

European Adventures with Identity

For Derrida, the problem of Europe is its lack of openness to the other (the non-European) within and outside the political entity of Europe. This unopen comportment has grounded European colonisation; the dominance of orientalist thinking not only within the arts and sciences, but also within politics; the strict regulation of immigration and the resistance to recognising immigrants as rightly belonging in Europe; and of course, various forms of racism and xenophobia such as anti-Semitism and Islamophobia. It is important to note here that what Derrida demands of Europe, and what he interprets as European responsibility (and in fact, responsibility as such) is not the mere implementation of policies that would be more 'hospitable' to the other. It goes without saying that Derrida, like many other thinkers of Europe, does want an end to the aforementioned European policies and yet, for him, the problem of Europe cannot be adequately addressed if Europe does not first come to terms with the manner in which its 'own' identity, its 'own' culture is constructed.

In *On Cosmopolitanism and Forgiveness*, Derrida argues that in order to be able to comport oneself ethically to the other (to approach the other with an openness that eliminates any possibility of violence against the singularity of the other), one must first come to terms with the omnipresent irruption of the other in one's own identity (Derrida 2001: 17). As Matthew Calarco argues, all identities are marked by their constitutive outside and therefore no culture can point to a pure identity after which the present and the future of the culture will be modelled (Calarco 2000: 53). Therefore, it is only by way of coming to terms with the inability to identify oneself as a self-same being, by non-identifying with oneself, and by being at home with difference to oneself, that we can imagine a relationship with the other that is characterised by the radical openness Derrida demands of European culture. As Derrida writes, 'there is no self-relation, no relation to oneself, no identification with oneself, without culture, but a culture of oneself as a culture of the other, a culture of . . . the difference to oneself' (Derrida 1992: 10).

This inability and unwillingness to say 'we' and to identify oneself (in the manner we traditionally understand) requires what Friedrich Nietzsche called a heroic attitude. It consists of simultaneously facing one's highest suffering (in this case, the inability to self-identify with the safe identities that provide a ground for being someone) and one's highest hope (the ability to truly open up to the other and the other's irruption within the self) (Heidegger 1984: 29; Nietzsche 1974: 219). What I mean by this is the following: if it is impossible for a subject to identify with a self-same identity that is at the same time shared by all members of a community, then we must conclude that any identity that we have invented in order to define ourselves is actually a construction, a tool whose major function is to reveal the very presence of the other within us (be it an individual or a community). The suffering involved comes from the fear of not being able to feel part of a uniform, stable, overarching communal identity. However, and parallel to Derrida's thinking on the coexistence of fear and hope, the same condition (the absence of such self-same identity) constitutes a subject's greatest hope, as it opens the space where the said subject can finally come to terms with his or her own singular being and with the irruptedness of the other within the self, which in turn enables one to comport oneself to the other in a truly ethical (and thus responsible) manner. As such, coming to terms with one's difference to oneself, for Derrida, opens up a space in which one can act responsibly, without evoking alibis in the name of which action is undertaken. In other words, it would be impossible for a subject to assert that the reason behind his or her actions is who he or she already is, his or her *a priori* defined identity. An example might clarify what I mean by this.

As Michel Foucault argues in his genealogy of sexuality, there exists in every modern society a set of rules that regulate death (Foucault 1998: 135–45). These rules legitimise some acts of murder while banning others. To put it very briefly, it is particularly when there is an existential threat to society that murder becomes not only legitimate, but in fact desirable (Foucault 1998: 137). It is, for instance, perfectly normal, and in fact heroic, to engage your enemies during times of war, to kill them, and if need be, to welcome your own death. It is, in this case, in the name of the nation that such acts are justified and constructed as desirable. Those who engage in such acts enact themselves as part of a nation, as they identify with the nation. This construction of a self-same national identity (which despite our differences creates an organic bond between us) creates a 'we' feeling which in turn provides those subjects who identify themselves with the nation with a feeling of safety. Within this logic, 'we' who form a unity are essentially different from the other who poses a threat to us (either by attacking us or, as Žižek (1993) argues, by symbolically threatening our way of life). During that moment of threat, 'we' are justified in committing violent acts against the other to protect 'ourselves', knowing that all of us will sacrifice everything for the protection of what makes us a 'we', the 'we-thing'.

It is this kind of safety that disappears if we think of identity and identification in the manner Derrida theorises them. Realising that there is no 'we' that we can easily identify with, we are enveloped by an existential fear. As Blaise Pascal argued, in the face of such fear, humans predominantly turn to anodyne to ease their pain (Barrett 1990: 110–19). The invention of the 'we' which we are supposed to identify with is one such anodyne. It should not come as a surprise then that Europe, especially in moments of crises (where this existential fear emerges very strongly), invents its own anodyne: a unified culture and an accompanying identity. Derrida's interpretation of Edmund Husserl's 'Europe as a spiritual unity' provides us a very strong example of how European identity and culture is invented in this manner.

The construction of a spiritual unity in Europe grounds this *eidetic* unity in the origin of Europe, almost always understood to lie with Greek philosophy. Derrida attempts to challenge this on two grounds. He shows, first, that at the origins of Europe lies nothing but multiplicity. He argues, second, that origins understood in the Greek sense do not imply a unity, but instead a coexistence with otherness.

For Derrida, if there is to exist a European spirit, there must exist a purity of essence, one that originates uniquely in Europe, and belongs only and exclusively to Europe. Exemplified in Husserl's exclusion of Gypsies from European humanity, such definition of pure spiritual unity not only forecloses all openness to the other (Derrida 1989: 120), but also presumes that unity as such is possible. As Rodolphe Gasché argues, the 'longstanding determination of Europe's identity as spiritual has its roots in the equally venerable assumption that Europe originates in one source alone, whether this source is held to be Greek philosophy or Medieval Christianity' (Gasché 2007: 6). What Derrida highlights, instead, is the differential unity and multiplicity at the origins of Europe (Gasché 2007: 7). In other words, Derrida's aim is not to replace the so-called Greek origin with another origin (Gasché 2007: 6) but to emphasise the effective coexistence of a multitude at the origins of Europe (Birmingham 2008: 115).

Derrida further claims that the only way to address the question of the silenced multitude at the origins of Europe is, in fact, through the language of the Greeks (Derrida 1978: 133). For Derrida what makes philosophy in its Greek form unique is that it inscribes within itself the place of the other (Gasché 2007: 9). What Derrida attempts, therefore, is to investigate the traces of otherness erupting into the Greek being (Derrida 1978: 253). This is crucial, as by way of this thinking Derrida locates alterity at the origins of Europe. What is more, he declares that alterity to be the heritage of Europe. From this heritage, argues Derrida, a new Europe, one that is unnameable and unforeseen, might arise (Derrida 1992: 9). This Europe, 'the new figure of Europe' as Derrida calls it in *Philosophy in a Time of Terror* (2003: 116), is a non-identity constituted by an openness not only to those who are constructed explicitly as non-European, but also to an unforeseeable, unpredictable otherness. It is a non-identity that comes into being by the irruption of the unforeseeable other. As Gasché aptly points out, this figure of Europe 'presupposes neither a prior identity to be overcome, nor a new one to be achieved' (Gasché 2007: 17). Rather, it exists only in so far as it is not crystallised, only in so far as it remains a non-identity. And it is in this non-identical form of existence, where a sovereign identity of Europe cannot be invented, that the hope (and chance) of Europe resides. To understand how the destruction of a self-same identity and a culture of unity generates hope, we need to turn to another concept Derrida worked with: autoimmunity.

Autoimmune Europe

Derrida argues that all identities and communities are haunted by autoimmunity, which 'at once threatens them and allows them to be perpetually rethought and reinscribed' (Naas 2006: 17). For Derrida, no community or identity is exempt from the autoimmune condition; 'the auto-immunitary haunts the community and its system of survival like a hyperbole of its own possibility. Nothing in common, nothing immune, safe and sound, *heilig* and holy, nothing unscathed in the most autonomous living present without a risk of autoimmunity' (Derrida 2002: 82). In other words, autoimmunity is at work everywhere (Derrida 1997: 75–6), destroying the integrity and self-identity of all forms, and as Michael Naas rightly points out, opening them up to their unforeseeable futures (Naas 2006: 18). Autoimmunity as such reveals the powerlessness and instability of all self-identification and exposes the fact that all living organisms are in desperate need of the 'other', the non-life (the technical apparatus, the prosthesis (Naas 2006: 23)), without which life would cease to exist. In the way Derrida talks about autoimmunity, then, it is of course a threat, as it compromises the immune system (the self-same identity). Yet it is at the same time a chance, as without autoimmunity at work our bodies would reject organs, transplants or other apparatuses that could be essential to survival (Naas 2006: 25).

This inherent openness to the other means that the identity or culture in question, Europe, cannot be definitively known as autoimmune forces always lay it open for unforeseeable reinscription and reinterpretation. This openness (to the future and to the other) results in the emergence of a Europe-to-come, not as an absolutely novel entity that had not existed before, but, by virtue of its autoimmune character, always open to rethinking and change. This is why the threat posed by autoimmunity does not cause a chance to emerge, but (along with the compromise and destruction of all self-same identities that follow) itself constitutes that chance. By destroying the forces of identity that sustain self-sameness, autoimmunity opens us to the other; it opens Europe to non-Europe.

This Europe that is always already open to the other, whose arrival cannot be foreseen or known, would not, for Derrida, break entirely with its past. The hope of Europe-to-come is not that it is entirely new, but that it is open to that which is heterogeneous to itself. It is a Europe that heads to the unknown while cherishing some of the values that have caused Derrida to retain the name of Europe (and retain its hopeful character). As such, this would be a Europe that is 'open to that which is not, never was, and never will be Europe' (Derrida 1992: 76); a Europe that would welcome foreigners not to integrate them but to recognise, accept, and celebrate their alterity (Derrida 1992: 77); a Europe that would be ill at ease with all forms of dogmatism (and the sovereign forms of identity that these dogmatisms construct) (Derrida 1992: 77); a Europe that would respect minorities and singularities while affirming the validity of universal opposition against racism, xenophobia and other forms of exclusion (Derrida 1992: 78). For Derrida, Europe bears this potential as despite the violence that marked its history, it also gave birth to values of enlightenment, such as democracy, freedom of thought and expression, critical engagement and liberal education (Naas 2005).

Derrida has insisted in numerous places that this vision of Europe (which builds on the very values of European enlightenment) was not Eurocentric, but was in fact based on a rejection of Eurocentrism. As he wrote in 2004 in 'A Europe of Hope' (for the fiftieth anniversary of *Le Monde Diplomatique*):

> Without Eurocentric illusions or pretensions, without the least European nationalism, indeed without even the abundance of confidence in Europe as it now is, or seems in the process of becoming ... we must fight for what this name represents today, with the memory of the Enlightenment, to be sure, but also with a complete awareness and full admission of the totalitarian, genocidal, and colonialist crimes of the past. We must thus fight for what is irreplaceable within Europe in the world to come, so that it might become more than just a single market or single currency, more than a neo-nationalist conglomerate, more than a new armed force. (Derrida 2004)

Why Europe?

Derrida has asserted in numerous places that he wanted to retain the name of Europe (and its promise) because of the birth and presence of values associated with enlightenment in Europe, including but not limited to democracy, hospitality and responsibility (Redfield 2007: 382). In this section, I offer another possible explanation for insisting on the name of Europe by engaging with Brague's conceptualisation of Europe as 'Romanity'. I argue that such an intervention strengthens the validity of Derrida's insistence on a 'Europe of Hope'.

Brague insists that we need to rethink being European as being Roman (Brague 2002; 1998: 254). Predominantly, studies on European history and civilisation neglect the Romans on the grounds that they invented nothing, and merely transmitted that which was not theirs (Brague 2002: 32). As such, the Roman contribution to European civilisation has not been original and has been nothing other than the transmittance of that which is foreign to itself. But for Brague, not only is this 'mere transmittance' of the foreign not a flaw, it is actually the characteristic that European culture should acclaim as its own.

For Brague, as for Derrida, one of the most troublesome aspects of European identity is the boastful claims about Europe as the place where all of the values that we cherish today were invented. Such a claim essentially distinguishes Europeans (as inventors and creators) from non-Europeans (who have never invented anything) (Brague 2002: 91). Furthermore,

> it is unhealthy to recall one's proper glorious past, to recall a glorious past that is one's own. A reflection of this genre cannot avoid fomenting resentment that will turn alternately toward oneself and toward others, and that will have paralyzing effects. For if what was great was already myself, it will be necessary for me to ask myself why I have fallen in relation to that greatness. To avoid morose soul searching, one will be tempted to find these reasons outside, in the malice of one or another 'other'. The accusation of the exterior permits one to turn away from the internal causes that are, however, the only causes one can treat. Thus one is saved the difficult effort regarding oneself such a treatment would require. (Brague 2002: 137)

In this rather long yet crucial quote, Brague is asserting the need for Europe to redefine itself in such a manner that the other will cease to be a scapegoat for its failures. This is a crucial remark for today, with the increasing dominance of xenophobic discourses accusing 'non-Europeans', 'immigrants' and 'foreigners' of the damage they have ostensibly caused Europe, and with the persistent fear of the 'invasion of the interior by an exterior of supposedly questionable purity' (Brague 2002: 185). Europe needs to rethink its relationship to its other and, for Brague, such rethinking can happen only by accepting the Romanity of Europeanness.

This acceptance of Romanity as the essence of Europeanness helps Brague transcend the opposition between the European and its other, opening the former to the latter. European culture comes to be characterised by a relation of appropriation of that which is perceived as foreign (Brague 2002: 92). In other words, the foreign, the other, becomes central to the very constitution of European identity, always already constituting what it means to be European. The question we face here is: what are the implications of this identification of Romanity with Europeanness?

For Brague, the immediate effect of developing a European consciousness of having sources and origins outside itself is the displacement of its cultural identity (Brague 2002: 133). This displacement – very close to what Derrida called an identity that is always different to itself – leads to the constitution of European identity and European culture as nothing other than eccentric. As an eccentric culture, the culture of Europe and its sources does not belong to Europe, and as such it is always already foreign to Europe itself. As such, every time European culture is enacted, every time European identity is constituted, Europe appropriates that which is not its own, that which is foreign to it. This Roman comportment, I argue, is what Derrida was demanding from Europe – a radical openness to the other at all times. Such a rethinking of what it means to be European results in a radical transformation of the relationship between Europe and its others.

When Europe is constructed as an exemplary entity, a heading to be followed, a culture to be imitated, a civilisation with the most glorious origins, non-Europeans are interpreted as peoples who either want to become European or who reject European culture in the name of their 'own', 'authentic' culture. This line of thinking is what led to various violent European projects, especially colonialism. Brague argues, like Derrida, that if we accept that European identity and culture are not self-same but always already different (or foreign) to themselves, Europe becomes nothing other than a constant movement of self-Europeanisation (Brague 2002: 147). In other words, one *is* not, but can only *become*, European. And as Derrida would put it, the call to become European, in this sense, is for anyone who hears it (Naas 2005). Europe (and accordingly non-Europe) does not precede Europeanisation; in fact, Europe is not the cause but the effect of Europeanisation. It is in this sense that Brague declares to both Europeans and non-Europeans, 'You do not exist!' (Brague 2002: 148–9) Rather, what exists is the work of Europeanisation, by and through which that which is foreign, or that which is deemed to be foreign, is appropriated incessantly.

A Europe to Come?

In his lectures on Friedrich Hölderlin's hymn 'The Ister', Heidegger wrote: 'The appropriation of one's own is only as the *Auseinandersetzung* with the foreign' (Heidegger 1996: 147–8). If by '*Auseinandersetzung*' we understand a relationship, an encounter whereby differences appear and are not reduced to one another, whereby issues are problematised, and whereby dreams of synthesis are replaced by trust in differential existence, we can argue that Heidegger's statement says a lot about the manner in which identity (and particularly European identity) should be thought. European identity, if we follow Heidegger, would then be where the foreign is always already at home and where, if one is to be, one must always already be with the foreign.

This would constitute the Europe of Hope, the Europe-to-come, a Europe whose identity and culture is never crystallised, but always subject to becoming (different to itself). This would be a Europe whose identity is never unitary and homogeneous but always already open to the irruption of the other and the foreign; a Europe which is not constructing itself as a heading to be followed thanks to its supreme origins, but is the other of the heading, relating to the other in a 'relationship no longer governed by a traditional logic of identity' (Calarco 2000: 55); a Europe which is responsible towards its 'own' Roman self; a Europe which is different to itself; a Europe that exists only by way of its openness to the other.

References

Barrett, William [1958] (1990), *Irrational Man: A Study in Existential Philosophy*, New York: Anchor.
Birmingham, Peg (2008), 'A Deceptive God of Dazzling Whiteness', *CR: The New Centennial Review* 8(3), 107–17.
Böll, Steven and David Böcking (2011), 'The myth of a lazy southern Europe: Merkel's clichés debunked by statistics', Spiegel Online International, 19 May, http://www.spiegel.de/international/europe/the-myth-of-a-lazy-southern-europe-merkel-s-cliches-debunked-by-statistics-a-763618.html (last accessed 20 June 2013).
Brague, Rémi (1998), 'Athens, Jerusalem, Mecca: Leo Strauss's "Muslim" Understanding of Greek Philosophy', *Poetics Today* 19(2), 235–59.
Brague, Rémi [1992] (2002), *Eccentric Culture: A Theory of Western Civilization*, South Bend, IN: St. Augustine's Press.
Calarco, Matthew R. (2000), 'Derrida on Identity and Difference: A Radical Democratic Reading of *The Other Heading*', *Critical Horizons* 1(1), 51–69.
Derrida, Jacques (1978), *Writing and Difference*, Chicago: University of Chicago Press.
Derrida, Jacques (1989), *Of Spirit: Heidegger and the Question*, Chicago: University of Chicago Press.
Derrida, Jacques [1991] (1992), *The Other Heading: Reflections on Today's Europe*, Bloomington: Indiana University Press.
Derrida, Jacques [1994] (1997), *Politics of Friendship*, London: Verso.
Derrida, Jacques [1997] (2001), *On Cosmopolitanism and Forgiveness*, London: Routledge.
Derrida, Jacques [1996] (2002), 'Faith and Knowledge: The Two Sources of "Religion" at the Limits of Reason Alone', in *Acts of Religion*, New York: Routledge.
Derrida, Jacques (2003), 'Autoimmunity: Real and Symbolic Suicides', in Giovanna Borradori (ed.), *Philosophy in a Time of Terror: Dialogues with Jürgen Habermas and Jacques Derrida*, Chicago: University of Chicago Press, pp. 85–136.
Derrida, Jacques (2004), 'Une Europe de l'espoir, *Monde Diplomatique*, November.
Foucault, Michel [1976] (1998), *The History of Sexuality, Vol. I: The Will to Knowledge*, London: Penguin.
Gasché, Rodolphe (2007), 'This Little Thing that Is Europe', *CR: The New Centennial Review* 7(2), 1–19.
Heidegger, Martin [1954] (1984), *Nietzsche, Vol. II: The Eternal Recurrence of the Same*, San Francisco: Harper & Row.
Heidegger, Martin (1996), *Hölderlin's Hymn 'The Ister'*, Bloomington: Indiana University Press.
Milchman, Alan and Alan Rosenberg (2003), 'Toward a Foucault/Heidegger *Auseinandersetzung*', in Alan Milchman and Alan Rosenberg (eds), *Foucault and*

Heidegger: Critical Encounters, Minneapolis: University of Minnesota Press, pp. 1–29.

Naas, Michael (2005), 'A Last Call for "Europe"', *Theory & Event* 8(1).

Naas, Michael (2006), '"One Nation ... Indivisible": Jacques Derrida on the Autoimmunity of Democracy and Sovereignty of God', *Research in Phenomenology* 36(1), 15–44.

Nietzsche, Friedrich [1882] (1974), *The Gay Science: With a Prelude in Rhymes and an Appendix of Songs*, New York: Vintage.

Redfield, Marc (2007), 'Derrida, Europe, Today', *South Atlantic Quarterly*, 106(2), 373–92.

Walker, Peter and Matthew Taylor (2011), 'Far right on the rise in Europe, says report', *The Guardian*, 6 November, http://gu.com/p/336z2 (last accessed 20 June 2013).

Žižek, Slavoj (1993), *Tarrying with the Negative: Kant, Hegel, and the Critique of Ideology – Post-contemporary Interventions*, Durham, NC: Duke University Press.

Chapter 4

Other Shores: Insularity, Materiality and the Making (and Unmaking) of 'Europe'

Stuart McLean

Prologue: A Different Today

Today is . . . 1926. A precarious peace ratified seven years previously at Versailles. A newly ascendant United States. A not-yet-rearming Germany. Black Tuesday and the ensuing Great Depression still three years in the future. A distinguished poet and essayist (what used to be called a 'man of letters'), newly elected to the Académie Française, representative of his country on cultural matters to the League of Nations, sits down to reflect upon the state of his native Europe after more than a decade of geopolitical upheaval. Surveying what he sees as the stagnation of contemporary European politics, he asks his readers: 'What are you going to do TODAY? (Valéry 1962c: 228)

Today is . . . 1992. A fallen wall. A dismembered onetime superpower. The End of History and/or the inauguration of a New World Order. Ethnic and free market fundamentalisms. A hundred thousand-plus corpses in waiting in the former Yugoslavia. A Midwestern American university press publishes, in English translation, a short book by an eminent, if sometimes controversial, French philosopher. Originally presented in 1990 in Turin to a colloquium ('European Cultural Identity') of fellow European intellectuals, it was subsequently published (October 1990) in what aspired to be a 'European' newspaper – *Liber* – inserted as a supplement into a number of 'national' European newspapers. The philosopher begins by observing that 'something unique is afoot in Europe' – if, indeed, there remains an entity to which the name 'Europe' can plausibly be applied – and reiterates the question posed by his predecessor: 'What are you going to do TODAY?' (Derrida 1992: 3)

Today is . . . 2012. The aftermath of another global economic collapse. Debt crisis. Threats of secession from the eurozone. A resurgent far right. Bank bailouts. Public spending cuts. Anti-austerity protests on the streets of Lisbon, Madrid, Paris, London, Brussels, Berlin, Rome, Athens . . . A much-criticised Nobel Peace Prize for an enlarged but ever more precarious-seeming European Union. A mid-career anthropologist, a native of a small island off continental Europe's western shore, currently a resident of the United States but still the holder of an EU passport, sits down to write about the philosopher's reflections twenty years after their first publication. Leafing through the pages of *The Other Heading* and scanning his own, recent field notes, he asks himself: 'What are you going to do TODAY?'

From My Notebooks

Leaving behind the settlements of Haroldswick and (further to the northeast) Shaw, the road climbs towards the headland, narrowing as it ascends. To the right is Burrafirth Beach and, further inland, the Loch of Cliff, separated from the incoming sea by a narrow strip of land. On the far side of the inlet is Hermanness National Nature Reserve, the seasonal nesting ground of gannets, puffins, great skuas and red-throated divers. To the right, looking out to sea on a clear day, you can see to the north the lighthouse on the small, rocky island of Muckle Flugga, once the most northerly inhabited outpost of Britain, but ceding that status to Unst itself when the lighthouse was automated in 1995. Further to the north is the still smaller islet of Out Stack (or 'Ooster'), commonly referred to in guidebooks as 'the full stop at the end of Britain'.

As the road gets steeper and narrower you begin to make out the dome and masts and the single-storey concrete huts in the distance and, as you move closer, the wire perimeter fence that surrounds them. A sign to the left, now faded, rusted and weather-beaten, announces:

RRS SAXA VORD

THIS IS A PROHIBITED PLACE WITHIN THE MEANING OF THE OFFICIAL SECRETS ACT – UNAUTHORISED PERSONS ENTERING MAY BE ARRESTED AND PROSECUTED.

Opened in 1957, Saxa Vord Royal Air Force Radar Station (to give it its full name) was an integral part of Britain's Cold War air defence network. Its motto – '*Praemoneo de Peliculis*' ('I forewarn of danger') – encapsulated its function: a cliff top outpost more than 200 metres above the North Sea sending out pulses of radio waves to give advanced warning of hostile incursions into Britain's northerly airspace. Following the fall of the Berlin Wall and the break-up of the Soviet Union, the station continued to operate until 2006, when it was closed with the loss of more than 100 jobs. Today the quarters at the foot of Saxa Vord hill that once housed the military personnel associated with the station are in the process of being converted into tourist accommodation, consisting of a hostel, self-catering holiday homes and a restaurant-bar. The station itself remains fenced off, but the headland is accessible by foot to those willing to brave the winds, grazing livestock from neighbouring farms and the often aggressive gulls who nest there. Adjacent to the approach road stand two further signs. One, dating from the time of the site's operational use and now barely legible, warns of the potential danger of radiation. Below it another, newer sign alerts walkers and motorists that a cattle grid lies ahead.

For almost half a century, the station's role was to mark and guard territory, including not only the terrestrial limits of the United Kingdom, but also their offshore extension into territorial waters and airspace. Today, visitors to Unst are invited to explore this northern extremity of Britain – 'the island above all others' in the words of the Saxa Vord Resort's tourist brochure, which has the following to say about the onetime defensive site: 'Quite simply, on the hill of Saxa Vord you are on the edge of the world – on the *Ultima Thule* of the Ancients' (Saxa Vord 2007–13).

In a sense, this could be anywhere – any randomly chosen fragment of the elusive and contested entity called 'Europe' that forms the subject of Derrida's reflections. But it isn't. It's a particular somewhere with a particular presence and history. Is it then an 'example', a term to which Derrida's text makes repeated reference? Certainly this island outpost of an island outpost, battered by the winds and waves of the North Sea, seems to resist the exemplary status often assigned to Europe's great urban centres, its contenders for the title of 'capital'. If the latter, as Derrida notes, have frequently been invoked as exemplifications not only of a 'European' history and identity but, more expansively, of 'civilisation', 'spirit', 'modernity', the 'West,' then perhaps Unst can be understood as a different kind, exemplary of that which disrupts such a smooth passage from the particular to the purported universal, a somewhere that remains stubbornly and recalcitrantly a somewhere, for all its wider implications in history and geopolitics. Perhaps Unst manifests a certain inescapable non-coincidence of any version of 'Europe' with itself.

Once upon a Time . . .

In a time before Europe, before Europeans (whoever they are) . . . According to the version of the story of the earth narrated by modern geological science, the islands of Shetland and its southerly neighbour, Orkney (my current field site), are the remnants of a mountain chain formed around 400 to 600 million years ago by a collision of continents – the great southern continent of Gondwanaland and the great northern one of Laurasia, both of which came to form part of the 'supercontinent' of Pangaea, the ongoing decomposition of which forms the basis of the current global deposition of continents and which was itself the product of the formation and break-up of a succession of earlier supercontinents, among them Nuna, Rodnia and, most recently, Pannotia (Auton et al. 1996: 4; Nance et al. 1988).

Stresses and fractures in the earth's crust following the collision created depressions that filled with drainage water, forming a giant freshwater lake – Lake Orcadie – that teemed with a variety of life forms whose sediment-trapped remains, geothermally heated and worked upon by anaerobic bacteria living below the lake floor, were transformed over millennia into the oil and gas now so profitably pumped from fields in the North Sea to BP's Sullom Voe terminal on Mainland, the largest of the Shetland islands (McKirdy 2010: 40) As the continents were forced apart by magma welling up from the earth's core – Europe separating from North America and the Atlantic Ocean opening up between them – the mountain ranges were eroded by the sea to form the present-day island chains, a process that continues today and will eventually cause the islands of Orkney and Shetland to disappear beneath the waters from which they first emerged (Auton et al. 1996: 10–15). Eighteen thousand years ago Shetland was entirely covered by ice sheets. More recently (7,900 years ago) it was temporarily submerged by a tsunami, possibly caused by an undersea earthquake off the coast of Norway, as a result of which marine fossils and other debris from the ocean floor continue to be found on cliff tops to a height of 9 metres above the present-day high-water mark.[1] The earliest evidence of a human presence in Shetland dates from 4320–4030 BCE and takes the form of a Mesolithic midden (domestic waste site) on the south coast of Mainland (Melton 2008; Melton and Nicholson 2004). Successive waves of incomers followed, including the builders of the settlement of Jarlshof, close to the southern tip of Mainland, which contains remains dating from 2500 BCE to the seventeenth century CE (Nicholson 1972: 33–5; Turner 1998). Norse settlers (some of whom would later make their way northward and westward to the Faroe Islands and Iceland) first appeared on the islands from the eighth century, becoming the dominant presence in Shetland and Orkney, and leading to the islands' annexation to the kingdom of Norway in 875. The Earldom of Orkney, comprising Orkney and Shetland, was transferred to the Crown of Scotland in 1468 as part of a marriage settlement and became, in turn, part of the British nation state with the Acts of Union of 1707, and of the then European Economic Community when Britain joined in 1973 (Thomson 2008).[2] Today Shetland is home to 22,500 people, variously employed in (among other things) fishing, aquaculture and agriculture, the petroleum industry and tourism (National Records of Scotland 2012).

Mediterranean Spirits and Westward Voyagers

The geographical focus of Derrida's essay, however, is not the islands of the North Atlantic, but the region surrounding the Mediterranean – Europe's 'inland sea.' For Derrida, as for his principal interlocutor, Paul Valéry, the Mediterranean furnishes an indispensable reference point for any reflection upon the question of Europe, past, present or future. Indeed, Valéry, the son of an Italian mother and a Corsican father, is described by Derrida as a 'Mediterranean spirit' (Derrida 1992: 35). If Europe was, for Valéry, 'a kind of cape of the old continent, a western appendix of Asia' (as he described it in his essay of 1919, 'The Crisis of Spirit') the expansionist ambitions of which had been predominantly westward in orientation, it was nonetheless bordered to the south by a 'famous sea' that had been 'wonderfully effective in the development of that European spirit with which we have been concerned' (Valéry 1962a: 311–12, quoted Derrida 1992: 21). Elsewhere he would describe the Mediterranean as 'a veritable machine for making civilization' – an enterprise involving the conjoint mobilisation of 'spirit', 'culture' and 'trade' through multiple and overlapping forms of exchange (Valéry 1962b: 196, quoted Derrida 1992: 64). The same sense of Mediterranean distinctiveness would later be echoed by Fernand Braudel, who, in his magisterial three-volume history of 1949, describes the region as the 'radiant center of the globe' (Braudel 1972, quoted Pagden 2002: 37).

Derrida too identifies himself as a product of the Mediterranean region, albeit its 'other shore', referencing his childhood spent in what was then still French Algiers. He describes himself as an 'old' European who has nonetheless sought to retain something of the 'impetuous youth' of that other shore and who can be classed, therefore, as 'a sort of over-acculturated, over-colonised European hybrid'. The Europe of the early

1990s is also, Derrida suggests, simultaneously old and young –poised on the brink of a new beginning that is also, in the view of some commentators (notably the then President of France, François Mitterrand), a return to itself and its history, a 'reunion', a 'homecoming' (Derrida 1992: 7–8). Derrida noted too that the colloquium that furnished the occasion for the initial delivery of his reflections on Europe took place in Turin, 'a Latin place of the northern Mediterranean' and that the European Union of his own day was 'predominantly Mediterranean' – a claim that, twenty years later, may require some revision following the accession of new EU member states from eastern and central Europe (Derrida 1992: 35, 23).

Recent scholarship has often followed Derrida in portraying the Mediterranean less as the wellspring of a quintessentially European history and identity than as a cultural ecumene – a zone of exchange where 'Europe' has opened itself to influences emanating from outside its self-designated borders. The historian and cultural theorist Iain Chambers has written of the Mediterranean and its environs as a space characterised by fluid interchanges and hybridisations involving a variety of Graeco-Latin, Arab, Jewish and Turkish currents. He writes:

> It is in this arduous combination of communication and difference, of shared encounters and marked distinctions, of resonance and dissonance, that the Mediterranean proposes a multiplicity that simultaneously interrupts and interrogates the facile evaluations of a simple mapping disciplined by the landlocked desires of a narrow-minded progress and a homogeneous modernity. (Chambers 2008: 25)

The Mediterranean, for Chambers, is a 'postcolonial sea' – a site, moreover, where the postcolonial can be encountered not 'out there' in extra-European spaces of alterity, but 'in here' as integral to and constitutive of who 'we' are, what 'Europe' is – a vision that he finds prefigured in the writings of 'a brilliant Jewish Algerian philosopher from the African shore of the Mediterranean' (Chambers 2008: 29, 10). For Chambers, as for Derrida, the Mediterranean stands in relation to Europe less as a unitary scene of origin than as one of plurality and cross-fertilisation, marked by the indelible presence of the various 'others' (Islamic, Jewish, African, Asian) that latter-day visions of European identity have often sought to exclude.

Derrida's writings provide a point of reference too for the Italian sociologist Franco Cassano in his elaboration of a counter-tradition of 'southern thought' defined in opposition to northern European-identified discourses of modernity and emphasising instead exchange, relationality and a multiplicity of viewpoints.[3] Cassano links the Greek 'invention' of philosophy to the physical topography of the Mediterranean, suggesting that there exists a 'structural homology' between the geographical configuration of the region (and of Greece in particular) and the emergence of an intellectual ethos of open-ended questioning and inquiry, founded upon the recognition that truth is always plural, that it can never be definitively and exhaustively defined. Such recognition, according to Cassano, finds its geographical counterpart in the interplay between land and sea, water and solid ground. If the Mediterranean itself is a body of water that has simultaneously conjoined and divided multiple populations, languages and traditions, enabling relationship and contact across distance and difference, so Greece is a land that has always been defined by its relation to the sea:

> Thus, from the beginning Greece exists on the borderland and internalises it, a place of meetings and clashes, where war, commerce, voyage and exploration alternate and overlap to the point of becoming indistinguishable. A land incapable of closing itself off, a society open and of borders, a 'fluid city', doomed to experience and contain within itself relationship and conflict; a great land precisely because it is a minor, coastal land, far away from the solipsism of continents. (Cassano 2012: 17)

The Greek example serves to counter not only the 'solipsism of continents' – seen as issuing in the fetishisms of fatherland, territoriality and exclusive and originary belonging – but also the contrasting valorisation of the sea as a zone of unconstrained freedom and becoming, a view that Cassano sees as underwriting both Europe's imperial expansion and the global diffusion of capitalism, along with the technological developments that have accompanied them. Unwitting support for these, Cassano suggests, is to be found in the writings of thinkers such as Friedrich Nietzsche (with his exhortation to philosophers to 'send your ships into uncharted seas!') and, later, Gilles Deleuze and Félix Guattari, whose invocation of nomadism is read, somewhat perplexingly, as an endorsement of 'people without land-based income' (Cassano 2012: 30–3).[4] In contrast, according to Cassano, 'Mediterranean man instead lives always between land and sea', restraining one through the other (Cassano 2012: 34).

Cassano seeks explicitly to distance the Mediterranean and its cultures from the universalising aspirations seen as emanating from Europe's western seaboard. It is the shores of the Atlantic – an 'ocean' rather than a terrestrially bounded 'sea' – that are understood as the launching ground for Europe's imperial expansion. Indeed, Italy's embrace of capitalism and modernity in the years following the Second World War is understood as a repudiation of its Mediterranean heritage, a trend that Cassano sees being challenged in recent years as Mediterranean Italy rediscovers a sense of its own history and cultural distinctiveness (Cassano 2012: 131–41).[5] Derrida too cites Valéry's claim that Europe 'looks naturally toward the west'. This westward orientation, for Valéry, derived from Europe's status as something less than a continent as geographers are accustomed to define one. Europe was, rather, more akin to a headland, 'a kind of cape of the old continent, a western appendix to Asia' (Valéry 1962a: 311–12, quoted Derrida 1992: 21). If this little promontory or headland (the cape that supplies the French title of Derrida's reflections, *L'Autre cap*) could appear (again in Valéry's words) as 'the elect portion of the terrestrial globe' it was, precisely, as a result of its westward drive towards self-universalisation, initially through the forcible acquisition of overseas territories and, later, through the global diffusion of its institutions, languages and traditions. By this means, Derrida suggests, Europe has been able to affirm itself as 'the avant-garde of geography and history', the manifestation of what is, or will be, the universal essence of humanity. For Derrida, as for Chambers and Cassano, the Mediterranean, in contrast, provides a potential alternative to Europe's frequently violent imposition of itself upon the rest of the globe by offering an image of Europe as open to and rendered non-coincident with itself by its others, by what is not and never will be Europe (Derrida 1992: 76–8).

Both Derrida and Cassano find one of the most emphatic formulations of Europe's westward orientation and directionality in the philosophy of G. W. F. Hegel, for whom the progression of world history was, precisely, a movement from east to west, from the Persian empire, via Greece and Rome, through the Middle Ages, Reformation and French Revolution, and culminating in the Prussian state of his own day (Hegel 1975). Such an assumed trajectory, as the anthropologist Michael Herzfeld has famously noted, has often led to the latter-day disparagement of Mediterranean societies (in particular Greece) as superseded waystations on the road to Europe's global historical self-actualisation (Herzfeld 1987: 1–27). For Hegel too the sea played a crucial role in the westward advance that marked 'Spirit's' coming-to-consciousness of its own freedom. Not only did the sea provide European states with an outlet that their despotically inclined Asiatic counterparts were seen to lack, but the very act of maritime voyaging, of venturing forth on the sea, marked a decisive break with the constraints of 'Nature' and thus an entry into the agentive freedom of 'History,' a freedom that carried with it the assumed right to reshape the non-European world in accordance with Europe's own dominant self-images:

> The European state is truly European only in so far as it has links with the sea. The sea provides that wholly peculiar outlet which Asiatic life lacks, the outlet which enables life to step beyond itself. It is this which has invested European political life with the principle of individual freedom. (Hegel 1975: 196)

For Cassano, the accession to freedom that Hegel associated with setting forth on the sea provides an image rather of the deterritorialising imperatives of capital and modernity as they sought to universalise themselves from their western European origins through a combination of territorial expansion, unrestricted economic growth and an increasing reliance on technology. He finds in the history of the Mediterranean an alternative ethos, one that avoids what he characterises as the 'fundamentalisms' of both sea and land, the latter including the sedentary and terrestrial orientation of such avowedly anti-maritime thinkers as Carl Schmitt and Martin Heidegger, both of whom are cited as examples of the centric, land-based thought of Germany, in contrast to the decentred thought of Greece (Cassano 2012: 28–9).[6] Crucially, in Cassano's description, the Mediterranean is a sea bounded by its adjacent land masses, a space of journeys and exchanges rather than definitive casting off, never to return.

Yet Cassano's formulation of a 'southern' alternative to the intertwined histories of capital, modernity and European expansion risks succumbing to its own version of European exceptionalism, rooted in an appeal to the geographical uniqueness of the Mediterranean region. In the achieved equilibrium between land and sea for which Cassano applauds classical Greece, the sea's role is to disrupt and undermine the uncritical certitudes of an exclusively land-based territoriality, while the land's role is precisely to contain and limit the deterritorialising power of the sea. Elsewhere in his writings, Cassano displays a multifaceted, indeed poetic appreciation of the sea as an ecosystem, a material presence, a source of livelihood and of wonder. In his discussion of Greece, however, the sea risks being reduced to the subordinate term of a binary contrast, the envisioned relationship between land and sea being, ultimately, weighted in favour of the land. The Mediterranean is applauded for being literally (and etymologically) an inland sea, that is, a sea surrounded by land. Indeed, it is precisely this boundedness that distinguishes the Mediterranean as a sea from the uncontained expansiveness of the Atlantic Ocean, on which generations of imperialist and capitalist voyagers have set sail.

But for all its importance as a physical barrier and a means of communication, there is little suggestion that the sea or ocean itself might play a productive rather than a merely dissipative role. In this respect, Cassano comes close to echoing the sentiments attributed to many of the writers he criticises, for example Schmitt, for whom 'the sea is only a principle of eradication: it represents diabolic temptation, the seducer that pushes us toward the fiercest bewilderment and toward the idolatry of technology' (Cassano 2012: 26). Is Cassano's view really so very different, given that the Mediterranean is understood to differ from the Atlantic principally because of its enframing land masses? If, however, we are to consider land and sea not only as metaphors or symbols but as material presences, we are bound to acknowledge that both have played an active role in shaping and transforming the geographical, political and cultural entity known as 'Europe'. Cassano himself cites the observation of the French historian Michel Mollat du Jourdin that Europe has an exceptionally long coastline relative to its total land mass – the ratio of coast to continental area being 4.0 kilometres per thousand square kilometres, compared with 1.7 kilometres in the case of Asia (Mollat du Jourdin 1993: 4). The involuted coastline of Europe (what has sometimes been called its 'fractal' character) is a feature to which many commentators have called attention (e.g. Cunliffe 2008). It is worth remembering, however, that Europe's many bays and inlets, along with its natural harbours and places of shelter, are themselves in large measure a creation of its seas, of their action over millennia in sculpting their adjacent land masses, not only through marine erosion but also through the laying down of sediments that would later become the basis of rock formations, sandbanks and beaches. The sea's role has, therefore, been not merely destructive or dissipative but also productive, helping to establish not only the physical contours of terrestrial Europe but also the conditions and possibilities of human access to maritime environments.

Might then the interplay between land and sea have assumed very different, if no less generative, forms outside the Mediterranean context? One striking contrast to Cassano's portrait of Greece and the Mediterranean is afforded by Europe's Atlantic islands. Here it is the ocean, the open sea, that surrounds the land. The history of human settlement is, therefore, not one of traversing an enclosed (or largely enclosed) sea, but of inter-island oceanic voyaging. Yet this history is one in which the relationship between land and sea has played no less conspicuous a part. Certainly, attempts have been made before to consider the Atlantic as a space of cultural exchange and hybridisation –

notably by Paul Gilroy. Yet Gilroy's explorations of the 'Black Atlantic' are concerned predominantly with specific circuits of cultural exchange linking Europe to west Africa, the Caribbean and North America (Gilroy 1993). In terms of such a vision, the Atlantic's northerly islands are apt to appear as belonging to a bygone historical moment, much as the Mediterranean and its lands appeared to Hegel and many of his northern European successors. Perhaps it's time to take another look.

Places Apart?

Surveying the Europe of the early 1990s, Derrida warns that the rejection of imperialistic and universalising visions of Europe and of the centralising authorities through which they are promulgated must not result in the countervailing embrace of wilful parochialism. European identity, he writes,

> cannot and must not be dispersed into a myriad of provinces, into a multiplicity of self-enclosed idioms or petty little nationalisms, each one jealous and untranslatable. It cannot and must not renounce places of great circulation or heavy traffic, the great avenues and thoroughfares of translation and communication, and thus of mediatization. (Derrida 1992: 39)

Do islands, particularly perhaps those of Europe's westwardly exposed Atlantic seaboard, represent precisely this danger? W. H. Auden, on a sea voyage to Iceland in 1936, in company with his fellow poet Louis MacNeice, wrote that 'islands are places apart where Europe is absent' (Auden and MacNeice 1937: 25) But perhaps islands – all islands – have a more complicated relationship to questions of territoriality, identity and belonging. At first glance, islands seem so obvious: clearly delineated land masses neatly circumscribed by sea – places where territorial boundaries and physical geography ought to coincide in the most straightforward and unambiguous way. It's curious to remind ourselves then that the status of islands has often been anything but unambiguous. Think of territorially divided islands, split between the jurisdictions of different nation states – Ireland, Cyprus, Hispaniola, New Guinea, Borneo, Timor, Usedom, Saint Martin, Isla Grande de Tierra del Fuego – or of the Faroe Islands, a self-governing part of Denmark but not part of the European Union, of which Denmark is a member. Think too of the frequency with which islands have been the subject of competing claims to sovereignty – the Falklands/Malvinas Islands, the Kuril Islands, the conflicts attendant upon the divided sovereignty of Ireland and Cyprus. Nor is it just a matter of definitional and jurisdictional elusiveness. Islands have a habit of appearing and disappearing too. Today they include some of the most recently formed and some of the soonest-to-vanish land masses on the globe. Auden and MacNeice's destination, Iceland, the most geologically recent land mass to be considered part of 'Europe' (at least culturally and linguistically), was formed between sixteen and eighteen million years ago by a series of volcanic eruptions along the rift separating the North American and Eurasian tectonic plates, a rift that continues to widen to the present, pushing the two continents gradually farther apart (Scherman 1976: 129–30). Conversely, the low-lying Pacific island nations of Tuvalu and Kiribati are currently faced with the prospect of becoming uninhabitable as the result of rising sea levels – a similar, although more protracted, fate awaits Britain's northernmost outposts, Orkney and Shetland, the combined result of anthropogenic climate change and ongoing marine erosion (Clark 2011: 107–8). Perhaps islands are not as straightforward as they seem.

More from My Notebooks

Standing on the hill of Saxa Vord, are we in the presence then of one of those western extremities from which 'Europe' has sought to universalise itself, one of the launch sites for its world historical project? Certainly Shetland and its southerly neighbour, Orkney, were crucial waystations in the westward diffusion of Norse settlers to Britain and Ireland, the Faroe Islands, Iceland, Greenland and, more fleetingly, North America. They would later participate in a burgeoning capitalist global economy through their involvement in fishing and whaling, in the trading activities of the Hudson Bay Company and, more recently, the drilling and distribution of North Sea oil (Thomson 2008). During its Cold War days of active service, the Saxa Vord radar station too played a conspicuous geopolitical role as a defensive frontline of the 'West' (which then included only part of Europe) – this time against the Eastern-identified threat of communism.

But was it ever that simple? To stand on the summit of Saxa Vord hill, with the waves crashing below and gulls circling above, is not, in fact, to stand at the edge of either Britain or Europe. Offshore there's Muckle Flugga, with its now automated, unmanned lighthouse and, further out still, Out Stack, 'the full stop at the end of Britain'. Perhaps what Unst reminds us is that neither nation states nor the entity called Europe, elusive yet of global historical consequence, ever come punctually to a stop, a full stop. Indeed, the present-day physical geography of Unst's northwest coast is more akin to an unfinished sentence, trailing off into an ellipsis, a series of dots . . . testifying too to the ongoing and perennially unfinished resculpting of Britain's and Europe's coastline by the action of the sea. Similarly, the efficacy of Saxa Vord as a onetime front line of Britain's air defence was never simply a matter of keeping watch over an already established territory. It was, equally, dependent upon a technologically assisted prosthetic seeing beyond territorial boundaries – radar pulses being sent out across the North Sea to give pre-emptive warning of impending incursions by Soviet aircraft or, in the worst case scenario, missiles. Here, at the once fortified edge of Britain, Europe and the West, physical borders appear to take on a curiously fragmentary and porous character.

Later that night, in the resort bar, I overhear an elderly local resident telling a group of English visitors – in English – that Shetland should rightfully be part of Norway.

Before and after Humankind

If Derrida chose to identify himself as a product (at least in part) of the terrestrially bounded waters of the Mediterranean, it was islands that fascinated his near contemporary Gilles Deleuze. In his early essay 'Desert Islands' (1953), Deleuze identified two kinds of islands: 'continental' ones – broken-off shards of existing land masses – and 'oceanic' ones – the result of the petrification of coral reefs or of magmatic upwellings from beneath the ocean floor, rising, cooling and solidifying to create new formations. Both kinds of island, he claimed, attested to the ongoing, elemental 'strife' between land and sea. As such, they affirmed that the forms of the actual, existing world were not and never would be definitively fixed. Islands, for Deleuze, were pre-eminently a source of creativity, of new beginnings. The creativity exemplified by islands was, however, always a matter of re-creation, of beginning again rather than beginning from scratch. The second creation, the act of re-creation, affirmed creativity itself as an ongoing and endlessly open-ended process, a capacity not to create *ex nihilo*, nor simply to repeat what had gone before, but to repeat and differ (to echo the title of one of Deleuze's later and best-known philosophical works). The beginning anew associated with desert islands usurped the privilege of any single, unique and self-identical origin, appealing instead to a principle of originary difference that remained inassimilable to chronologically marked time:

> In the ideal of beginning anew there is something that precedes the beginning itself, that takes it up to deepen and delay it in the passage of time. The desert island is the material of this something immemorial, this something most profound. (Deleuze 2004: 13–14)

Human engagement with the creativity, the *élan*, associated with islands required, therefore, a studied alignment with material processes and potentialities that were always in excess of human projects and understandings and evocative of a time-span vastly more expansive than that of humans' fleeting presence on earth: 'Islands are either from before or for after humankind' (Deleuze 2004: 9).

It is instructive to juxtapose Deleuze's conjuration of the pre- and posthistorical time of islands with Derrida's claim that to be European in the present (his and ours) is to be simultaneously old and young. The rocks of Unst are old – older than any humanly conceivable vision of Europe, older than humanity itself. Some of them, indeed, are among the oldest rocks on the planet – Lewisian gneisses, formed between 3,000 and 1,500 million years ago and once forming part of the original crust of the continent of Laurentia, of which present-day Scotland was also once a part.[7] The time-span evoked by Unst's rocks is one that encompasses and outstrips the much briefer history of human settlement indexed by the archaeological record and the more recent history in which Saxa Vord played its part. The vistas of prehuman time opened by the geology of Orkney and Shetland suggest too the possibility of a posthuman future in which neither the political landscape of Europe nor its physical contours will be recognisable. Fifty million years from now, for example, Africa will have collided with Europe, the Mediterranean will have disappeared and a mountain range will have been forced up in its place (Press et al. 2001). In 250 million years' time, according to one possible scenario, further continental collisions will produce a single supercontinent circling what remains of the Indian Ocean (Scotese 2012). Even this, though, cannot be regarded as a definitive ending to the earth's story as seismic upheavals and currents within the earth's mantle will continue to generate further shifts and realignments. The strife of land and sea will continue irrespective of any human presence to witness or document it.

The imperative to envision a world from which humanity is radically absent, a world that demands, therefore, to be grasped as existing radically independently of its being given to a knowing, perceiving human subject, has been asserted in a number of recent philosophical writings (e.g. Brassier 2007; Meillassoux 2008). I have chosen here to engage in this detour via the geological past and future of the North Atlantic islands as a reminder that the materiality of the entity known as 'Europe' – the physical 'stuff' that successive conceptualisations of Europe have taken as their referent – is itself marked by an irreducible heterogeneity that resists encompassment by any single discursive elaboration of what Europe is or might be. It is, I suggest, this all too palpable heterogeneity that is the indispensable counterpart to the definitional openness and receptivity towards an unspecified outside for which Derrida's essay argues so passionately. It is Europe's offshore islands that reveal, perhaps more emphatically than its Mediterranean heartlands and continental thoroughfares, that the materiality of Europe will always exceed any possible version of 'Europe'. Islands are not so much places apart where Europe is absent as places where Europe becomes external to itself, other to itself, where the phallic directionality of its westward expansionist drive fragments and dissipates. Yet they are not isolates but, rather, as both Deleuze's reflections and the histories (prehuman, human and posthuman) of the North Atlantic islands suggest, scenes of encounter, of engagements across difference, of beginning again, continuously ... To affirm such heterogeneity is to refuse the proclaimed self-sufficiency both of parochial nationalisms and of universalising visions of historical progress as they continue to hold sway over much of the early 21st-century present.

Derrida's essay itself raises on a number of occasions the question of Europe's materiality. He refers, for example, to the upheavals shaking eastern and central Europe in the 1990s as a seismic event – an 'earthquake' (Derrida 1992: 19). He questions too the tendency of many self-identified European writers to deploy interchangeably the terms 'Europe' and 'Spirit', rendering the former exemplary of the latter. If this gesture is subjected to more sustained scrutiny in Derrida's study of Heidegger (published prior to the 'earthquake'), it should perhaps prompt us also to re-examine the later volume's labelling of Valéry as a 'Mediterranean spirit' (Derrida 1989; 1992). Is it not, ultimately, the unassailable materiality of Europe, including Mediterranean Europe – its mountains, valleys and plains, its waterways, its built environments, its flora and fauna – that, as a presence subsisting independently of human discourses and designs, perennially disrupts any such attempt to pass seamlessly from the history of Europe to the history of Spirit?

A Conclusion amongst Other Things

Derrida suggests, in bringing his reflections to a close, that he wishes to be considered – and to consider himself – 'more or less European' or 'European amongst other things' (Derrida 1992: 83). What, then, are the 'other things' amongst which one might be European, whether in the 1920s, the 1990s or in our very different but no less seismically disturbed today? Clearly, the constitutive others of the more or less European must include a plurality of human presences and projects that continue to press upon Europe's internal and external borders, demanding an openness to lives and futures that can never be prescriptively ranged under the rubric of a European history and identity. They must also include a range of other-than-human presences, both 'animate' and 'inanimate' as conventionally described, in relation to which 'we' Europeans are obliged to negotiate our habitation of the earth, the small part of it known as Europe and beyond. Finally, not the least of the other things to be reckoned with is the certainty of our own and Europe's eventual demise. Such a perspective necessarily cuts down to size the universalising pretentions of Europe and Euro-America, revealing their moment of self-proclaimed global ascendancy to be no more than a transitory one, just as the career of humanity itself forms only a fleeting episode in a vastly more expansive planetary chronology.

Unlike Valéry, or Derrida, or Cassano I am no Mediterranean spirit, being the product, by birth, of an offshore outpost of Europe's other, Atlantic shore and, by ancestry, of a still smaller offshore outpost (the island of Mull in the Inner Hebrides, off the west coast of Scotland). Doubtless too, my own more or less Europeanness has been further inflected by almost two decades spent studying and teaching in the United States, latterly in a part of it (the 'Midwest') more remote from the sea than any location in insular or continental Europe. Perhaps it is these considerations that impel me to reread Derrida's reflections in the light not only of a different present but of a different geography, a geography of scattered, shifting yet intercommunicating fragments, the material density and opacity of which are, for me, a forceful reminder not only of the elemental strife of land and sea that subtends the making and unmaking of human worlds but also of the impossibility of a Europe definitionally secured against incursions of alterity. Twenty years after its initial publication, surely one of the most powerful and enduring provocations of Derrida's *The Other Heading* is, precisely, its exhortation to engage unceasingly with such incursions from both within and without, that is, with the transformative impingement of other things. Only amongst other things have we ever been or could we ever be European.

Notes

1. The tsunami, known as the Storegga tsunami, was precipitated by a build-up of sands and muds on the continental shelf offshore from Norway. The earthquake shifted a quantity of sediment equal to the size of present-day Scotland from the continental shelf into the deeper waters of the North Sea, displacing vast quantities of sea water and causing enormous and fast-moving waves. (McKirdy 2010: 32).
2. Although the islands had come increasingly under Scottish influence during preceding centuries, not least through their predominantly Scottish clergy, the transfer of sovereignty was not intended, initially, to be a permanent one. Rather, it amounted to the pawning or impignoration of the islands by Christian I of Norway and Denmark, who lacked the funds to provide an adequate dowry for his daughter on the occasion of her marriage to James III of Scotland. The ostensibly temporary nature of this arrangement has continued to be invoked by local activists. In the 1980s campaigners against the disposal of radioactive material at the Dounreay power station in Caithness drew up a declaration calling on the Danish monarchy to challenge Orkney's constitutional status as part of the United Kingdom. Around the same time, the Orkney and Shetland Movement, a group seeking devolution for the northern isles, unsuccessfully contested the Orkney and Shetland Parliamentary seat in the 1987 general election, polling just over 3,000 votes (Thomson [1987] 2008: 189–205).
3. Cassano's *Southern Thought* was first published in Italian in 1996 and in English translation (with four additional essays) in 2012.
4. Despite Deleuze and Guattari's repeated emphasis on the collective and relational dimensions of becoming, Cassano insists on reading their arguments as a validation of an individualistic conception of freedom: 'Deleuze's nomadism is the space of individual freedom, the Dionysian notion of a world dominated, unified and organized by economic principles' (Cassano 2012: 110).
5. Cassano discusses the relationship of the Mediterranean to northern Italy in the context of the 'Southern Question', which first arose following the unification of Italy in 1860 with denunciations of the conditions of the south by writers such as Pasquale Villari, Leopoldo Franchatti and Sydney Sonnino and was famously taken up in the early twentieth century by Antonio Gramsci, a native of the Mediterranean island of Sardinia, in his essay of 1926, 'Some Aspects of the Southern Question' (Cassano 2012: 181; Gramsci 1995).
6. Schmitt, for example, writes in his book *Land and Sea* that 'man is a terrestrial, a groundling. He lives, moves and walks on the firmly grounded earth' (Schmitt 1997: 1, quoted Cassano 2012: 26). Heidegger, a professed Graecophile, presents a somewhat more complicated case, although, for Cassano, his admiration for Greece is always inflected by a distinctively German partiality for *terra firma*: 'the Greece described here is heavily Germanized; in it, being has dried out the sea, and water serves only as support for the land' (Cassano 2012: 28).
7. These earliest rocks were subsequently added to by Dalradian rocks – metamorphic rocks subject to refolding and recrystallisation at high temperatures and pressures and formed between 700 and 600 million years ago from sediments laid down at the edges of an ancient, long-since-vanished ocean (the 'Lapitus' ocean). At a later date magma was injected into the metamorphic rocks to form igneous rocks of various types, like the Saw granite that is a conspicuous feature of northeast Unst (McKirdy 2010: 10).

References

Auden, W. H. and Louis MacNeice (1937), *Letters from Iceland*, London: Faber & Faber.
Auton, Clive, Terry Fletcher and David Gould (1996) *Orkney and Shetland: A Landscape Fashioned by Geology*, Perth: Scottish Natural Heritage / Edinburgh: British Geological Survey.
Brassier, Ray (2007), *Nihil Unbound: Enlightenment and Extinction*, Basingstoke: Palgrave Macmillan.
Braudel, Fernand [1966] (1972), *The Mediterranean and the Mediterranean World in the Age of Philip II*, vol. I, New York: Harper and Row.
Cassano, Franco [1996] (2012), *Southern Thought and Other Essays on the Mediterranean*, New York: Fordham University Press.
Chambers, Iain (2008), *Mediterranean Crossings: The Politics of an Interrupted Modernity*, Durham, NC: Duke University Press.
Clark, Nigel (2011), *Inhuman Nature: Sociable Life On A Dynamic Planet*, London: Sage.
Cunliffe, Barry (2008), *Europe between the Oceans: Themes and Variations 9000 bc–ad 1000*, New Haven, CT: Yale University Press.
Deleuze, Gilles [2002] (2004), *Desert Islands and Other Texts 1953–1974*, Los Angeles: Semiotext(e).
Derrida, Jacques [1987] (1989), *Of Spirit: Heidegger and the Question*, Chicago: University of Chicago Press.
Derrida, Jacques [1991] (1992), *The Other Heading: Reflections on Today's Europe*, Bloomington: Indiana University Press.
Gilroy, Paul (1993), *The Black Atlantic: Modernity and Double Consciousness*, Cambridge, MA: Harvard University Press.
Gramsci, Antonio [1926] (1995), *The Southern Question*, West Lafayette, IN: Bordighera.
Hegel, G. W. F. [1822] (1975), *Lectures on the Philosophy of World History*, Cambridge: Cambridge University Press.
Herzfeld, Michael (1987), *Anthropology through the Looking Glass: Critical Ethnography in the Margins of Europe*, Cambridge: Cambridge University Press.
McKirdy, Alan (2010), *Orkney and Shetland: A Landscape Fashioned by Geology*, 2nd ed., Perth: Scottish Natural Heritage.
Meillassoux, Quentin [2006] (2008), *After Finitude: An Essay on the Necessity of Contingency*, London: Continuum.
Melton, Nigel D. (2008) 'West Voe: A Mesolithic-Neolithic Transition Site in Shetland', in Gordon Noble, Tessa Poller, John Raven and Lucy Verrill (eds), *Scottish Odysseys: The Archaeology of Islands*, Stroud: Tempus, pp. 23–33.
Melton, N. D. and R. A. Nicholson (2004), 'The Mesolithic in the Northern Isles: The Preliminary Evaluation of an Oyster Midden at West Voe, Sumburgh, Shetland, UK', *Antiquity* 78(299).
Mollat du Jourdin, Michel (1993), *Europe and the Sea*, Oxford: Blackwell.
Nance, R. Damien, Thomas R. Worsley and Judith B. Moody (1988), 'The Supercontinent Cycle', *Scientific American*, July, 72–9.
National Records of Scotland (2012), *Shetland Islands Council Area: Demographic Fact Sheet*, http://www.gro-scotland.gov.uk/files2/stats/council-area-data-sheets/shetland-islands-factsheet.pdf (last accessed 21 June 2013).
Nicholson, James R. (1972), *Shetland*, Newton Abbot: David & Charles.
Pagden, Anthony (2002), 'Europe: Conceptualising a Continent', in Anthony Pagden (ed.), *The Idea of Europe: From Antiquity to the European Union*, Cambridge: Cambridge University Press, pp. 33–54.

Press, Frank, Raymond Siever, Jeremy Dunning and J. Lawrence (2001), *Understanding Earth*, 3rd ed., New York: W. H. Freeman.
Saxa Vord (2007–13), 'About Unst', Saxa Vord website, http://www.saxavord.com/about-unst.php (last accessed 21 June 2013).
Scherman, Katharine (1976) *Iceland: Daughter of Fire*, London: Victor Gollancz.
Schmitt, Carl [1942] (1997), *Land and Sea*, Washington, DC: Plutarch Press.
Scotese, Christopher R. (2012), Paleomap Project, www.scotese.com (last accessed 21 June 2013).
Thomson, William P. L. [1987] (2008), *The New History of Orkney*. Edinburgh: Birlinn.
Turner, Val (1998), *Ancient Shetland*, London: B. T. Batsford.
Valéry, Paul (1962a), 'The European [*La Crise de l'esprit, Note* ou *L'Européen*]', in *History and Politics*, New York: Pantheon.
Valéry, Paul (1962b), 'The Freedom of Spirit', in *History and Politics*, New York: Pantheon.
Valéry, Paul (1962c), 'Notes on the Greatness and Decline of Europe', in *History and Politics*, New York: Pantheon.

Chapter 5

Europe's Constitution for the Unborn

Matthias Fritsch

Introduction

In this chapter I will draw out what Derrida's work – in particular as it concerns law, democracy and intergenerational justice in the context of European heritage – can contribute to constitutionalism and law in relation to future people, at the national and supranational levels of the European Union. In its first section, the chapter will outline some of Derrida's contributions to legal scholarship and European identity, and then, in the following two sections, argue for two main points. First, Derrida can help us understand the much-discussed constitutional double bind with regard to future people as merely an instance of a more general aporia. The double bind consists in the fact that the constitutional promise to safeguard future freedom also limits and binds future people. I will show how this aporia results from the temporal structure of the making of constitutional law. Accordingly, the double bind cannot be resolved, either conceptually or in constitutional practice, but only negotiated with greater awareness. Second, the same aporia of time entails that future generations are already implicated in the formulation and reformulation of law here and now. Because the present moment is constitutively related to the past and the future, the meaning of a constitutional formulation can become legible only from the future. Hence, the present generation, whose unity is never given, cannot but draw an advance credit on the future, whose cooperation it anticipates. As a result, the political promise of Europe depends on its relation to its geographical, but also to its temporal, others.

A Constitution for the Unborn

In October 2004, the month of Derrida's death, representatives of the then twenty-five EU member states signed the European Constitution, an international treaty that, if ratified by the parliaments of the member states, would have integrated Europe politically in a new way. Many commentators, including Jürgen Habermas and Derrida, demanded such political unification, not only to present a counterweight to US hegemony, but also to submit to better democratic control the economic unification that had been the dominant aim of the Union. The treaty's fortune was sunk in 2005, by which time eighteen members had ratified the treaty, by the referenda in France and the Netherlands. In response a less wide-ranging treaty was drawn up, signed in Lisbon in 2007 and eventually ratified in 2009. The Lisbon Treaty contains many of the changes that were originally placed in the Constitutional Treaty, now formulated as amendments to the existing treaties. However, it does not mention future people specifically.[1] By contrast, the failed 2004 European Constitution did so in two ways: by adopting the Charter of Fundamental Rights of the European Union (the EU Charter), whose preamble we will discuss below, and by devoting the constitutional text, again in a preamble, to the 'consciousness of its responsibility toward future generations and the earth' (for a detailed analysis, see Häberle 2006).

In a jointly signed newspaper article, published in the *Frankfurter Allgemeine Zeitung* and in *Libération* in May 2003, both Habermas (the author) and Derrida (the co-signatory) called for the political unification that the planned constitution was to accomplish. They welcomed what they saw at the time as the 'future constitution', for they thought it would 'endow Europe with certain state-like properties', such as a 'common policy in external affairs, security, and defence', as resolved in Nice in 1999 (Habermas and Derrida 2006: 272). As Derrida put it shortly thereafter, 'we must fight for what of Europe remains irreplaceable for the world to come, for it to become more than a market or a single currency, more than a neo-nationalist conglomerate, more than a new armed force' (Derrida 2006: 410). In the Habermas-authored article of 2003, 'the mechanisms of "strengthened cooperation" created in Nice' would be shored up by a new European identity generated by 'a shared political fate and the prospect of a common future' (Habermas and Derrida 2006: 273).

The European identity needed for this unification is understood to rely on the projection of a 'common future', and such a projection must include, and seek to integrate, future citizens. Political identity-building by way of a constitution must reference the unborn, those who are to be bound, but also to be constituted, by the constitution as Europeans, no matter that the rights and liberties to be enshrined in it are universal.[2] In this sense, it may be no accident that the EU Charter, welcomed by Habermas and Derrida in response to the threat of unilateral American military action in Iraq and thus against non-European hegemony, is considered by constitutional scholars a 'quantum leap' when it comes to including future generations (Häberle 2006: 219). By explicitly mentioning future people, the preamble of the EU Charter does what very few constitutional texts have done before: 'Enjoyment of these rights entails responsibilities and duties with regard to other persons, to the human community and to future generations' (EU Charter, Preamble).

This formulation gives a special status to future generations: they are singled out as a third category such that one may suspect they are not included in the first two, other persons and the human community. Nonetheless, we should note that this formulation addresses future people as beneficiaries of present responsibilities, and not, or not yet, as duty bearers. No doubt the explicit reference to duties to future people responds to a growing awareness of increased human abilities to affect even distant future generations, given that not only nuclear waste but also many environmental problems and greenhouse gas emissions remain problematic for tens of thousands of years. In fact, many of the new constitutions passed recently, before and after the EU Charter, by European nations, especially in the postcommunist east, and by subnational states and provinces, enshrine environmental protection and sustainable development, at times explicitly mentioning future generations (see Häberle 2006).

Given that they figure in the EU Charter as the responsibility of the present population, future people are not primarily seen as charged with the duty to continue the project of European integration. And yet, mentioning them explicitly reveals their dual status: on the one hand as objects of concern whose wellbeing is to be safeguarded, and on the other as subjects of action, to be constituted and addressed as legal subjects continuing the project of Europe, including its economic, political, constitutional and thus intergenerational unification. It is the logic of this dual status that we will be concerned to espouse by means of reading Derrida.

The contention in this chapter is that Derrida can help us rethink the European world in its generational, discontinuous connectedness. Derrida's work is of genuine interest in this context because it extensively reflects on both Europe and constitution-making as well as on intergenerational justice. Regarding the European heritage, his work reinterpreted, beyond Eurocentrism, its political and cultural 'exemplarity' and democracy (*The Other Heading*), its religion and concept of responsibility ('Faith and Knowledge' (Derrida 1998), *The Gift of Death* (Derrida 1995)) and its scientific rationality ('The World of the Enlightenment to Come' in *Rogues* (Derrida 2005)). As regards constitution-making and state-founding or nation-building, these were of particular interest to Derrida, from his reading of the Declaration of US Independence (Derrida 1986) and of Walter Benjamin's 'Critique of Violence' in 'Force of Law' (Derrida 1990), to his many discussions of Carl Schmitt (Derrida 1997 in particular). One of the most outstanding of Derrida's arguments regarding law is that it must try for but can never attain justice (Derrida 1990). Justice, however, must be thought intergenerationally from the start, all justice relating us and the law both to the dead and the unborn:

> If I am getting ready to speak at length about ghosts, inheritance, and generations . . . it is in the name of justice. Of justice where it is not yet, not yet there, where it is no longer . . . present, and where it never will be, no more than law, reducible to laws or rights . . . No ethics, no politics . . . seems possible and thinkable and just that does not recognise in its principle the respect for those others who are no longer or for those others who are not yet there, presently living, whether they are already dead or not yet born. (Derrida 1994: xix–xx)

For Derrida, then, to think – but also to make – law, including constitutional law, is to think its irreducible reference to non-presence and to justice, and to think justice is to think the relation to the unborn. Hence, the role of intergenerational relations in Europe's constitutionalism stands to gain from reflections on the connections we may reconstruct in Derrida's wake. On this basis, I will draw out what Derrida can contribute to European constitutionalism and the moral and political implication for its relation to future people.

The Constitutional Double Bind

Many scholars believe that the inclusion of future people in a constitution is a 'double-edged sword' (Gosseries 2008: 32) or even an 'aporia' (Häberle 2006: 221). The difficulty consists in the fact that a frequent constitutional motif, in a certain respect the very *raison d'être* of a constitution, is to safeguard future freedom, including the freedom of future people. The point of constitutional law is precisely to build a political and legal structure capable of enabling individuals to form a community around a common identity, a community that is able to govern itself and pass more particular, more revisable laws. However, future legal subjects are thereby also constitutionally limited and bound. Hence, we have a legal-political version of the famous double bind most succinctly expressed in the command 'Be free!' Here are two formulations of the problem in the literature:

> On the one hand, generation protection implies norms and values that must be eternally valuable. On the other hand, these norms must not constrain the coming generations' liberty to design their future world. Thus, a compromising middle course between a certain degree of 'eternity clauses' and sufficient flexibility is needed for generation contracts. (Häberle 2005: 28)

> For a constitution to be successful – to organise a political society and guarantee the freedom of its citizens and their participation in the process of government, in short, to secure liberal democracy as such – it needs to last through many generations. Yet perpetual constitutions seem to subvert one of the foundational principles of liberal democracy, namely that political legitimacy rests on the consent of the governed and that 'the people' are the source of all political authority. (Muniz-Fraticelli 2009: 379)

Seeking to protect future people means asking for their consent before they are able to give it, in fact, proceeding as if they had consented, anachronistically, before their time. (I will return to this drawing on the future in the present, presuming the other's countersignature in anticipation.) The protection can only come in the form of a restriction on an autonomy that is first of all to be enabled. For this reason, Thomas Jefferson famously suggested to James Madison in 1789 that the US Constitutional Convention ought to be reconvened at the start of a new generation, which he calculated, on the basis of contemporary mortality statistics, to be every nineteen years: 'Every constitution, then, and every law, naturally expires at the end of 19 years. If it be enforced longer, it is an act of force and not of right' (Jefferson 1904).

The first constitution to address this aporia comes from France. Four years after Jefferson wrote from Paris to Madison – and two years after Thomas Paine discussed the problem in similar terms in his *Rights of Man* (Paine 1906: 11, 26), siding with the French Revolution against Edmund Burke's attack on it – the French Constitution was passed in 1793, stating in Article 28:

> *Un peuple a toujours le droit de revoir, de réformer et de changer sa Constitution. Une génération ne peut pas assujettir à ses lois les généra-*

tions futures [A people always has the right to revisit, reform, and change its Constitution. One generation may not subject future generations to its laws]. (Godechot 1984)³

Much would have to be said here about the debate between Paine and Burke, among Jefferson and his fellow 'Founding Fathers', and also about the ways in which the aporia must be seen to shape political modernity, given that it implicates the crucial relations between liberal individual rights and democratic collective self-determination, between freedom and education, between being constituted and constituting, and so on. Let us single out here from among these the crucial relation between autonomy, including the self-identity it presupposes, and time in its unfolding.

Most scholars who discuss this aporia see it as occurring once the constitution explicitly seeks to address, to include so as to protect, future people (Häberle 2005, 2006; Gosseries 2008; Tremmel 2006). As long as the law addresses only those presently living, it seems, there is no aporia, for the (collective) self that passes the law is the very self that is subject to it, preserving, in fact exemplifying, the idea of autonomy. The idea supposes that the self (the common identity expressed by a constitution) coincides with itself, as does time more generally. There may thus be an intrinsic connection between Enlightenment autonomy and presentism, the favouring of the present among the three modalities of time (past, present, future), as has in fact been suggested in relation to democracy (Thompson 2005, 2010). But if the present time is not identical to itself, and is no longer thought to be either separated by a gulf from past and future or bridged by an underlying substance remaining identical to itself over time (*hypokeimenon, subiectum*), does not this aporia affect every law and every constitution, whether or not it explicitly addresses future people?

It is for this reason that we may fruitfully bring Derrida into this discussion by focusing on what he says about the relation between 'today' and European identity. As may be expected – for deconstruction's explicit target has always been the 'metaphysics of presence' – Derrida begins his reflections on Europe by questioning the unicity of 'today' as well as of identity. As noted, a common cultural and political identity is seen, by Derrida and others, as central to the political integration of Europe by means of a constitution. In this context, Derrida's *The Other Heading* argues, in its 'second axiom', that identity is never proper or identical to itself. On Derrida's understanding, an identity 'may take the form of a subject' – an entity sufficiently unified so as to act in its own name, for example, politically or legally in founding a union – only 'in the difference with itself [*avec soi*]' (Derrida 1992: 9). Such a difference demands – indeed, non-coincidence with oneself gives rise to a normative demand – that the future direction of the political subject be both envisioned and remain contestable, so both anticipated and unanticipatable (Derrida 1992: 18).[4]

In the language of *The Other Heading*, Europe must have a heading to be a 'subject' in the first place, but this heading must – a must both normative and ontological – also be exposed to the heading of the other, to another heading. The attempt to destroy the other is in the end self-destructive (Derrida 1992: 15). In part as a consequence of this exposure, however, difference from oneself as a condition of self-identification also means that the subject's future direction is essentially unknown. For if the heading, the future direction, is exposed to, and must in fact for its self-constitution in difference welcome, contestation by other headings, other ideas as to what Europe should do and where it should go, then Europe must also not know its heading (Derrida 1992: 75–6). It must be responsible not only to other subjects, both within and without, but also to what is other than a subject, other than itself. It must be responsible to the other of the heading, to what is other than 'the *telos* of an oriented, calculated, deliberate, voluntary, ordered movement' (Derrida 1992: 14). European identity, like every identity and every constitution, thus comes with a 'double bind', a 'double injunction' or a 'double duty' (Derrida 1992: 29, 38, 80) to anticipate the future so as to protect it from 'the worst' while leaving it to its alterity, that is, to the 'unanticipatable, the non-masterable, non-identifiable', on pain of a destructive ego-centrism (Derrida 1992: 18, 15). As a result, ethics and politics, but also responsible law-making, must begin with 'the experience and experiment of the aporia' (Derrida 1992: 41). As the art of the possible, politics takes place as the impossible.

To the extent that political subjectivities are internally divided collectives owing themselves to both historical chance and wilful human institution, constitutions are primary sites to find at work the central but also divided reference and exposure of political subjectivity to a future both calculated and incalculable, both willed and involuntary. It is in this context that Europe could learn from the other heading, the other shore, rerouted through a reading of Jefferson's Declaration of Independence by that 'European hybrid' over-colonised in French Algeria (Derrida 1992: 7). For in Jefferson, too, it may appear that the idea of a voluntary refounding of the Constitution every nineteen years is dependent on a certain Enlightenment presentism, a favouring of the rights of the present with no ties to past or future: 'No society can make a perpetual constitution, or even a perpetual law. The earth belongs always to the living generation,' Jefferson writes to Madison (Jefferson 1904).

This presentism would find further expression in the wilful founding of a new republic, a cutting of ties with the British colonisers by the self-assertion of the present in constitutional form. However, 200 years after the fact, Derrida sought to show that the Declaration's performative, law-making power is so divided against itself that it cannot do without the decidedly non-performative, constative reference, with which the text indeed opens, to a transcendent source, 'the Laws of Nature and of Nature's God' (Derrida 1986). The signatories to Jefferson's Declaration should thus not be accused of a 'failure of nerve', as Hannah Arendt charged, bemoaning the Founding Fathers' lack of faith in their own pure constitutive power (see Honig 1991), but should be said to sense that the autonomous power of communal self-building is constituted in heteronomy. Heteronomy here means that constitutional founding takes place in response to an unmasterable, unanticipatable force that is, however, also reified and hypostasised in being called 'God' or 'Nature'. It is this force that the title of Derrida's 'Force of Law' names, and that the subtitle calls, with Blaise Pascal and Michel de Montaigne, the 'mystical foundation of authority' (Derrida 1990: 937). The mysticism stems from the 'aporia' of law in general (Derrida 1990: 947). To put it schematically, the aporia consists in law's mandate to cover future cases whose singularity cannot but also escape law's generality – no 'case' fits its law perfectly, whether constitutional or not. A future application is never fully justified by the law under which it is claimed to fall, an inadequation that implies both the threat of illegitimate violence and the chance for justice beyond the law, a justice that law may seek to anticipate in perfecting itself, but that cannot ever be fully captured in law.[5] Each future application thus reinterprets the law it is meant to merely apply, thereby adding to and refounding the law made in the past (Derrida 1990: 957–71).

The aporia of the time of constitutional founding, an aporia that Jefferson addressed by oscillating between the performative ('We hold . . .') and the constative ('. . . these truths to be self-evident'), is, according to this argument, repeated in each act of law-making and law-applying. It is an aporia of a time that will not coincide with itself. The law-making, constitutional force at work even in alleged mere applications springs precisely from the 'inadequation to itself of the present', and thus from the non-coincidence of the subject with itself:

> There was no signer, by right, before the text of the Declaration [the US Declaration of Independence], which itself remains the producer and guarantor of its own signature. By this fabulous event, by this fable, which implies the structure of the trace and is only in truth possible thanks to the inadequation to itself of a present, a signature gives itself a name. (Derrida 1986: 10)

The aporia of including future people in the European constitution is thus an aporia of both law and time more generally (cf. Beardsworth 1996, ch. 3). Colonial people, in this case British subjects, can declare themselves independent only by anticipating, in the present, their future independence, which is only accomplished (although not once and for all, as we will see) by the signature. That is what Derrida calls the 'fabulous retroactivity of the signature' (Derrida 1986: 10): The signatories draw, in the future anterior and not the grammatical time of the present indicative, on their future independence: 'we who will have been free', rather than 'we who are free'. Thus with the European Constitution: its failure in 2005 and quasi-resurrection in 2009 (when the Treaty of Lisbon came into effect) could be considered its 'normal' process of living and dying, one death calling for another birth, another attempt. Nor should we think that the disappearance of the explicit dedication to future generations removes the aporia of freeing and binding, for the constitutional treaties, precisely in never quite being over, still address future people. Let us look at this implicit or explicit address in greater detail.

The Role of Future People in Law-making

In his reading of the Declaration of Independence, Derrida calls the retroactivity – we could also say anteriority – of the signature 'fabulous'. The reason for this lies in the fact that such founding in anachronism cannot but cover over its illegitimacy, its mysticism, its lack of authority. It does so by telling fables about itself, for example, by assuming the garb of the past – a practice Derrida defends, in the case of the French Revolutions of 1789 and 1848, against Marx's critique of the ghosts of the past (Derrida 1994, ch. 4) – but also, now in relation to the future, by providing interpretive models geared to showing its own legitimacy, however problematic it may otherwise seem. The US Constitution – particularly in relation to its racist exclusions and violent dispossession of Amerindians, the many broken treaties with First Nations forming its enduring context – certainly remains contestable, and in fact contested, and the Europeans should therefore be cautious today of the exclusions and dispossessions attending their own constitutional project. Let us consider a long passage from 'Force of Law' that makes this point about 'fables' and relates it to future generations:

> All revolutionary situations, all revolutionary discourses, on the left or on the right ... justify the recourse to violence by alleging the founding, in progress or to come, of a new law. As this law to come will in return legitimate, retrospectively, the violence that may offend the sense of justice, its future anterior already justifies it. The foundation of all states occurs in a situation that we can thus call revolutionary. It inaugurates a new law, it always does so in violence. Always, which is to say even when there haven't been those spectacular genocides, expulsions or deportations that so often accompany the foundation of states, great or small, old or new, right near us or far away. In these situations said to found law [*droit*] or state, the grammatical category of the future anterior all too well resembles a modification of the present to describe the violence in progress. It consists, precisely, in feigning the presence or simple modalization of presence. Those who say 'our time,' while thinking 'our present' in light of a future anterior present do not know very well, by definition, what they are saying ... A 'successful' revolution, the 'successful foundation of a State' (in somewhat the same sense that one speaks of a '"felicitous" performative speech act') will produce *après coup* what it was destined in advance to produce, namely, proper interpretative models to read in return, to give sense, necessity and above all legitimacy to the violence that has produced, among others, the interpretative model in question, that is, the discourse of its self-legitimation. Examples of this circle, this other hermeneutic circle, are not lacking ... There are cases in which it is not known for generations if the performative of the violent founding of a state is 'felicitous' or not. (Derrida 1990: 991–3)

Let us put this last point in somewhat stronger form (stronger because not just epistemic), and then defend it. The felicity of constitutional state-building depends on future generations, and the present must bind them for the purpose of this felicity. As we heard, the lack of knowledge, this epistemic unanticipatability of the future, is not an accident: rather, constitution makers must be committed to it in the present. For if no time is simply identical to itself, then any project, including the 'revolutionary' attempt to begin something unheard of, like a trial *de novo*, must promise to continue itself in the future. According to the logic of 'double affirmation', to say 'yes' to something in a present time that is not simply present means to already promise to say 'yes' to it tomorrow.[6]

While this holds for any project, even one that could be accomplished in a lifetime and so need not involve future people, a constitution, one may argue, is an intrinsically transgenerational project. It involves more than one generation, either because we define 'generation' in such a way that several generations coexist at any one time (minors, adults, elders), all of which would be addressed simultaneously by a constitution, or because we accept, against Jefferson, that the very point of a constitution is to be 'perpetual' (or at least to last for more than one generation), for it is distinguished from ordinary legislation by its resistance to change and its foundational nature (cf. Muniz-Fraticelli 2009). With this transgenerational premise in place, the obligation – the 'double duty' to carry on the project and to alter it so as to adapt it to new circumstances – is imposed, willy-nilly, on future generations. That is why a freedom-enabling constitution cannot but also restrict and bind the future, charging it with the duty to carry on the project. If we will have been free rather than simply being so, then we – including the future others whose inclusion in the 'we' is not guaranteed – must repeat it, this projection upon the future from which we seek to retroactively constitute ourselves as free. Our future 'self' must collaborate with our present 'self' – where the continuity here, the one that covers up all the difficulties, is in this formulation assured by the 'we'.

The retroactivity or temporal non-coincidence of the constitutional signature with itself is, then, the reason that the founding of a republic must appeal, from the inside, to an outside (which thus does not quite remain outside). Rather than owing itself to the pure performative power of humans to construct their own world, constitutions reveal that human freedom depends on a countersignature from others. These others must, and this is how we most often understand it, be other entities, other states recognising for example a Europe thus constituted, recognising, in word and deed, a common foreign policy, and so on. However, for the reasons we discussed, these others must also include future others. The same temporal and aporetic structure that allows but complicates self-identification entails that the future is already implicated in the founding and refounding of law here and now. Because the present moment is constitutively related to the past and the future, so that 'we' do not quite know what 'our time' is, the meaning of a constitutional founding can become legible only from the future. Hence, the present generation draws an advance credit on the future, with which it must seek to collaborate before its time.

While it is tempting to avoid the infinite regress of constitutions – their drawing their legitimacy from other constitutions or models of interpretation that they have given themselves – by appeal to God, nature, tradition, and so on, Derrida seeks to show that the founding act is not over 'for generations'. The constitutional act needs to be repeated in different circumstances, and then too, promised to be reaffirmed in yet other contexts, thus drawing on the future in advance. And given this perpetuity, a perpetuity in discontinuity, the future anticipated in advance never coincides with generations of future European citizens.

This is how we should now, after the quasi-failure or quasi-success of the European constitution of 2004, understand Derrida's conclusion to *The Other Heading*:

> Hence the duty to respond to the call of European memory, to recall what has been promised under the name of Europe, to re-identify Europe ... This duty also dictates opening Europe, from the heading that is divided because it is also a shoreline: opening it onto that which is not, never was, and never will be Europe. (Derrida 1992: 76–7)

The promise of Europe includes, then, both the duty to reidentify Europe and the duty to open it to that which cannot be identified with it, the other of the heading –which is nonetheless needed for its identification.

Conclusion: The Other of the Heading

I have argued for two implications of Derrida's work on Europe, law and future generations. The first is that the constitutional double bind applies to all identity and to all law, not only when it explicitly seeks to include future people in some way. Constitutions always involve the contributions of other generations, both past and future. This is why the seemingly stalled project of a European constitution should be placed – in a 'deconstructive genealogy' (Derrida 1992: 77) that could not be carried out here – in a longer historical view, stretching back to at least the French and the American revolutions and their debates regarding the constitutional inclusion of future people, and perhaps reaching forward another 200 years or so. The second conclusion focuses more explicitly on the contribution of future people to present European constitutionalism. For the double bind that I have traced to the non-coincidence of time also shows that we must inherit and pass on the law in double affirmation. Double affirmation is double not only because it calls right away for its repetition, but also because identity must welcome its other. Thereby it entails a responsibility to oneself and to the other, the non-European required for self-identification. Mandated of every identity, such affirmation responds to an ineluctable temporal-spatial dispersion by calling for reunification, a call to reaffirm a heritage by promising to reunify it, and that means to move it beyond itself.

Hence, Europe needs to think of itself not only as constitutionally and politically unified in the face of its presently existing, presently identifiable others, let alone as a merely economic counterweight to the US and China. Rather, it must also see itself as an intergenerational project in which its constitutions and its institutions are to be shared with the unborn. Given that the future cannot unproblematically be projected as a constitutionally guaranteed identity or unity, but must be permitted to be fundamentally other – not only to permit future people their autonomy, but to give present constitutionalism a chance to succeed – appreciating the constitutive role of intergenerational sharing is part and parcel of Europe learning to open itself to its spatial other as well, beyond closed borders and the ideal of the natural-born brother. Perhaps future Europeans will not be European, in any case not in a way recognised by present Europeans. It is only along this path of a geographical opening induced through and inflected by intergenerational discontinuity, and of a respect for future people mediated by the experience of living others, that Europe may become a political model, what Derrida discusses as an 'exemplary' universal (Derrida 1992: 72–3), beyond Eurocentrism. Such is the hope shared by both Derrida and Habermas in their call for European renewal by way of a constitution.

Notes

1. Yet it may be no accident that, on the official webpage for the Treaty of Lisbon, the twelve stars on the EU flag are replaced by twelve infants in yellow outfits: http://europa.eu/lisbon_treaty/take/index_en.htm (last accessed 24 June 2013).
2. This may not be the place to discuss Habermas's idea of constitutional patriotism, that is, a common and particular identity formed around universal values, despite the fact that it has become standard reference in the context of European constitutionalism (Lacroix 2002). Yet it would be helpful to discuss it in relation to Derrida's promise of Europe as an 'exemplary' universalism, which similarly seeks to bridge the singular and the universal (Derrida 1990: 73–4).
3. For a recent version of Jefferson and Paine's argument, see Otsuka (2003); for discussion of this 'voluntarism', see Muniz-Fraticelli (2009).
4. For a more detailed exposition of this double, and indeed contradictory, relation to the future, see Fritsch (2011a).
5. I have tried to show this in relation to discourse ethics and its distinction between discourses of justification and application (Fritsch 2010).
6 Having analysed this 'double affirmation' in Fritsch (2011b), I permit myself to refer to it here.

References

Constitutional texts

Charter of Fundamental Rights of the European Union, available at http://www.europarl.europa.eu/charter/pdf/text_en.pdf (last accessed 24 June 2013).

Treaty establishing a Constitution for Europe, available at http://eur-lex.europa.eu/JOHtml.do?uri=OJ:C:2004:310:SOM:en:HTML (last accessed 24 June 2013).

Treaty of Lisbon, available at http://europa.eu/lisbon_treaty/full_text/index_en.htm (last accessed 24 June 2013).

Other texts
Beardsworth, Richard (1996), *Derrida and the Political*, London: Routledge.
Derrida, Jacques (1986), 'Declarations of Independence', *New Political Science* 7(1), 7–15.
Derrida, Jacques (1990), 'Force of Law: The "Mystical Foundation of Authority"', *Cardozo Law Review* 11(5–6), 919–1078.
Derrida, Jacques [1991] (1992), *The Other Heading: Reflections on Today's Europe*, Bloomington: Indiana University Press.
Derrida, Jacques [1993] (1994), *Specters of Marx: The State of the Debt, the Work of Mourning, and the New International*, New York: Routledge.
Derrida, Jacques [1992] (1995), *The Gift of Death*, Chicago: University of Chicago Press.
Derrida, Jacques [1994] (1997), *Politics of Friendship*, London: Verso.
Derrida, Jacques [1996] (1998), 'Faith and Knowledge', in Jacques Derrida and Gianni Vattimo (eds), *Religion*, Stanford, CA: Stanford University Press, pp. 1–78.
Derrida, Jacques [2003] (2005), *Rogues: Two Essays on Reason*, Stanford, CA: Stanford University Press.
Derrida, Jacques (2006), 'A Europe of Hope', *Epoché* 10(2), 407–12.
Fritsch, Matthias (2010), 'Equality and Singularity in Justification and Application Discourses', *European Journal of Political Theory* 9(3), 328–46.
Fritsch, Matthias (2011a), 'Deconstructive Aporias: Quasi-transcendental and Normative', *Continental Philosophy Review* 44(4), 439–68.
Fritsch, Matthias (2011b), 'Taking Turns: Democracy to Come and Intergenerational Justice', *Derrida Today* 4(2), 148–72.
Godechot, Jacques (ed.) 1984, *Les Constitutions de la France depuis 1789*, Paris: Garnier-Flammarion.
Gosseries, Axel P. (2008), 'Constitutions and Future Generations', *Good Society* 17(2), 32–37.
Häberle, Peter (2005), 'A Constitutional Law for Future Generations: The "Other" Form of the Social Contract – The Generation Contract', *Intergenerational Justice Review* 3, 28.
Häberle, Peter (2006), 'A Constitutional Law for Future Generations: The "Other" Form of the Social Contract – the Generation Contract', in Jörg Chet Tremmel (ed.), *Handbook of Intergenerational Justice*, Cheltenham: Edward Elgar.
Habermas, Jürgen and Jacques Derrida (2006), 'February 15, or What Binds Europeans Together: A Plea for a Common Foreign Policy, Beginning in the Core of Europe', in Lasse Thomassen (ed.), *The Derrida–Habermas Reader*, Chicago: University of Chicago Press.
Honig, Bonnie (1991), 'Declarations of Independence: Arendt and Derrida on the Problem of Founding a Republic' *American Political Science Review* 85(1), 97–113.
Jefferson, Thomas (1904), *The Works of Thomas Jefferson*, New York and London: G. P. Putnam's Sons.
Lacroix, Justine (2002), 'For a European Constitutional Patriotism', *Political Studies* 50(5), 944–58.
Muniz-Fraticelli, Victor M. (2009), 'The Problem of a Perpetual Constitution,' in Axel Gosseries and Lukas H. Meyer (eds), *Intergenerational Justice*, Oxford: Oxford University Press.
Otsuka, Michael (2003), *Libertarianism without Inequality*. Oxford: Clarendon Press.

Paine, Thomas [1791] (1906), *The Rights of Man*, London: Watts.
Thompson, Dennis F. (2005), 'Democracy in Time: Popular Sovereignty and Temporal Representation', *Constellations* 12(2), 245–61.
Thompson, Dennis F. (2010), 'Representing Future Generations: Political Presentism and Democratic Trusteeship', *Critical Review of International Social and Political Philosophy* 13(1), 17–7.
Tremmel, Jörg Chet (2006), 'Establishing Intergenerational Justice in national Constitutions', in Jörg Chet Tremmel (ed.), *Handbook of Intergenerational Justice*, Cheltenham: Edward Elgar.

Chapter 6

The Borders of Contemporary Europe: Territory, Justice and Rights

Tracey Skillington

This chapter explores how border practices within Europe today have become the centrepiece of a much-politicised debate on where the parameters of Europe, as both a territorial entity and a cultural project of belonging, ought to begin and end. In particular, the chapter will assess how universally applicable rights, including rights to free movement and safe haven or asylum, are interpreted through this dialogue as secondary to the territorial privileges and vetoing powers of Europe's self-determining sovereignties. Defined in its most general terms, this is a dialogue aimed at restricting entry to, appropriation of, or control over the spaces of European belonging. What it also represents is an attempt to collapse the reciprocal nature of cosmopolitan rights into a one-sided interpretation of Europe's duties to the other.

Maria Rovisco (2007) notes a clear lack of correspondence between narratives defining contemporary Europe as a sphere of tolerance, openness and cosmopolitan belonging on the one hand and the growing empirical realities of Europe's 'fortress' mentality (Habermas 2006) on the other. A number of reports produced by the European Commission against the backdrop of ongoing EU enlargement, including *The Spiritual and Cultural Dimensions of Europe* (Biedenkopf et al. 2005), explore utopian understandings of Europe as 'a project of the future', subject to ongoing 'questioning and debate' (Biedenkopf et al. 2005: 12). Europe, as this report explains, 'is not a fact. It is a task and a process' (Biedenkopf et al. 2005: 8), engaged in a largely unfinished project of democracy and unification. Throughout this and similar literature, the EU explores interpretations of a Europe that does not yet fully exist (Derrida 1992: 7), a space of intercultural understanding and inclusion, with boundaries that are negotiable and subject to ongoing revision. While the concept of the cosmopolitan is rarely presented through this literature in an explicit fashion (one exception is the recently published

Commission report *The Development of European Identity/Identities: Unfinished Business* (European Commission 2012b)), promises of peace, solidarity or human rights offer a moment of reflection when Europe can gather memories of itself as a champion of cosmopolitan justice and universal ethics. Having emerged initially from European traditions of law and trade (Therborn 2002), such memories now impose certain duties and obligations upon Europe, including a duty to resist totalitarianism, crimes of xenophobia, racism and extreme nationalism (see Text of the Berlin Declaration 2007), as well as obligations 'to contribute, in accordance with its ability, to the securing of world peace' (Biedenkopf et al. 2005: 12) and the struggle against 'war, terrorism and violence' (Text of the Berlin Declaration 2007). Paralleling this exploratory discourse of world openness is another expressing fear and uncertainty regarding the future of a Europe 'under siege' (see European Commission 2010: 5). Such uncertainty comes to be articulated most clearly through debates on border practices, security and migration policies. Here, the emphasis shifts to Europe as a culturally, spiritually and territorially bounded heading (Derrida 1992: 24). Above all, this uncertainty hints at a Europe not fully at home with difference or even the possibility of radical future transformation. As Derrida poignantly states:

> We ask ourselves in hope, in fear and trembling, what this face is going to resemble. Will it still resemble? Will it resemble the face of some persona whom we believe we know: Europe? And if its non-resemblance bears the traits of the future, will it escape monstrosity? (Derrida 1992: 6)

The arguments presented here draw mainly upon the work of Derrida to explore how contradictory logics of openness and closure are played out through contemporary European policy discourse and articulated in various position papers produced by the European Commission, the European Council and the European Parliament. A rights discourse, while upholding an image of Europe as a space of cosmopolitan solidarity and openness, frequently finds itself in conflict with a more communitarian logic of closure. Under the growing influence of this second logic, especially in a world of resource scarcity and climate and economic instability, Europe's citizenry is encouraged to use more traditional principles of sovereignty (mainly rights to self-determination, territorial as well as citizen rights) to impose limits upon the rights of others to free movement, safe haven or asylum. Commitments to human rights on a worldwide scale or the global fight against 'poverty, hunger and disease' (Text of the Berlin Declaration 2007) are played down. Instead what is prioritised is the overlap between the membership boundaries of rights communities and the geographical boundaries of a European community of sovereign states.

Given the prominence and largely unquestioned nature of this prioritisation, many ethical issues arising in relation to Europe's policies of security, immigration, detention and border control have not been addressed adequately. For one, obligations to humanity at large or the interrelationship between a European and global commons remain largely unspecified (for instance, unfulfilled universal rights to food, water or health for millions). Also requiring greater clarification and perhaps justification is the notion that the cumulative territories of Europe's sovereign states 'belong' to their peoples as an intergenerational and somehow unchanging community. Underlining such claims is the notion that contemporary European citizens, as descendants of early European settlers, can legitimately deny others rights of residency or temporary sojourn on the basis of their claims to 'first labour' or cultivation of the lands of Europe beyond a 'state of nature', and a resultant claim to what become the 'formative territories' (Gans 2001) of Europe.

In his account of Immanuel Kant and the limits to hospitality, Derrida (2001: 21) notes how 'our common right of possession on the surface of the earth' (Kant 1972: 137–8) is conditioned by transformations (for example, cultivation of arable lands, construction of cities and sovereign state borders) brought to bear on a portion of land by its occupants. When those who occupy lands gradually cultivate them through their joint efforts, such land acquires a significance that surpasses material advantages thereby accrued. Land also accumulates cultural, political and historical value or 'formative ties' (Gans 2001) for its inhabitants. The common use of a parent analogy, such as 'motherland', 'fatherland' or even 'homeland', to describe such territories captures the deeply significant ties they accumulate for a people not only in terms of occupancy but also group identity and shared memories of war, tragedy or victory (see Gans 2001: 58–79). Territorially based definitions of belonging delimit hospitality predominantly to a right of visitation. Under the law of the land, hospitality becomes heavily dependent upon state sovereign rulings on the right of residence. There is no denying the extent to which the 'splendid cathedrals, cloisters and city halls' that mark the territories of Europe 'from Sicily to Britain, from Spain to Poland' (Hänsch 2006) are seen to suggest a certain 'cultural unity' to 'Europe's heritage'. Together with certain intellectual and artistic traditions, this architectural legacy is presented as one of the most defining features of Europe's 'living brotherhood of Christian philosophers, artists and architects' (Hänsch 2006). Not only are Europe's cities, monuments, even its former Nazi death camps, promoted as important 'landmarks' in the rich historical legacies of an expanding Europe, they also act as mnemonic bordering mechanisms, creating clear distinctions as to the most 'relevant' civilisational constellations in Europe's histories of violence, suffering, war, enlightenment, democracy and peace.

Even in the face of such efforts to impose greater unity of interpretation, official definitions of a European common culture and identity remain notoriously vague and often conflicting (as in, for instance, memories of World War II). Given that the compositional and geographical reach of this community continues to evolve, the notion that historical claims to Europe ought to remain the primary basis upon which collective imaginaries of European belonging and identity are defined into the future proves objectionable for a number of reasons. For one, it does not allow for the fact that the compositional mix of a European commons is subject to ongoing change and in that, it largely denies the possibility of difference. Second, it ignores the distinctly eclectic quality that has always marked Europe's intellectual and cultural histories. Historical claims to belonging ultimately 'depend on where in history one starts and whose history one accepts' (Moore 1998) as relevant to, in this instance, the origins of a broadly European community of identity. Cultural reconstructions of this identity still remain heavily laden with exclusionary political imaginaries of ethnic lineage and territorial belonging. Problems arise when such historical claims are used to reify distinct aspects of 'our European heritage' (Biedenkopf et al. 2005: 12) 'as a compact, bounded, localised and historically rooted set of traditions' (Stolcke 1995: 4) whose exclusivity to particular peoples becomes the primary justificatory basis upon which practices of exclusion, discrimination and non-recognition are performed.

Criteria for inclusion within dominant definitions of European belonging today and accompanying stipulations regarding membership privileges remain firmly rooted within specific monocultural traditions. In spite of the increasing diversification of its populations, Europe's 'identity and destiny' is still distinctly Christian (Bekemans 2008: 2). The question remains as to whether such criteria provide a truly democratic basis for an adjudication of core elements of Europe's identity as a 'task' or 'unfinished project'. This and similar questions prove all the more pertinent given the contemporary global realities of deepening humanitarian crises (the effects of war, poverty, climate change, famine, drought and so on). Can historical claims to community belonging continue to be used in the future as universally legitimate grounds for the exclusion of increasing numbers of displaced persons worldwide?

Not only should secular Enlightenment values of equality, solidarity and freedom be considered relevant to Europe's historical narratives as a 'Europe of rights', but so also should more contemporary encounters with the other. Human rights and cosmopolitan ethics in the context of global war, climate change and humanitarian crises demand new thresholds of public justification (beyond traditional sovereign borders). Entitlements to spaces of refuge and tolerance, as well as access to basic, life-sustaining resources, will acquire greater social urgency in the years ahead as climate conditions deteriorate further and grave resource deficiencies for millions force us to reconsider our obligations to the citizen of the world. Reading hospitality as a way of life, as Derrida (2001: 16) recommends, or as a state of being in which the relation of self to other is conditioned by our shared creation of home or 'the familiar place of dwelling' (as opposed to the privatising tendencies inherent in the notion of homelands), Derrida's ethics of cosmopolitanism may well prove the only possible and truly human ethical basis upon which a universal human rights agenda can move forward in the future.

The Social Integration of Europe's Migrant Communities

Almost in denial of the radical potential embedded in Derrida's cosmopolitan ethics for shaping a more peaceful and just future world, governments across the European Union today seek out a clearly identifiable limit to European hospitality. Refuge from the other is sought in 'the deepest layers' of a Christian secular European identity and more exclusive principles of European selfhood. The civic integration of immigrant communities is presented as especially important given the undeniable and anxiety-provoking presence of the non-Christian other. Policy initiatives in Germany, for instance, include a new integration law introduced in 2005. Accompanying such legislative changes is a lively debate as to the essential elements of *deutsche Leitkultur* (or 'German guiding culture') and the desirable/undesirable presence of certain immigrant communities within Germany, in particular the 2.2 million Turks residing there. *Leitkultur* promotes the idea that cultural change on the part of the immigrant is necessary for the granting of full membership rights. According to Friedrich Merz, a former member of the Christian Democratic Union (CDU) in the Bundestag, German *Leitkultur* must remain firmly rooted in Christian values and traditions, and supportive of the notion that cultural difference is counterproductive to the project of integration (Ehrkamp 2012: 159). 'Germany is not a classical country of immigration and must not become one in the future,' according to the Christian Socialist Union (CSU) in Bavaria. In an official statement made recently, the CSU describes how 'foreigners living in Germany' must embrace 'values rooted in Christianity' (see Migration News 2000). Although definitions of *Leitkultur* remain largely unspecified, certain secular religious notions of belonging are taken for granted (that is, secular Christianity) in arguments supportive of more 'regulated' practices of integration or 'limited' immigration (see Migration News 2000). In Denmark, where a similar discourse prevails, the parliament considered legislation that would grant social workers the authority to place immigrant children whose parents 'forbid them to integrate into Danish society' in foster care on the grounds that the child's 'best interests are not being served by raising them to be hostile to Danish society' (Fekete 2005: 8).

Integration measures that reinforce monocultural definitions of a guiding *Leitkultur* are problematic for a number of reasons. In a truly open democratic environment, emphasis ought to be upon the recognition and acceptance of alterity as an enduring characteristic of Europe (past and present) rather than integration into some historically skewed representation of European 'exemplarity' (Derrida 1992: 24) associated with its 'motherlands'. What is advocated by various European states is more akin to the latter. According to Fekete (2006: 7), new integration measures legitimise the practice of a 'cultural fundamentalism' where those who embody religious, ethnic or racial otherness are discriminated against on the basis of their perceived cultural inferiority, over and beyond any socially assigned racial or ethnic inferiorities. If otherness is recognised in this instance, it is only in terms of its distance from dominant norms.

Underlying the reasoning of a multicultural society is the celebration of many ways of life, beliefs or values. What unites such a people is not some universal secular or ethnic ideal, but rather a shared commitment to pluralist democratic principles, cultural values and human rights. Mixed with contemporary expressions of xenophobia, social Darwinism and racist feelings of supremacy (like those expressed recently in conjunction with the publication of Thilo Sarrazin's *Germany Does Away with Itself: How We Are Gambling Away Our Country* (Sarrazin 2010)), appeals to *Leitkultur* represent 'a rearguard action', one applying 'the reactions of yesterday' to the problems of today (Habermas 2010).

Across the continent, a concerted backlash against the notion of a multicultural Europe is clearly evident. From the late 1960s through to the mid-1990s, the trend had been towards greater accommodation of ethno-cultural and religious diversity and recognition of the importance of minority and human rights more generally. Europe's multicultural experiment was promoted initially as a vital component of postwar democratic transformations, including the expansion of human rights legislation and the rejection of illiberal or undemocratic relationships of authority. For many, however, Europe's postwar celebration of diversity and desire to dismantle its historical cultures of totalitarianism, discrimination and exclusion have, quite simply, 'gone too far', or, as Angela Merkel put it in October 2010, have 'failed, utterly, failed' (see also Telegraph 2011). Multiculturalism, according this more contemporary discourse, has become the main threat to the preservation of a distinctly European way of life (Kymlicka 2012: 3). Since the late 1990s, in particular, more progressive models of democratic liberalism have gradually come under assault from politically conservative elements spearheading 'regressive' trends towards the substitution of social with security policies for the regulation of relations between minorities and the state (see Saggar and Somerville 2012: 11). Populist anti-foreign sentiments feed off a gross mischaracterisation of what European multiculturalism over the last four decades has achieved (for instance the inclusion of ethnic representation in the mandate of public media; constitutional or at least parliamentary affirmation of multiculturalism at all levels of government; and the funding of ethnic group cultural activities, as well as policies of affirmative action). What current efforts at 'civic integration' focus on instead is the realisation of wider objectives to reterritorialise markers of European inclusion and exclusion (a shift away from post-territorial, more cosmopolitan models of citizenship). Older prewar ideologies of exclusion (illiberal relationships of hierarchy and discrimination) are annexed to newer, more diffuse border mechanisms centred on emerging civilising currents within an expanding Europe. If anything, such additional mechanisms of bordering represent a more explicit attempt to 'contain' Europe's possible future civilisational clusters, especially those perceived as being insufficiently 'Western'. The question of rights and the possibility of accommodating the stranger become utterly conditional on the degree to which the presence of this stranger is desired.

'A Europe That Protects'

Ambivalences regarding the desirability of the stranger coincide with a deliberate narrowing of conceptualisations of where the boundaries of Europe's commons lie. The enjoyment and activation of membership rights is more conditioned today by notions of a bounded geographical jurisdiction (rather than any genuinely cosmopolitan community of rights) than it ever was in the four previous decades – a prioritisation deliberatively defended in spite of Europe's legal institutional endorsement of 'the inherent dignity' as well as 'the equal and inalienable rights of all members of the human family' (United Nations 1948, Preamble). When we take into consideration the fact that the basic human rights of many members of this 'human family' today are violated by the climatically destructive practices of high-polluting states (including those of the EU), that the total global number of refugees is predicted to increase six-fold by 2050 (to 150 million) or even that 58 per cent of the current global refugee population (twenty-five million people) are classified as ecological refugees (that is, victims of globally sustained practices of ecological destruction) (see Friends of the Earth 2007; International Federation of Red Cross and Red Crescent Societies, 2001), efforts to fortify the borders of a self-professed 'Europe of rights' (European Parliament 2009) seem somewhat contradictory and out of step with the greater humanitarian necessities of an ethos of hospitality and global solidarity.

Crafting a doctrine of cosmopolitan right during Europe's great 'Age of Discovery', Kant wrote that every individual has a fundamental right to freedom (Kant 1972). Combining this right with the fact that the lands of the earth are scarce, each individual is said to have a further right to reside somewhere in this world, 'to present oneself to society by virtue of the right of common possession of the earth' and lay legitimate claim to a universal right to hospitality. In principle, those fleeing persecution have 'the right to seek and to enjoy in other countries asylum from persecution' (United Nations 1948, Article 14). In practice, however, this is a right too often denied in European states (Derrida 2001: 13). Figures produced by the United Nations High Commissioner for Refugees (UNHCR) show that the number of people seeking asylum in the EU-27 was just over 300,000 in 2011, a notable decrease from numbers seeking asylum in 1992 in the EU-15 (670,000 applications) (see Eurostat 2012).

> At a time when we claim to be lifting internal borders, we proceed to bolt the external borders of the European Union tightly. Asylum seekers knock successively on each of the doors of the European Union states and end up being repelled at each one of them. Under the pretext of combating economic immigrants purporting to be exiles from political persecution, the states reject applications for the right to asylum more often than ever. Even when they do not do so in the form of an explicit and reasoned juridical response, they often leave it to their police to enforce the law. (Derrida 2001: 13)

There is by now no doubt of the future impact of globalising and crisis-ridden ecological, economic and political worlds on a 'Europe under siege' (Zolberg 1993; see also European Council 2010). Rather than responding to such challenges through a spirit of global cooperation and hospitality, Europe activates a whole new range of 'modalities of violence', including intensive policing, surveillance, military threat (see European Commission 2008: 12) and legally regulated states of closure against the other. For a 'Europe that protects' its citizens against the threat of illegal immigration, trafficking or global terrorism, for instance (see European Parliament 2009: 21), policing is as much a part of the promoted mentalities of justice as it is a social practice (for example, the role of FRONTEX, Europol or the EU's new Eurosur in border surveillance). Police jurisdiction becomes ever more 'formless' and 'faceless' (Derrida 2001: 14). The increasing surveillance of civilian populations together with the further militarisation of border practices are promoted in the interest of building 'a Europe for citizens' (European Commission 2012a), a Europe that also interprets a common policy on the 'removal and return' of illegal persons fleeing persecution, famine and sometimes even death as congruent with 'respect for the human person and human dignity, freedom, equality, and solidarity' (European Commission 2010: 53).

There is something fundamentally anti-cosmopolitan about a regime that denies the extent of its own refusal of cosmopolitan duties to those fleeing ecological persecution, torture, hunger, poverty or warfare. The borders of European belonging must be explored openly through processes of democratic deliberation that speak to changing political, economic, ecological and cultural circumstances. Without such a dialogue, we affirm the legitimacy of what have become 'repressive' forms of tolerance (such as the assimilation of migrants into some static definition of European belonging or the denial of the right of growing numbers to asylum), a move neo-conservatives describe as necessary to counter Europe's 'over-tolerance' of people from foreign cultures or territories (see Fekete 2006: 10). According to their critics, new integration measures and border policies do not foster real hospitality, but rather, openly promote a non-recognition and exclusion of the other as a 'legitimate' response to the issue of 'security'. How might a 'Europe that protects' address such anti-cosmopolitan tendencies?

If the democratic core of Europe is to continue to flourish it cannot shy away from the more radical potential embedded in its full range of political and cultural models of the cosmopolitan, especially those that define membership from the perspective of the universal subject of rights. The universal in this instance is not the antithesis of Europe's national particularisms but rather, their complement. This realisation, however, requires a more critical self-awareness of the generalisability of human interests and responsibilities not only within or even between the sovereign communities of Europe, but also beyond them.

Conclusion

This chapter offers a critical assessment of two parallel discourses of European identity and belonging at work in contemporary European policy. One discourse is classically cosmopolitan, with an emphasis on the importance of world openness, human rights and global solidarity. The other is supportive of a communitarian 'territorialism' (Benhabib 2011: 119) and protracted moments of closure. Its focus on national prerogatives breeds forms of cultural fundamentalism, perpetuates logics of exclusion and captures the essence of Europe as an ipseity (Derrida 2002: 420). The paradox underlying the presence of these two discourses is that both, in fact, are relevant to the peculiar character of contemporary Europe. The latter, far from embodying an enclosed or particularly coherent consciousness, recreates the aporetic nature of European identity through ongoing encounters with the other. Europe epitomises both limits and possibilities – violent and non-violent manifestations of subjectivity towards the other. Today, an expanding Europe proudly celebrates its identity as a community of demoi. Yet in actively preserving the primacy of a peculiarly western Christian ethos, it also promotes new varieties of 'illiberal nationhood' and non-recognition (Kymlicka 2006).

The contrasting elements of Europe's identity project today may not be unique to this period in its histories. However, the current assertion of 'formative ties' to a Europe based primarily upon recalcitrant claims to territory or some monocultural definition of historical belonging will prove extremely difficult in the future, as human mobility and ecological destruction become ever more prominent features of social life. Under these conditions, accommodating the other will become a necessity if relations of international peace are to be maintained. As Europe along with other climate powers such as the USA, China, Australia and Canada contributes most to climate change and natural resource depletion, the question arises as to whether these communities in particular owe hospitality privileges to the world's ecological refugees. As climate change continues to become a socially embedded reality, its contribution to our awareness of humanity as a globally interconnected and equally threatened community also grows. Notions of belonging to a commons, therefore, need to be adjusted accordingly, as do justifications for practices of exclusion.

In light of such immanent threats now facing a global humanity, will Europe be forced to reconsider its cosmopolitan legacy? Although traces of this legacy are clearly evident (for instance the European Charter of Rights and Freedoms, the European Court of Justice, the European Committee for the Prevention of Torture, the Human Rights Commissioner, the Council of Europe Parliamentary Assembly's Committee on Migration, Refugees and Population, and to a lesser degree, in official representations of collective European identity and belonging), in the areas of border control and security, Europe's record is highly questionable. For a 'Europe of rights' that 'stands up for liberties and civil rights also in the struggle against those who oppose them' (Text of the Berlin Declaration 2007), the threads connecting citizenship entitlements and civic responsibilities with international human rights obligations need to be critically reassessed. Clearly missing is sufficient empirical evidence of a principle of reciprocity at work in Europe's more contemporary 'intercultural dialogue' (see European Communities 2009) with alterity. With firm moves towards a 'postmulticultural Europe' steadily underway, Europe is in danger of losing sight of the practical necessity of such a dialogue, one that has always in the past proven pivotal to processes of collective moral learning and democratic innovation.

However, illiberal trends can be reversed and the democratic spirit of Europe revived if cosmopolitan ethics of solidarity are successfully pluralised beyond the petty nationalisms of a fortress Europe, and the alterity inherent in Europe's character is embraced as a positive creative force. Ultimately, it is the translation of, or experimentation with, the interminable, even paradoxical nature of the European that is most likely to preserve Europe's status as an unfinished project of democracy and enlightenment.

References

Bekemans, Léonce (2008), 'The Christian Identity in the Pluralistic Europe', European Forum of National Laity Committees, Bratislava, 1–6 July, http://www.europ-forum.org/dateien/alt/Bekemans.engl..pdf (last accessed 24 June 2013).
Benhabib, Seyla (2011), *Dignity in Adversity: Human Rights in Troubled Times*, Cambridge: Polity Press.
Biedenkopf, Kurt, Bronisław Geremek and Krzysztof Michalski (2005), *The Spiritual and Cultural Dimensions of Europe: Concluding Remarks*', Luxembourg: Office

for Official Publications of the European Communities, http://cordis.europa.eu/documents/documentlibrary/104214451EN6.pdf (last accessed 24 June 2013).

Derrida, Jacques [1991] (1992), *The Other Heading: Reflections on Today's Europe*, Bloomington: Indiana University Press.

Derrida, Jacques [1997] (2001), *On Cosmopolitanism and Forgiveness*, London: Routledge.

Derrida, Jacques [1996] (2002), *Acts of Religion*, New York: Routledge.

Ehrkamp, Patricia (2012), 'Migrants, Mosques, and Minarets: Reworking the Boundaries of Liberal Democracy in Switzerland and Germany', in Marc Silberman, Karen E. Till and Janet Ward (eds), *Walls, Borders, Boundaries: Spatial and Cultural Practices in Europe*, New York: Berghahn, pp. 153–72.

European Commission (2008), 'Climate Change and International Security: Recommendations of the High Representative on Follow-up to the High Representative and Commission Report on Climate Change and International Security', http://www.glogov.org/images/doc/eucouncilfollowup2008.pdf (last accessed 24 June 2013).

European Commission (2010), 'Communication from the Commission to the European Parliament, the Council, the European Economic and Social Committee and the Committee of the Regions: Delivering an Area of Freedom, Security and Justice for Europe's Citizens – Action Plan Implementing the Stockholm Programme', http://eur-lex.europa.eu/LexUriServ/LexUriServ.do?uri=COM:2010:0171:FIN:EN:PDF (last accessed 24 June 2013).

European Commission (2012a), *The Citizen's Effect: 25 Features about the Europe for Citizens Programme*, Luxembourg: Publications Office of the European Union, http://ec.europa.eu/citizenship/pdf/citizens_effect_en.pdf (last accessed 24 June 2013).

European Commission (2012b), *The Development of European Identity/Identities: Unfinished Business*, Brussels: European Commission, http://ec.europa.eu/research/social-sciences/pdf/development-of-european-identity-identities_en.pdf (last accessed 24 June 2013).

European Communities (2009), *Highlights of the European Year of Intercultural Dialogue 2008*, Luxembourg: Office for Official Publications of the European Communities.

European Council (2010), 'The Stockholm Programme: An Open and Secure Europe Serving and Protecting Citizens', *Official Journal of the European Union* C115, 1–38, http://eur-lex.europa.eu/LexUriServ/LexUriServ.do?uri=OJ:C:2010:115:FULL:EN:PDF (last accessed 24 June 2013).

European Parliament (2009), 'European Parliament Resolution of 25 November 2009 on the Communication from the Commission to the European Parliament and the Council: An Area of Freedom, Security and Justice Serving the Citizen – Stockholm Programme',http://www.europarl.europa.eu/sides/getDoc.do?pubRef=-//EP//NONSGML+TA+P7-TA-2009-0090+0+DOC+PDF+V0//EN (last accessed 24 June 2013).

Eurostat (2012), 'Asylum Statistics', Eurostat website, http://epp.eurostat.ec.europa.eu/statistics_explained/index.php/Asylum_statistics (last accessed 24 June 2013).

Fekete, Liz (2005), 'Immigration, Integration and the Politics of Fear', *IRR European Race Bulletin* 52, http://www.irr.org.uk/pdf/immigration_and_elections.pdf (last accessed 8 July 2013).

Fekete, Liz (2006), 'Enlightened Fundamentalism? Immigration, Feminism and the Right', *Race & Class* 48(2), 1–22.

Friends of the Earth (2007), *A Citizen's Guide to Climate Refugees*, http://www.safecom.org.au/pdfs/FOE_climate_citizens-guide.pdf (last accessed 25 June 2013).

Gans, C. (2001), 'Historical Rights: The Evaluation of Nationalist Claims to Sovereignty', *Political Theory* 29(1), 58–79.

Habermas, Jürgen (2006), 'Opening Up Fortress Europe', Signandsight.com, 16 November, http://www.signandsight.com/features/1048.html (last accessed 25 June 2013).
Habermas, Jürgen (2010), 'Leadership and Leitkultur', *New York Times*, 28 October, http://www.nytimes.com/2010/10/29/opinion/29Habermas.html (last accessed 25 June 2013).
Hänsch, Klaus (2006), 'Reflections on the Constitution', keynote speech, Conflicting Memories and European Integration, New York University, 20 April.
International Federation of Red Cross and Red Crescent Societies (2001), *World Disasters Report 2001: Focus on Recovery*, Geneva: International Federation of Red Cross and Red Crescent Societies, http://www.ifrc.org/PageFiles/89755/2001/21400_WDR2001.pdf (last accessed 25 June 2013).
Kant, Immanuel [1795] (1972), *Perpetual Peace: A Philosophical Essay*, New York: Garland.
Kymlicka, Will (2006), 'Liberal Nationalism and Cosmopolitan Justice', in Seyla Benhabib, *Another Cosmopolitanism*, ed. Robert Post, Oxford: Oxford University Press.
Kymlicka, Will (2012), *Multiculturalism: Success, Failure and the Future*, Washington, DC: Migration Policy Institute, http://www.migrationpolicy.org/pubs/Multiculturalism.pdf (last accessed 25 June 2013).
Migration News (2000), 'Germany: Culture, Immigration', *Migration News* 7(12), December, http://migration.ucdavis.edu/mn/comments.php?id=2259_0_4_0 (last accessed 8 July 2013).
Moore, Margaret (1998), 'The Territorial Dimension of Self-determination', in Margaret Moore (ed.), *National Self-determination and Secession*, Oxford: Oxford University Press, pp. 134–57.
Rovisco, Maria (2007), 'Cosmopolitanism, Collective Belonging and the Borders of the European Union', in Chris Rumford (ed.), *Cosmopolitanism and Europe*, Liverpool: Liverpool University Press, pp. 202–20.
Saggar, Shamit and Will Somerville (2012), *Building a British Model of Integration in an Era of Immigration: Policy Lessons for Government*, Washington, DC: Migration Policy Institute, http://www.migrationpolicy.org/pubs/uk-countrystudy.pdf (last accessed 25 June 2013).
Sarrazin, Thilo (2010), *Deutschland schafft sich ab: wie wir Land aufs Spiel setzen*, Munich: Deutsche Verlags-Anstalt.
Stolcke, Verena (1995), 'Talking Culture: New Boundaries, New Rhetorics of Exclusion in Europe', *Current Anthropology* 36(1),1–24.
Telegraph (2011), 'Nicolas Sarkozy declares multiculturalism had failed', Telegraph website, 11 February, http://www.telegraph.co.uk/news/worldnews/europe/france/8317497/Nicolas-Sarkozy-declares-multiculturalism-had-failed.html (last accessed 25 June 2013).
Text of the Berlin Declaration (2007), BBC News website, 25 March, http://news.bbc.co.uk/2/hi/europe/6491487.stm (last accessed 25 June 2013).
Therborn, Göran (2002), 'The World's Trader, the World's Lawyer: Europe and Global Processes', *European Journal of Social Theory* 5(4), 403–17.
United Nations (1948), The Universal Declaration of Human Rights, http://www.un.org/en/documents/udhr/index.shtml (last accessed 25 June 2013).
Zolberg, Aristide R. (1993), 'Are the Industrial Countries under Siege?', in Giacomo Luciani (ed.), *Migration Policies in Europe and the United States*, Dordrecht: Kluwer, pp. 53–82.

Chapter 7

We, the Non-Europeans: Derrida with Said

Engin F. Isin

If in fact the crisis of Europe is more fundamental than the current crisis that engulfs it, then how do we diagnose that fundamental crisis? How do we address the question 'What is called Europe?'? The question is made even more challenging when we further ask what the referent 'Europe' refers to and what the forces are that use that referent. When, in May 1990, Derrida delivered his lecture on 'the other heading' during a colloquium in Turin on European cultural identity he was in many ways responding to these questions and outlining possible ways of approaching them. But Derrida's problem of Europe is much older than that. Europe had been a 'problem' for Derrida – at least philosophically – from the moment he encountered Edmund Husserl and engaged with a cluster of problems that Husserl had articulated as 'the crisis of Europe', a cluster which gave also rise to various thoughts on Europe by Martin Heidegger, Jean-Paul Sartre and Emmanuel Levinas. So there is a danger in beginning with 'the other heading' and forgetting that Derrida's ethical and political problem of Europe had exercised him practically all his public life.

There are other scholars, especially Rodolphe Gasché (2009), who attend to the problem of Europe as Derrida's problem. What I wish to address in this chapter is how Derrida's problem of Europe can be brought into sharper relief with Edward Said's problem of orientalism. Said too was exercised by the question of Europe or 'what is called Europe?', albeit from a different angle. Said's Europe was one which articulated itself through what Derrida would later call its 'wholly other'.

It is true that Derrida and Said rarely, if at all, are brought or read together. There are good reasons for this (Karavanta and Morgan 2008). Said himself reacted strongly to what he considered a 'crippling limitation in those varieties of deconstructive Derridean readings that end (as they began) in undecidability and uncertainty' (Said 2004: 66). For Said, the readings that Derrida provides 'defer too long a declaration that the actuality of reading is, fundamentally, an act of perhaps modest human emancipation and enlightenment that changes and enhances one's knowledge for purposes other than reductiveness, cynicism, or fruitless standing aside' (Said 2004: 66).

How Said came to associate these attitudes with Derrida and to assume that Derrida would not recognise the demand that we as citizens 'enter into the text with responsibility and scrupulous care' remains a problem for me (see Spivak 2005). Its beginnings can be traced to an early essay where Said considered Derrida and Michel Foucault as occupying opposed positions on reading (Said 1978). Marzec (2008) and Radhakrishnan (2010) discuss Said's vexed relations to Derrida and Foucault respectively. However, these issues are not my concern here. I am not interested in consigning Derrida and Said to their separate posts – postcolonialism and poststructuralism. Nor am I really concerned with making Derrida and Said speak to each other. Rather, my aim is to selectively read, or at least invite you to read, Derrida with Said on the question of the non-European. In a nutshell, for both Derrida and Said the fundamental crisis of Europe is an inability to approach the non-European with the openness that is required. To put it differently, the question is not quite 'what is called Europe?' but 'what is called non-European?' This question is simultaneously an ethical, political, psychoanalytical and philosophical question, each aspect irreducible to the others and yet each complicating the others. Let me start with Said's reflections on Freud and the non-European, then discuss the problem of the non-European in Derrida and draw these readings together with Étienne Balibar to conclude the chapter.

Said begins with the observation that Sigmund Freud's knowledge of other cultures was deeply inflected by his education in Judaeo-Christian tradition, especially European humanism and scientism. Said says that Freud was not bothered much by the problem of the other. This may appear a strange statement since Freud can arguably be considered the classic figure in the invention of the other. Yet the other that preoccupied Freud, Said suggests, is a 'European' other (Said 2003: 14). According to Said,

> Freud was deeply gripped by what stands outside the limits of reason, convention, and, of course, consciousness: his whole work in that sense is about the Other, but always about an Other recognisable mainly to readers who are well acquainted with the classics of Greco-Roman and Hebrew Antiquity and European languages. (Said 2003: 14)

Yet, in both *Totem and Taboo* (Freud 2001a) and *Moses and Monotheism* (Freud 2001b) Said detects a refusal by Freud to establish an insurmountable difference or gap between the European and the non-European (Said 2003: 19). It is this refusal, albeit implicit, that can be said to constitute Freud's ethics towards the non-European. Politically Freud goes even deeper and claims that the very fabric of the European is made up of non-European elements. Said notes, for example, that Freud was adamant about Moses's identity: 'Moses was an Egyptian, and was therefore different from the people who adopted him as their leader – people, that is, who became the Jews whom Moses seems to have later created as his people' (Said 2003: 35). What Said observes is not so much the historical accuracy of Freud's interpretation – in fact he remains unconvinced and unsatisfied – but its audacity given how aware Freud was of the dangers of his interpretation and how uncertain he was about it (Said 2003: 39). What Said highlights, and this is of utmost importance to us when we discuss Derrida's articulation of the question of non-Europeans, is that

> in excavating the archaeology of Jewish identity, Freud insisted that it did not begin with itself but, rather, with other identities (Egyptian and Arabian) which his demonstration in *Moses and Monotheism* goes a great distance to discover, and thus restore to scrutiny. (Said 2003: 44)

Freud's audacity was to have argued that the founder of Jewish identity was himself a non-European Egyptian. Said concludes from this that 'identity cannot be thought or worked through itself alone; it cannot constitute or even imagine itself without that radical originary break or flaw which will not be repressed, because Moses was Egyptian' (Said 2003: 54).

It is this political stance that Derrida considers as the problem of the non-European. For both Said and, as I shall now discuss, Derrida, the European is always already the non-European. This is not a thesis of identity. It is not a claim that European is equivalent to non-European or that there is no difference between the European and the non-European. It is a thesis of impurity. It is the assertion of an impossibility of any social group – a people, a nation or a profession – being able to identify itself with itself without any relation or reference to the other.

As mentioned earlier, Gasché closely examines how Derrida approaches Europe. He will be my guide in what follows. Gasché illustrates how Derrida inherits a tradition in which Europe never figures as a geographic or political entity but is always something other, which has been called by various names. Husserl calls Europe an idea or concept.

Gasché (2009: 9) makes reference to other names such as 'figure', an image (Valéry), a category (Badiou), a schema (Guénoun), and 'a little thing' (Derrida); he could have also included a 'vanishing mediator' (Balibar).

If Europe is not merely an entity, what are its origins as an idea? As Gasché says, although 'Europe' as a name originates in the seventh century BC, it is doubtful that it meant the same thing in subsequent centuries. Arguably, the name was inherited by the Greeks from Asia, where its possible meaning – 'dusk' – designated the 'land of evening'. Intriguingly, Gasché surmises, the Greeks may well have not thought of themselves as Europeans but those who were glancing towards dusk, looking towards the land of evening. Thus, in later centuries, by naming itself as Europe, Europe arguably constituted itself with a name that originated outside itself. In a very strong sense, and following Derrida, Gasché says this is perhaps the character of Europe: it calls itself by the name of the other (Gasché 2009: 10). Europe comes to name itself, is able to name itself, only through the other, or the name inherited from the other. It comes to itself from outside itself.

> What the name Europe refers to is thus not primarily the proper name of a land but a name for a movement of separation and tearing (oneself) away in which everything proper has always already been left behind. It is thus an extension prior to all confinement within oneself, thus constituting an exposure to the foreign, the strange, the indeterminate. (Gasché 2009: 11)

'Europe' is not a proper name and the name comes to Europe from outside. The name 'Europe' designates an obscure part of the world where the sun sets. 'The name itself names Europe's origin in a movement of departure from everything native' (Gasché 2009: 13). Europe always glances towards the distance, being always ahead of itself with the other (Gasché 2009: 14). Europe is, or rather stands for, a fundamental openness to the world.

> To elicit the name Europe is not only to evoke the continent and its history – Europe as a geographical and political entity, as well as the history of its many accomplishments and its many failures – but something else as well (even though one does not know exactly what this is). (Gasché 2009: 16)

Perhaps unfairly, Gasché criticises postcolonial thought for creating a blind spot of Europe by assuming its unity and hegemony instead of articulating it as a question. But articulating Europe as a concept that takes its name from outside Gasché also provides a strong sense of the kind of project Europe is (Gasché 2009: 17). This sense is clearly indebted to Derrida, as Gasché readily admits, but it also locates Derrida within a project, or rather, as belonging to a project, or better still, as inheriting a task, a task that is Europe.

Derrida himself intimated this with his emphasis on the relationship between inheritance and responsibility, or rather, inheritance as responsibility. For Derrida, being European means taking responsibility for the heritage of thought that reflects upon what Europe is. This is not a responsibility that is chosen. It imposes itself upon us. For Derrida, being what we are is first of all this inheritance and this inheritance is our task (Gasché 2009: 265). Derrida goes as far as to say that 'we are insofar as we inherit' (Derrida 1994: 68). Taking responsibility for this inheritance means keeping the openness of the concept of Europe through its relation to the other, non-Europe. The task consists in a double movement of being faithful to the concept of Europe and remaining committed to its openness (Gasché 2009: 266). It requires recognising that Europe is the name of an identity involving conflicting demands and that it produces a mode of being that is infinitely open to what is other than itself. It is in this sense that Europe is a project that is yet to come (Gasché 2009: 286).

It is also in this sense that Europe is a question of non-Europeans. We, the non-Europeans, are a problem for Europe, Derrida (of Algerian-French and Jewish upbringing) and Said (of Arab-Christian and Palestinian upbringing) seem to announce, only in so far as Europeans are already contaminated by non-Europeans. It is also in this significant sense that 'the question of Europe is not merely one question among others' (Gasché 2009: 287). It is a question that projects itself beyond its boundaries and beyond its limits, especially those of a geographical, political and cultural nature. The question of Europe is always 'at once a chance and a danger' (Gasché 2009: 287). To capture this aspect of Europe as a concept it is never adequate to recall the question as a question of crisis. To begin with 'crisis', Gasché says, would suggest that Europe as a concept and idea was once stable or intact and that now it is destabilised. As a starting point for reflecting on Europe, the trope of crisis is equivalent to the idea that Europe is identical with itself.

The starting point of reflecting on Europe cannot be its ostensible unity or stability. If the starting point, its originary promise, is its openness, or rather, its commitment to openness, defining itself with other than what it is, placing itself always under question, then the name of this task is at once Europe and non-Europe. The question is not about Europeans as such but Europeans as non-Europeans. Europe is that name which signifies the commitment to place itself under question regarding what it itself is not. That is why Europe is not a geography, a polity, a culture or even a civilisation, but stands for the radical openness of that space which took as its name as the name of the other. That is also why we, the non-Europeans, are a historical problem of Europeans.

Derrida therefore insists that it is 'essential to study and take seriously into account ... beginning with the Greece of Plato and Aristotle, of Hellenism and Neoplatonism, what gets passed on, transferred, translated from Europe by pre- and post-Koranic Arabic, as well as by Rome' (Derrida 2005: 31). Derrida declared that he had neither the competence nor the time to undertake such a study. Yet

> we feel strongly the seriousness of the question of whether philosophy was born in Greece or not, whether it is European or not, whether one can speak of Chinese philosophy, whether one can speak of African philosophy, or whether the destination of philosophy is marked by a singular source, thus by a singular language or a network of singular languages. (Derrida 1995: 377)

For Derrida, then, the fact that Europe's origin is not identical to itself should lead to a historical understanding of the multiple sources of its identity. Derrida was convinced that it is wholly inappropriate to regard the identity of Europeans historically as solely Greek, with some additional Jewish, Christian and Islamic elements. Rather, Europeans are all these things and these things are all open to them at once.

The openness that Said anticipates in his reflections on Freud and the way Derrida approaches Europe as an open project (Derrida 1992b) are radical in the sense that they place demands on us Europeans and non-Europeans alike to reconfigure our relations with our multiple sources of identity and identifications. For Europeans the urgency of this reconfiguration becomes immediately apparent with regard to the ancient Greeks.

For major European philosophers Europe always comes into existence with the ancient Greeks. The birth certificate of Europe as philosophy is staged as inescapably Greek (Gasché 2009: 291). Derrida complicates this relationship with Greece as Europe's birth certificate. It is not that he disowns that originary moment. It is that he multiplies the sources of Europe as philosophy. Derrida accepts that what we rigorously recognise as philosophy as such does not exist elsewhere than Greece. Philosophy, as thought of as being and existence, was born in Greece. To make this recognition requires neither orientalism (or occidentalism depending on the point of view of evaluation) nor historicism. But it means also to recognise that it will have traces of non-Europeans in it.

A year after his Turin lecture Derrida was invited to respond to two contributions by Éric Alliez and Francis Wolff, who had discussed the relations of Derrida, Foucault and Gilles Deleuze to ancient Greeks during a colloquium organised by Barbara Cassin. His oral response was subsequently published as 'Nous autres Grecs' (Derrida 1992a) and has been recently translated into English as 'We Other Greeks' (Derrida 2010). As the translators note, the phrase Derrida uses in the original title can mean 'we who are Greek', but can also mean 'we too are Greeks', as an affirmation, or 'we Greeks of another kind', as a claim of difference (Derrida 2010: 17, n1). As the editor notes, this is perhaps the most extensive if not the most explicit of Derrida's reflections on his relationship to ancient Greeks (Derrida 2010: 17).

This piece clearly illustrates that the Greek question for Derrida is just that, a question. When addressing that question we are inevitably in the presence of

> an intrusion of the other, of the wholly other, who forces the limits of identification and the relationship of language, the corpus, or the system to itself. It is thus a question of locating the traces of this intrusion (traumas, inclusion of the excluded, introjection, incorporation, mourning, and so on) rather than defining some essence or self-identity of the 'Greek', the originary truth of a language, corpus, or system. (Derrida 2010: 19, n2)

Derrida welcomes the efforts to see resonances and resemblances within contemporary thought to identify a configuration or a generation of approaches to the Greek question but also declares that this is not enough. 'We and the Greeks' as a question is too fractured and impure to enable the shaping of a configuration or generation. For Derrida it is urgent to recognise the limits of these resonances and analogies (Derrida 2010: 21). By saying that he has his own Greeks, followed with a pun, 'to each according to his Greeks', Derrida, in my view, signals the impossibility of a configuration that will delimit all the resonances and analogies (Derrida 2010: 19–20). He notes, for example, his difficult relationship to the way Nietzsche or Heidegger relates to the 'Greek thing'. He then wonders why in the twentieth century many scholars have chosen Greek words to name historical formations such as 'epoche' (Heidegger), 'paradigm' (Kuhn), 'episteme' (Foucault) and 'themata' (Holton) (Derrida 2010: 22, n11). He argues that this usage indicates or evokes three powers at once:

> (1) the invention of the new, namely, a concept that is irreducible to those circulating in everyday language; (2) the supposed invention of the new as archaeological rediscovery: restoration, reactivation, or liberation of an

occluded or even a forbidden memory; (3) finally, the authority attached to the use of rare words or of ancient languages considered to be learned languages. (Derrida 2010: 22, n11)

All three are gestures that, despite their claims to discontinuity, establish continuity with the Greeks as their source of authority. As for his own Greeks, Derrida resolutely and emphatically asserts:

> It is not only the non-Greek that attracted me in/to (*chez*) the Greek (it's a question of knowing in short what *chez* means), not only the other of the Greek (the Egyptian, the Barbarian, or whoever is determined by the Greek as his other, and so is excluded-included, posed as opposable), but the wholly other of the Greek, of his language and his *logos*, this figure of a wholly other that is unfigurable by him. This wholly other haunts every one of the essays I have devoted to 'Greek' things and it often irrupts within them: under different names, for it perhaps has no proper name. (Derrida 2010: 25)

Derrida insists that we must resist an either/or injunction where we as Europeans are obligated to announce ourselves as Greeks by an automatic inheritance or as having broken with them by a law of liberation. 'If we are still or already Greeks, we ourselves, we others (*nous autres*), we also inherit that which made them already other than themselves, and more or less than they themselves believed' (Derrida 2010: 27). It follows that

> if the legacy of the thought (of truth, of being) in which we are inscribed is not only, not fundamentally, not originarily, Greek, it is no doubt because of other convergent and heterogeneous foliations, other languages, other identities that are not simply added on like secondary attributes (the Jew, the Arab, the Christian, the Roman, the German, and so on); it is no doubt because European history has not simply unfolded what was handed down to it by the Greek; it is especially because the Greek himself never gathered himself or identified with himself. (Derrida 2010: 31)

Approaching it from another angle, Said articulates this openness well. He says:

> If you know in advance that the African or Iranian or Chinese or Jewish or German experience is fundamentally integral, coherent, separate, and therefore comprehensible only to Africans, Iranians, Chinese, Jews, or Germans, you first of all posit as essential something which, I believe, is both historically created and the result of interpretation – namely the existence of Africanness, Jewishness, or Germanness, or for that matter Orientalism and Occidentalism. (Said 1994: 31)

Moreover,

> you are likely as a consequence to defend the essence or experience itself rather than promote full knowledge of it and its entanglements and dependencies on other knowledges. As a result, you will demote the different experience of others to a lesser status. (Said 1994: 31–2)

I mentioned earlier that for both Derrida and Said the fundamental crisis of Europe is the inability to approach the non-European with the openness it demands. This may have sounded like a call for hospitality. Yet, notwithstanding Derrida's work on hospitality, Derrida's call, with Said's, is in my view more radical than that gesture. Calling attention to the fundamental crisis of Europe is no less than re-evaluating the multiple origins that constitute Europeans and their relationships to non-Europeans. It requires not only revisiting the 'Greek thing' and the inheritance that it implies but also re-evaluating a whole series of ostensible differences that have been put into play especially over the last few decades. It also requires exposing a whole series of differences that have been concealed within Europe as the question of others within Europe.

The infinite task of Europe is infinite not because it is over the horizon beckoning us to orient ourselves towards it. It is infinite because many contemporary problems are rooted in the fundamental crisis of Europe's inability to approach the non-European with the openness it demands. I have already mentioned the problem of others within Europe and the problems of non-Europeans as being distinct but related problems of this fundamental crisis. The symptoms of these problems are all around us.

One such symptom, for example, is the way in which European social and political thought always begins with its distinctiveness as the originary place of democracy, liberty, rights and citizenship. European thought has been unable to open itself up to the possibility that such fundamental institutions are not originary but connected with non-European histories, or rather, originate from dialogical relations between European and non-European histories. European social and political thought has not been able to approach non-European forms of thought with the openness they demand because it has created an insular aura about its origins and distinctiveness, and even (and this is something that Said has taught us) superiority. Examples from its history are many but the contemporary difficulty of creating at least a modicum of comparative political thought, for example, attests to its continuing hold on the life of the European mind (Freeden and Vincent 2013).

When this insularity and closeness persists in European social and political thought it is not surprising to find xenophobia not as prejudice against non-Europeans both within Europe and without but as an endemic condition of relatedness (Bonjour at al. 2011). Today differences among Europeans generate responses that are just as xenophobic and interlaced with resentment as responses to non-Europeans (El-Tayeb 2011). From the acrimony surrounding the accession of Turkey to the European Union to utterly ignorant and disingenuous approaches to China and India, and from disparaging statements about Greek, Italian, Spanish or Portuguese political cultures to the treatment of the Roma and Sinti peoples in Germany, France and elsewhere, yet again the contemporary symptoms of the fundamental crisis of Europe that Derrida and Said invite us to see are clearly visible.

How do we respond to this task? How do we assume responsibility for it despite its immense challenge? Let me conclude with Balibar's idea of Europe as a vanishing mediator. I will translate it into a demand of 'us, the non-Europeans'. Balibar proposes the idea of Europe as a vanishing mediator – apparently belatedly inspired by Fredric Jameson (1973) – to mean a figure that enables an imaginary of the new during the process of transformation of a society, as the old gradually fades away (Balibar 2004: 233). It is an imaginary of the moment between no longer and not yet. Balibar thinks that this idea of the vanishing mediator is not much different from the process of translation of ideas from one idiom to another.

For Europeans – Balibar now speaks as belonging to 'us, the people of Europe' – this might well constitute the exceptional character of Europe, as translator or mediator of cultures. He admits that Europe is not the only space in the world to translate cultures from one language to another, but argues that 'nowhere – not even in India or in China – was it necessary to organise to the same degree the political and pedagogical conditions of linguistic exchanges' (Balibar 2004: 234). Let us leave aside the question of whether finding an exceptional character for Europe brings back the spectre that haunts European thought, which Derrida and Said warned against. What Balibar has in mind points towards the openness that the fundamental crisis of Europe demands. For Balibar, the practice of translation is European but it cannot be enclosed within the borders of Europe since these languages can never remain within the national cultures of Europe. Balibar expands this task of Europe as vanishing mediator in two ways. First, it can be broadened to include Arabic, Turkic, Urdu and other languages that are already spoken within Europe. It can also be expanded by stretching the idea of translation from language to culture. For this utopia or myth – for

Balibar admits its enigmatic character and its impossibilities – Europe can become an interpreter of the world, translating cultures and languages in all directions (Balibar 2004: 235).

Both Derrida and Said were attentive to the questions of linguistic and cultural translation and offered significant insights on relays of translation between the European and the non-European. That each performed these insights as a non-European makes them especially European in the sense we have seen in this chapter. Derrida (1992b: 7) called himself an over-colonised European hybrid and Said (1999: 295) described his life as always out of place with dissonances. Throughout this chapter, you will have noticed, I alternated between their voices as Europeans and non-Europeans. While Balibar calls this multidirectional linguistic and cultural translation a utopia or a myth, to indicate perhaps the impossibility of the task, it also places urgent and immediate demands on both Europeans and non-Europeans. For those intellectuals practising in social sciences and humanities especially, the demand is no less than to re-evaluate many of the central concepts with which we perform ourselves as Europeans and others as non-Europeans: democracy, rights, citizenship, law, territory and state. Tracing the impure histories of these concepts, the ways in which they traversed different cultures and spaces, and the ways which each rationalised and justified pure origins while masking other differences is now a responsibility.

Acknowledgements

The research leading to these results has received funding from the European Research Council under the European Union's Seventh Framework Programme (FP7/2007-1013) / ERC grant agreement No. 249379. I am grateful to Jack Harrington for reading an earlier draft and providing insightful comments. I would also like to thank Agnes Czajka and Bora Isyar for their diligent queries and corrections on a later draft.

References

Balibar, Étienne (2004), *We, the People of Europe? Reflections on Transnational Citizenship*, Princeton, NJ: Princeton University Press.
Bonjour, Saskia, Andrea Rea and Dirk Jacobs (eds) (2011), *The Others in Europe*, Brussels: Université de Bruxelles.
Derrida, Jacques (1992a), 'Nous autres Grecs', in Barbara Cassin (ed.), *Nos Grecs et leurs modernes: les stratégies contemporaines d'appropriation de l'antiquité*, Paris: Seuil, pp. 251–76.

Derrida, Jacques [1991] (1992b), *The Other Heading: Reflections on Today's Europe*, Bloomington: Indiana University Press.
Derrida, Jacques [1993] (1994), *Specters of Marx: The State of the Debt, the Work of Mourning, and the New International*, New York: Routledge.
Derrida, Jacques (1995), *Points . . .: Interviews, 1974–1994*, ed. Elisabeth Weber, Stanford, CA: Stanford University Press.
Derrida, Jacques [2003] (2005), *Rogues: Two Essays on Reason*, Stanford, CA: Stanford University Press.
Derrida, Jacques (2010), 'We Other Greeks', in Miriam Leonard (ed.), *Derrida and Antiquity*, Oxford: Oxford University Press, pp. 17–39.
El-Tayeb, Fatima (2011), *European Others: Queering Ethnicity in Postnational Europe*, Minneapolis: University of Minnesota Press.
Freeden, Michael and Vincent, Andrew (eds) (2013), *Comparative Political Thought: Theorizing Practices*, New York: Routledge.
Freud, Sigmund [1955] (2001a), *The Complete Psychological Works of Sigmund Freud, vol. 13: Totem and Taboo and Other Works*, ed. J. Strachey, New York: Vintage.
Freud, Sigmund [1964] (2001b), *The Complete Psychological Works of Sigmund Freud, vol. 23: Moses and Monotheism, an Outline of Psychoanalysis and Other Works*, ed. J. Strachey, New York: Vintage.
Gasché, Rodolphe (2009), *Europe, or the Infinite Task: A Study of a Philosophical Concept*, Stanford, CA: Stanford University Press.
Jameson, Fredric (1973), 'The Vanishing Mediator: Narrative Structure in Max Weber', *New German Critique* 1, 52–89.
Karavanta, Mina and Morgan, Nina (2008), 'Introduction: Humanism, Hybridity and Democratic Praxis', in Mina Karavanta and Nina Morgan (eds), *Edward Said and Jacques Derrida: Reconstellating Humanism and the Global Hybrid*, Newcastle: Cambridge Scholars, pp. 1–21.
Marzec, Robert P. (2008), 'Said, Derrida and the Undecidable Human: In the Name of Inhabitancy', in Mina Karavanta and Nina Morgan (eds), *Edward Said and Jacques Derrida: Reconstellating Humanism and the Global Hybrid*, Newcastle: Cambridge Scholars, pp. 304–23.
Radhakrishnan, R. (2010), 'Edward Said and the Possibilities of Humanism', in Adel Iskandar and Hakem Rustom (eds), *Edward Said: A Legacy of Emancipation and Representation*, Berkeley: University of California Press, pp. 431–47.
Said, Edward W. (1978), 'The Problem of Textuality: Two Exemplary Positions', *Critical Inquiry* 4(4), 673–714.
Said, Edward W. (1994), *Culture and Imperialism*, New York: Vintage.
Said, Edward W. (1999), *Out of Place: A Memoir*, London: Granta.
Said, Edward W. (2003), *Freud and the Non-European*, London: Verso.
Said, Edward W. (2004), *Humanism and Democratic Criticism*, Basingstoke: Palgrave Macmillan.
Spivak, Gayatri (2005), 'Thinking about Edward Said: Pages from a Memoir', *Critical Inquiry* 31(2), 519–25.

Chapter 8
Of Europe: Zionism and the Jewish Other

Sherene Seikaly and Max Ajl

In Greece, we are at the world's cradle.

Theodor Herzl[1]

In *The Other Heading*, Jacques Derrida reflects on Europe as both possibility and danger. He poses the idea of Europe as at once 'old' and 'virgin' (Derrida 1992: 5). For Derrida, the question of Europe, as the home and origin of philosophy in particular, belongs to the past, but is also perpetually recurring (Chakrabarty 2000). Because of the danger of what Europe is and has been, and the promise of what it can become, Derrida wrote, 'We are younger than ever, we Europeans, since a certain Europe does not yet exist' (1992: 7). For him, the hope of a Europe-to-come lies in its capacity to embrace the other as its 'non-identity', that is, as the difference that constitutes the self. At the core of the 'impossible possibility' of Europe is the question of the example and the exemplary (Redfield 2007: 382). Will the Europe of the past, the present, and the future, asks Derrida, be an example among others, or the example – and so an exemplar? The danger of the example lies in its universalising impulse, an impulse that necessitates the erasure of difference. But there is a promise in the example as well, one that reintroduces irreducible singularity and the particular.

For many centuries, the 'internal other' of Europe was the Jew. In that Europe, the figure of the oriental within was not a subject to embrace, but an object of persecution and erasure. In the best of cases, Jewish belonging in Europe was conditional on the cleansing and reform of otherness, on the erasure of the particular. In the worst of cases, the European 'we' required the very annihilation of the Jew. In the face of this violence a group of Jews in nineteenth-century Europe sought to combine two theretofore contradictory tasks: the salvation of the Jews and the salvation of the idea of Europe. Part of that meant an embrace of the core premise of anti-Semitism: Jews could not assimilate in Europe. Zionists did not turn away from this idea of Europe. They sought, instead, to become a part of it. To do so, they postulated, required their physical departure from its shores; through this process the Jew could be (finally) of, even if not in, Europe. What can Zionism teach us about the ambiguities of the example, the 'irruption of the other,' the hope of the singular, the danger of the universal and the idea of Europe?

The Oriental Within

As Amnon Raz-Krakotzkin argues, 'from the Enlightenment onward, the discussion of the civil status of the Jews has been formulated in clearly orientalist terms' (2005: 162). For many centuries, the Jew was 'an oriental migrant into Europe's heartland' (Kornberg 1993: 18). Dirty, foreign, money hungry, Semitic, Eastern, swarthy, marked by immiscible difference, Jews could never become an organic part of Europe. The image of the Jew 'as a nomad . . . rootless and parasitic . . . shaped modern European sensibilities' (Kornberg 1993: 18). Hannah Arendt traces this explosive concatenation of foreignness, unnaturalness and otherness to the uneasy relationship between aristocrat and bourgeois in Prussia. The aristocrat defended his property on the grounds that 'being and having coalesce as historical property'. The aristocrats' privileges came from 'God and eternity itself' (Arendt 2007: 108). Arendt juxtaposes this natural privilege, closely linked to Romantic nationalism and the race theory that developed with it, to the manifestly acquired status of the merchant. The aristocracy, she argued, considered the bourgeoisie 'deceitful because the way it earns its living is illegal', since it had an '"original" lack of property'. The bourgeoisie was 'unpatriotic' and 'equally at home in all nations' (Arendt 2007: 108). This idea of rootless cosmopolitanism concentrated the entire ideological representation of the bourgeois into a few key reference points. As Arendt argues, this 'malicious description of the bourgeoisie [was] the historical wellspring of almost all antisemitic arguments', the political parry through which the European bourgeoisie defended itself and displaced political anger (Arendt 2007: 108). Thus it was only the Jews, not the bourgeoisie as such, that were 'crassly materialistic, unpatriotic, revolutionary, destructive, speculative, and deceitful, living only for the moment and lacking any historical ties to the nation' (Arendt 2007: 108–9). Later, the need to 'other' the Jews found potent ideological material in European race theory, which turned the European Jews and particularly the *Ostjuden*, the Eastern Jews, into a foreign irritant in an otherwise unified national body. This was part of the efflorescence of Romantic ideologies – *Blut und Boden* ('blood and soil') nationalisms – then in force in central Europe.

Zionist ideologues absorbed this idea and turned it on its head. They agreed that the Jews were indeed a race, even if a low race, but capable of uplift and in need of cleansing. For Arthur Ruppin, the Zionist planner, sociologist and founder of Tel Aviv, the problem was one of racial degeneration. In this conception, as Etan Bloom writes, the 'original Jewish' gene stock had worsened with the 'increase of the Semitic element in the Jewish *Volkskorper*', what Ruppin defined as the 'Bedouin' or 'Oriental type' (Bloom 2008: 116). Thus 'original Jews actually belonged to non-Semitic Indo-Germanic tribes' (Bloom 2008: 116). Over time, the 'Semitic element' had become predominant within the European Jewish race. This was due to Jews becoming 'detached' from their 'native soil', from their productive agricultural life-world. This process incubated within them 'their uncontrollable mercantile instinct' (Bloom 2008: 116). The tropes of Asiatic bazaaris and Moloch melded seamlessly.[2] Eliminating the mercantile tendency was a priority.[3] Similarly, for Theodor Herzl, the founder of political Zionism, 'the Jews of the medieval ghetto in Germany were an "Oriental tribe" ... they wore "Oriental costume"; their speech was Oriental' (Kornberg 1993: 24). It was this orient that had to be purified and erased.

The Mediterranean

The broad disparity between the promise of Derrida's Europe and the danger of Europe's past and present can perhaps best be illustrated in the form of the Mediterranean. For Derrida, the Mediterranean was a gateway to the promise of Europe – perhaps because he came from its southern coast and was 'not quite European by birth' (Derrida 1992: 6). The power and promise of the Mediterranean as a 'machine for making civilization' explains why Paul Valéry is a primary interlocutor in *The Other Heading* (Derrida 1992: 64). As Michael Naas points out, Valéry saw 'in the European spirit an exemplary value for humankind and in the Mediterranean an exemplary value for Europe' (Naas 1992: xxv). The Mediterranean is a gateway to thinking and rethinking Europe; it 'designates at once a limit, a negative limit, and a chance' (Derrida 1992: 35).

For a long time, the Jew had marked the internal oriental border of Europe, a border marked most powerfully by the Mediterranean. While Arendt traced the material origins of a strand of anti-Semitism in central

Europe, institutionalised anti-Semitism goes back further still – at least to the thirteenth century. The 'othering' of Jews as irredeemably oriental reached a pre-Nazi apotheosis during this period, in which one of the earliest frontiers of the East–West conflict unfolded in the very heart of Europe and on the shores of the Mediterranean. However, the *limpieza de sangre*, or blood-cleaning, the expulsions, the violence and the annihilation were directed at not just Jews but also Muslims, hundreds of thousands of whom were expelled in 1609. The remnants and inflections of that Mediterranean culture, that historic potentiality, *al-Andalus*, were expelled and suppressed, and nowhere more so than in the Spanish imaginary. As Ammiel Alcalay explains, it is no coincidence that modern Spain's most feared writers directed their work towards disrupting the destructive 'myths of a "pure" Spanish history whose only logical outcome could be Franco, fascism, and sterility', replacing austere purity with textured hybridity and messy remembrance (Alcalay 1993: 184–5). In this one can see the dual face and common origin of orientalist discourse: in 'western and central Europe' it was 'directed primarily toward Jews, whereas in Middle Eastern and North African countries it played out in the relationship between the European colonizer and the Arab colonized' (Raz-Krakotzkin 2005: 163).

Clearly, the Mediterranean is central to the paradoxes of the Zionist understanding of Europe. After all, until the twelfth century a majority of Jews lived in the eastern Mediterranean. Zionist destruction of Jewish history, and the destruction of the Mediterranean as the border and site of that history, fostered a 'comfortable illusion of a Judeo-Christian heritage' (Bronner 2000: 9). This illusion was shattered at various moments, such as with the publication of the canonical anti-Semitic tract *The Protocols of the Elders of Zion*. As Stephen Eric Bronner argues, 'as Jews rid themselves of their traditional garb and their religious habits, and entered civil society, characterizing Jews as a race became an ever stronger temptation' in modernising European nation states (2000: 57).

For Zionists, departing from Europe into the Mediterranean was the very 'means of joining the Christian West' (Raz-Krakotzkin 2005: 168). Departure was a return to the 'the proverbial cradle of Western (Judaeo-Christian) civilization, imagined and constructed in opposition to the real Arab-Muslim world' (Raz-Krakotzkin 2005: 168). Jews' location on this threshold space – physically of Europe yet rejected by it – and the turn to Zionism required the physical transgression of the Mediterranean and the foundation of a settler colony on its shores. At the same time, Zionism necessitated turning one's back to the Mediterranean, and to the figure of Europe's other within. Thus the Mediterranean was at once a physical refuge and a cultural threat.

This explains David Ben-Gurion's famous fear of the Levant as a cultural model. For along with the Jewish populations a certain conception of civilisation had come to Palestine. As Daniel Boyarin writes, 'Zionism [was] the ultimate project for an honorable conversion of the Jews to Christianity, understood as it always was for Herzl as not a religion, but as *Kultur* itself, as civilization' (1997: 294). It was crucial to Zionists' self-understanding that the Jewish nation be an adamantine shield of Europe on the Mediterranean littoral. As the father of Revisionist Zionism, Vladimir Jabotinsky, put it, 'if there is one outpost on the Mediterranean shore in which Europe has a chance of holding fast, it is Palestine, but a Palestine with a Jewish majority' (cited in Finkelstein 2003: 18). A Jewish Palestine had to be a European Palestine. But its human material was not, in fact, wholly European. Certainly, the Zionists had (and continue) to struggle with the persistent reality of building a Jewish state on a land whose natives were not Jewish. But the spectre of the oriental threat did not merely hover in what Zionists understood as the inferior Palestinian. Nor did it lie only in the oriental residue still remaining within the Jew from Europe.

It was the Jew from the East, in his irreducible singularity, that would pose one of the greatest threats to the rehabilitated, and now supposedly European, Jewish body. The Israeli politician and diplomat Abba Eban explained it best: 'The object should be to infuse the Sephardim' – he meant all of the non-Ashkenazi Jews – 'with an Occidental spirit, rather than allow them to drag us into an unnatural Orientalism'(cited in Alcalay 1993: 31). Since Zionism meant to reprise the construction of a white European identity, 'Levantisation', or the 'infusion' of the spirit of the orient, would be its downfall. The great danger was that 'the predominance of immigrants of Oriental origin [would] force Israel to equalize its cultural level with that of the neighboring world' (Eban, cited in Alcalay 1993: 31). And that would be intolerable.

For this reason, as Ella Shohat has shown, Zionism imagined and attempted to construct a Mediterranean scene without Palestinians or Mizrahim. Thus the massive (and ongoing) dispossession of hundreds of thousands of Palestinians and the erasure of the Jewish cultures of the East – Kurdish, Turkish, Indian, Algerian – were necessary for the consolidation of the Jewish state. These traditions denigrated the pursuit of a Europe that was always on a receding horizon, and kept it in sight only through the relentless material and symbolic rejection and refusal of integration with the surrounding region. To become fully European,

Zionism rejected the promise of the Mediterranean as a space of 'non-identity'. Zionism's Europe is not a space of possible alterity. Zionism's Europe requires the erasure of alterity.

Historicality

In his critique of Edmund Husserl's *The Origin of Geometry*, Derrida explains that Europe's status as the good example makes it an incarnation of 'all historicality' and 'universality' (cited in Naas 1992: xvii). In this sense, then, the non-European is 'only more or less historical; at the lower limit' (Derrida, cited in Naas 1992: xvii). Indeed, for Husserl, the non-European 'tends toward non-historicity' (Derrida, cited in Naas 1992: xvii). Rodolphe Gasché explains how Derrida 'highlights the multiplicity of sources and identities that intersect in the European heritage' (2007: 7). Derrida reads ancient Greek philosophy against the grain of traditional interpretation: he sees it as offering Europe the idea that the other is always already part of the self, a self that cannot exist but for its constitution through and with the other. Indeed, for Derrida, the 'totally other' of Greek philosophy is Judaism (cited in Gasché 2007: 9).

But Europe does not live up to this legacy. It has concealed the constitutive power of the other, the 'non-identity' that Greek philosophy has to offer. This is why Europe orientalised the Jew, constructing its identity against rather than through the other. Zionists replicated this rejection of the other in the self. They wanted to irreversibly erase this distinction of 'totally other' that Europe had bequeathed to them. In this sense, Zionism reproduced the same problematic discourse about ancient Greece that Derrida was committed to deconstructing. For Herzl, Greece, not Jerusalem, was at the core of history and civilisation: 'Culture began at Mount Olympus, not Sinai' (Kornberg 1993: 18). Zionism, in the formulations of Herzl, Ruppin and other ideologues and practitioners, was not simply a transplantation of Jewish communal existence, but was also its reconstruction. Only through this reconstruction could Zionists envision Jewish history as of Europe and its universalising and modernising impulse.

The reconstruction required a multilayered destruction of 2,000 years of exile culture. Zionists internalised Europe as the origin and the model of history itself. As a result, they proceeded to erase Jewish culture and replace it with a neo-Hellenic revival. First came the erasure of Yiddish and its substitution with Hebrew as the national Jewish language. Yiddish was sodden with the rank and rejected culture of the eastern European Jew: his poverty, his ghettoisation, his weakness and his perpetual victimisation in the face of recurrent pogroms. For the 'new Hebrew men' gestating in the educational system of the Jewish settlers in Mandate Palestine, Yiddish was a 'rejected language . . . the sign of a low culture' (Bloom 2008: 35). The destruction of the language was to be a 'radical and absolute cut'; Yiddish was to be 'erased from memory', as a component of the historical process through which European understandings of the oriental (in the Jew) shaped Zionist practice as it solidified in Palestine (Bloom 2008: 35–6). The erasure of Yiddish was crucial to the negation of exile.

The 'negation of exile', as Raz-Krakotzkin points out, was 'the negation of all that was considered "Oriental" in the Jews' while demonstrating 'the desire to integrate the Jews and their history into the narrative of the West' (2005: 167). This contempt for history rehearsed Europe's relationship to Jews. It despised and attempted to annihilate the other within. As pointed out in Boyarin (1997: 33), the German-speaking Jews, who had such a powerful impact on Zionism's trajectory, lathered anti-Semitic stereotypes on the Yiddish-speaking *Ostjude* in 'an uncanny analog to the "evolved" colonial subject, with his contempt for his native people, language, and culture'.

Another axis of destruction and reconstruction was Jewish masculinity. Zionists, like many Europeans, saw Jewish males as effeminate, and so subjected them to a misogynistic contempt. The need to reinstate the Jewish man as a figure of courage, honour and masculinity was one of the driving forces behind Herzl's early proposal for Jewish assimilation. Before his later proposal of a Jewish state, Herzl suggested three possible solutions to the Jewish question in Europe. One was mass baptism. The second was mass Jewish enlistment in socialism, which, given Herzl's elite liberalism and his 'supreme distrust of the masses as the enemies of freedom', reflected in some ways a growing desperation (Kornberg 1993: 46). The third of these early proposals was participation in duels, which Herzl hoped would both bring about and evidence a transformed Jewish masculinity. He hoped to introduce 'new modes of Jewish self-assertion, audacious, heroic modes' that would break with 'old Jewish habits' (Kornberg 1993: 126). Even as Herzl moved away from his earlier commitment to assimilation, he retained European understandings of a deformed Jewish masculinity.

The vision of the 'new Hebrew man' internalised and nourished notions of a stained and corrupt Jew who required geographic displacement to become truly rehabilitated. Zionists enveloped this rehabilitative project in the folds of history. They turned to the ancient Maccabees, who were models for the Crusaders for their willingness to die for their beliefs. This warrior-peasant ideal constituted the core of the Jewish – and crucially, the Hebrew – state. As the Zionist leader Chaim Weizmann, the first President of Israel, put it, 'the time has come when the spirit of the Maccabees will penetrate all layers of Judaism and solve the Jewish problem' through a kind of transhistorical cultural transfusion (cited in Bloom 2008: 136).

For thinkers like Ruppin, and in line with theories of social Darwinism percolating throughout central Europe at that time, Jews could be purified of their debilitating traits only in their ancestral port of call. The key to this endeavour was the revival of the 'Maccabean type', a revival which had already taken place in Christian European culture through, for example, the Maccabean martyrs' entrance into the Christian calendar of saints and their appropriation by the medieval bishopry (Joslyn-Siemiatkoski 2009).[4] The Maccabees offered, then, the promise of genetic and racial rehabilitation. They were outside Europe, but only in the literal sense, and connected to it through a thick and invented pan-Hellenism. As an exemplar of strength, the Maccabee was in opposition to the weakened Jew living in exile. Indeed, Zionists derided the weakness of the Jewish victims of the Kishinev pogroms as most famously recounted in Haim Bialik's *City of Slaughter*:

> Do not fail to note
> in the dark corners of Kishinev
> crouching husbands, bridegrooms, brothers
> peering through the cracks of their shelters,
> watching their wives, sisters, daughters
> writhing beneath their bestial defilers,
> suffocating in their own blood,
> their flesh portioned out as booty.
> And what did these watchers
> cradle in their hearts?
> Did they pray for a miracle:
> Lord, Lord, spare my skin this day?
> These are the sons of Maccabees? (Bialik 1995: 329–33)

Physical labour, self-sacrifice and settlement on ancestral land would redeem this passive, acquiescent figure, and ensure a return to the authentic, national, masculine Jew. This self-conscious transmogrification was at base an 'adoption from the Christian-European and nationalistic repertoires, of legitimate and positive "Jewish" images' (Bloom 2008: 140–2).

But the Jews could not become what Ruppin, Herzl and so many others demanded and fought for in Europe. The racial type – Hebrew, not Jewish – could only come into full flower in the appropriate soil. The more enthusiastic European settlers would, then, be the ones in the direct lineage of the correct 'germ plasma,' more likely to be tied genealogically to the 'pure race Jews' (Bloom 2008: 208). The quiescent or latent features lying dormant in the plasma would flourish in their natural element, transforming Jews once again into a 'vital race', with their best features rescued from quietude, not 'permanently erased' and thus capable of reappearing (Bloom 2008: 208–9).

The conception of historicality as inextricable from the European was crucial to Zionism's trajectory. Zionism, its proponents argued, would propel Jews' entry into history by becoming almost but never quite fully European. But by geographically displacing the Jewish question instead of resolving it politically, Zionism ended up keeping that question alive. It maintained 'Jews' as a distinct entity from Europeans, perhaps provisionally members of the metropolitan race but also with an air of difference, as liminal to modernity. 'European cultures represented male Jews as "female"'; the new Hebrew culture relentlessly worked to overturn this representation, and part of how it did so was by turning its back on old Jewish intellectual traditions and replacing them with a worship of virility, productivisation and war (Boyarin 1997: 34). In doing so, Zionism erased a history of learning, reading and intellectualism. Zionism's reclamation of Jewish pride and honour was premised on understanding the Jewish past just as Europeans did, deformed and oriental. In this discourse, becoming European depended on leaving Europe and the history of penury, supposed effeminacy, intellectualism and all else that was linked with exile. The historical erasure was nearly total.

If Derrida's definition of Europe is the 'irruption of the other', something that is already constituted by the other, then we can see in this 'example' of the oriental Jew not only Europe's potential but, more crucially, its failure. Zionism rehearsed this failure, first by accepting the premise that to become European, Jews had to leave Europe, and then by engaging in the very 'enlightening' and colonising projects that had brutalised them.

Europe as a Heading

Derrida hoped for a Europe that would advance 'itself in an exemplary way toward what it is not' (cited in Naas 1992: lvi). For Derrida, it is not enough to abandon the notion of exemplarity. He works instead to reinscribe it. As Naas suggests, it is this critique of the example 'that has remained the same in Derrida's political thought' (1992: xxxi). It is clear that the question of the example and the exemplary is linked to the 'value of universality' (Naas 1992: xxvi). In this lies the example's danger. Its promise, for Derrida, is in reintroducing 'not only the personal and the particular – the possibility of the other heading – but the irreducible singularity that would allow for the "unification" – although never the subsumption . . . of these particulars' (Naas 1992: lvi). As Naas explains, Derrida is working both within the logic of the example and against it.

Is the question of the example, as Naas proposes, the very question of politics? What can Zionism teach us about the example, its possibilities, promises and dangers? What does it leave open or foreclose about how 'we might invent a politics' (Naas 1992: xxxi)?

The universal in the renditions of men such as Herzl, Ruppin and Ben-Gurion could only mean the enlightened European. The Enlightenment plays a crucial role as a 'centrism' of its own both in *The Other Heading* and in texts about it. For Naas, the Enlightenment has given us human rights, political liberties and responsibilities. It would not make sense to do away with these gifts, he advises. The task is to rethink them. But to what extent is such a rethinking possible? One of the legacies of the Enlightenment was the understanding of Jews as religious dissenters and ethnic outsiders, as we have discussed above. The possibility of Jewish equality was contingent on Judah Leib Gordon's famous formulation: 'Be a man in the streets and a Jew at home!' (1995: 312–13). The erasure of the appearance of difference in the public sphere was an imperative. In the Enlightenment vision, Jews required transformation to be useful moral agents to civilisation. Zionism did not challenge this premise of transformation. Instead, it institutionalised it.

Derrida identified himself both with the Enlightenment and also with its deconstruction. As John Caputo points out, 'while Derrida is often made out to be the sworn enemy of the Enlightenment, he would contend, and we with him, that in fact the deconstruction he advocates is a continuation of what is best about the Enlightenment, but by another means' (1997: 54). In a posthumously published piece, Derrida wrote: 'We must fight for what this name [Europe] represents today, remembering the Enlightenment, certainly, but also consciously accepting the totalitarian, genocidal and colonialist crimes of the past' (cited in Redfield 2007: 373). Where do we locate the totalitarian, genocidal and colonialist crimes of the past in our understanding of the Enlightenment?

This question resonates in Marc Redfield's discussion of Eurocentrism, Husserl, and Derrida. Derrida is critical of Husserl for positioning the United States as belonging to Europe's spiritual geography but deeming the 'Eskimos and Indians ... or the Gypsies, who constantly wander around Europe' as outside it (cited in Redfield 2007: 377). Redfield argues that Husserl's Eurocentrism

> is not in the first instance a racism; such a 'unity of a spiritual life' offers in principle a certain limited hospitality to others, so long as these others, Eskimos, Indians, Gypsies, and so on, obliterate themselves as other by 'Europeanizing' themselves. (Redfield 2007: 377)

But this 'so long as' stands for the will to obliterate the other in the self. This 'limited hospitality' does not embrace or embody the irruption of the other. It is most certainly racism, for it requires the annihilation of alterity. It is that will, that interpretation of the Enlightenment, which has so far won out amid Zionism's pursuit of a European salvation. Derrida teaches us that in the Europe of today, 'hope, fear, and trembling are commensurate with . . . the worst violences, those we recognise all too well without yet having thought them through, the crimes of xenophobia, racism, anti-Semitism, religious or national fanaticism'. These crimes and violences, he explains, are 'mixed in with the breath, with the respiration with the very "spirit" of the promise' (Derrida 1992: 6). Thus, they are the Enlightenment's internal other: colonial crimes, anti-Semitism and racism constitute the Enlightenment just as much as human rights and liberal democracy do.

For well over a century Zionism has denied – indeed, made impossible – Palestinian rights. To some extent, this is an ongoing legacy of the Enlightenment. Jews, subject to the exclusive will of the Enlightenment, embraced in Zionism the ongoing exclusion of another people. Ultimately, Zionism in Palestine

> was made (a) by a European power (b) about a non-European territory (c) in flat disregard of both the presence and the wishes of the native majority resident in that territory and (d) it took the form of a promise about this same territory to another foreign group. (Said 1979: 9)

Zionism posited the Palestinians as well as the Jews of Alexandria, Baghdad and Istanbul as outside history. In Palestine, as Ella Shohat puts it, the 'Ostjuden . . . realized their desire of becoming European . . . on the back of their own "Ostjuden"' (1988: 306).

Conclusion

Derrida argues for the duty to respond to the call of European memory, to recall what has been promised under the name of Europe, to reidentify Europe, to open Europe to 'that which is not, never was, and will never be Europe' (1992: 77). We cannot fulfil this duty without naming, explicating and disavowing Europe's violence.

For the victims of Zionism, Palestinian and non-European Jews among them, Zionism's ideology, history and practices have been and continue to be profoundly unjust.[5] For its proponents too, it was violent. It required the imperative of cultural uplift and the improvement of flawed genetic-racial material; it entailed the notion that the infusion of spirit was possible through the right techniques; it warned of the dangers of pulling the Jews to the orient and the 'unnaturalness' of that orient; and finally, it located Palestine as the ancestral soil of the Maccabees already conceived as the locus of the Jewish future.

Zionism promised Jews who lived in Europe full and emancipated membership of the categories of the Western, the European and the enlightened. But that membership was to be conditional. To become fully European, the Jew had to leave Europe. He had to cross the Mediterranean. Only there and then would he become equal and enlightened. He would find others on the land. In this Zionist (and European) vision, these others were not a people but a disparate group, not a collective but a motley bunch of itinerant field-workers and migrants. They would be easily whisked away to make room for him and his brethren. These natives were inferior to his now-realised European self – that self which Europe had categorised as the dark, backward and superstitious oriental. Through his newly endowed civilisational force, he could take part in building and securing an 'outpost of civilization as opposed to barbarism' (Herzl 1988: 96). After all, becoming fully European required a hierarchical understanding of humanity – the 'clash' between the enlightened and the benighted. The Zionist thus 'othered' and 'inferiorised' the other to become European, just as the European had done to him. Zionism did not merely constitute Jews as being outside Europe. In accepting that Europe, geographically, could only hold certain kinds of political communities, it constituted Europe. And in embracing the task of moulding a territorially displaced European society, dependent on the continual displacement of native Palestinians, it has continued constituting that Europe, culturally and politically. It is, in every sense, its legacy.

Notes

1. Herzl (1983), cited in Kornberg (1993: 22).
2. Joseph Holt Ingraham represented the figure of the money-hungry Jew in his

story *Moloch, the Money-Lender; or, The Beautiful Jewess* (1845), deploying the stereotype of the Jewish usurer in the figure of Enoch Moloch; for discussion, see Harap (1974: 56–7). This in turn flowed into the notion of the Jew as both an import from the orient, from outside Europe, while at the same time identified with mercantilist practices; for the term itself, see Loewenstein (1995: 160).
3. Israel itself has been a massive boon for those seeking material gain; see Nitzan and Bichler (2002).
4. This Europe, too, was an invention: see *inter alia* Graeber (2007: 329–74).
5. See here specifically Said (1979) and Shohat (1988).

References

Alcalay, Ammiel (1993), *After Jews and Arabs: Remaking Levantine Culture*, Minneapolis: University of Minnesota Press.
Arendt, Hannah (2007), 'Antisemitism', in *The Jewish Writings*, ed. Jerome Kohn and Ron H. Feldman, New York: Schocken, pp. 46–121.
Bialik, Haim (1995), 'The City of Slaughter', in Paul Mendes-Flohr and Jehuda Reinharz (eds), *The Jew in the Modern World: A Documentary History*, 2nd ed., New York: Oxford University Press, pp. 329–33.
Bloom, Etan (2008), 'Arthur Ruppin and the Production of the Modern Hebrew Culture', dissertation, Tel Aviv University.
Boyarin, Daniel (1997), 'What Does a Jew Want? or, The Political Meaning of the Phallus', *Discourse* 19(2), 21–52.
Bronner, Stephen Eric (2000), *A Rumor about the Jews: Reflections on Anti-Semitism and the Protocols of the Learned Elders of Zion*, New York: St. Martin's Press.
Caputo, John (ed.) (1997), *Deconstruction in a Nutshell: A Conversation with Jacques Derrida*, New York: Fordham University Press.
Chakrabarty, Dipesh (2000), *Provincializing Europe: Postcolonial Thought and Historical Difference*, Princeton, NJ: Princeton University Press.
Derrida, Jacques [1991] (1992), *The Other Heading: Reflections on Today's Europe*, Bloomington: Indiana University Press.
Finkelstein, Norman (2003), *Image and Reality of the Israel–Palestine Conflict*, 2nd ed., London: Verso.
Gasché, Rodolphe (2007), 'This Little Thing that Is Europe', *CR: The New Centennial Review* 7(2), 1–19.
Gordon, Judah Leib (1995), 'Awake My People!', in Paul Mendes-Flohr and Jehuda Reinharz (eds), *The Jew in the Modern World: A Documentary History*, 2nd ed., New York: Oxford University Press, pp. 312–13.
Graeber, David (2007), *Possibilities: Essays on Hierarchy, Rebellion, and Desire*, Oakland, CA: AK Press, pp. 329–74.
Harap, Louis (1974), *The Image of the Jew in American Literature: From Early Republic to Mass Immigration* (Philadelphia: Jewish Publication Society of America).
Herzl, Theodor (1983), *Briefe und Tagebücher, Bd. 1: Briefe und Autobiographische Notizen, 1866–1895*, ed. Johannes Wachten, Frankfurt-am-Main: Propyläen.
Herzl, Theodor [1896] (1988), *The Jewish State*, New York: Dover.
Joslyn-Siemiatkoski, Daniel (2009), *Christian Memories of the Maccabean Martyrs*, Basingstoke: Palgrave Macmillan.
Kornberg, Jacques (1993), *Theodor Herzl: From Assimilation to Zionism*, Bloomington: Indiana University Press.
Loewenstein, Andrea Freud (1995), *Loathsome Jews and Engulfing Women:*

Metaphors of Projection in the Works of Wyndham Lewis, Charles Williams, and Graham Greene, New York: NYU Press.

Naas, Michael (1992), 'Introduction: For Example', in Jacques Derrida, *The Other Heading: Reflections on Today's Europe*, Bloomington: Indiana University Press, pp. vii–lix.

Nitzan, Jonathan and Shimshon Bichler (2002), *The Global Political Economy of Israel*, London: Pluto Press.

Raz-Krakotzkin, Amnon (2005), 'The Zionist Return to the West and the Mizrahi Jewish Perspective', in Ivan Davidson Kalmar and Derek J. Penslar (eds), *Orientalism and the Jews*, Waltham, MA: Brandeis University Press, pp. 162–81.

Redfield, Mark (2007), 'Derrida, Europe, Today', *South Atlantic Quarterly* 106(2), 373–92.

Said, Edward (1979), 'Zionism from the Standpoint of its Victims', *Social Text* 1, 7–58.

Shohat, Ella (1988), 'Sephardim in Israel: Zionism from the Standpoint of its Jewish Victims, *Social Text* 19/20, 1–35.

Chapter 9

The European Ideal in the Face of the Muslim Other[1]

Zeynep Direk

In both *Origin of Geometry* (1989) and *Voice and Phenomenon* (2011b), Jacques Derrida noted that a philosophical idea of Europe, as responsibility for knowledge, played a constitutive role in phenomenology as a form of transcendental philosophy. In *The Other Heading*, he undertook to think of Europe as an ethico-political ideal, as a relation with alterity, both within and outside Europe. Through a critical encounter with the Kantian ideas of cosmopolitanism and hospitality, Derrida then inquired into the possibility of Europe as the name for 'democracy to come'. This chapter focuses on the relationship between Europe and Turkey as the Muslim other, and takes it as a deconstructive site of Europe's theologico-political sovereignty. Such a deconstruction raises the question of whether present-day Europe lives up to Derrida's idealisation of it. I argue that Europe calls for deconstruction, and that the best deconstructive strategy would be to point to the manner in which Europe's theological politics and its technocratic governance are constitutive of one another, which accounts for its becoming a place of democracy without democracy.

Turkey's efforts over the past fifty years to become a part of Europe – at first through the institutional mechanism of the European Economic Community, and now through the EU – have given rise on the Turkish intellectual scene to debates about Turkish identity and the essence of Europe. For a long time, in Turkey, political ideologies determined the various positions on Turkey's relationship to Europe. On the one hand, Kemalists, the cosmopolitan democratic left and liberals supported Turkey's participation in the EU, even if for different reasons: Kemalists supported it because they have always conflated modernisation and Europeanisation;[2] the cosmopolitan democratic left supported it because after the fall of the communist bloc they contested nationalist identity politics in the name of enlightenment and human rights;[3] and liberals supported it because they were in quest of a modernity that is not statist, paternalistic and authoritarian (Keyder 1997: 48; Mutman 2001). On the other hand, as Tanıl Bora argues, Islamic and nationalist right ideologies rejected Turkey's Europeanisation (Westernisation), which they saw as cultural self-betrayal and loss of political independence (Bora 2002).

In the last decade, however, the tables have turned and positions on Turkey's relationship with Europe have dictated political ideologies. Its pro-EU discourse and efforts for membership made the Justice and Development Party (AKP) look like a politically 'progressive' party, despite its socially conservative agenda. In the meantime, the left was divided into nationalist and internationalist factions. The nationalist left wing defined itself by its opposition to the EU, and sided with the nationalist right in sharing its perception of Kurdish and Armenian human rights and justice claims as threats to Turkish political sovereignty. In contrast, the internationalist left continued to support membership of the EU and found itself on the same side as the AKP.

In this decade, the Turkish experience of European accession requirements has transformed the terms of political discourse, making human rights, minority rights and ethnic and cultural rights increasingly central to political debates in Turkey. In this context, it is also important to note the existence of various non-party organisations or NGOs in Turkey that are supportive of EU membership. And one must add that recently, the tides seem to have turned again, as Turkey's interaction with Europe has created a resentment within the AKP, making it seem much less pro-EU.

It is remarkable that in the last decade Derrida's philosophy has contributed to intellectuals' and activists' reflections on political problems in Turkey. Appeals to the politics of respect for alterity and to ethical responsibility for the other have often been made using the conceptual apparatus provided by Derrida's philosophy. Derrida's philosophy has been central to an increasingly sophisticated interrogation of Europe and Turkey's positions vis-à-vis Europe (Mutman 2002; Direk 2006). Questions such as 'What is Europe?', 'What is the West?' and 'What is meant by Western culture and morality?' have been increasingly asked and answered using concepts furnished by Derrida. Deconstruction was evoked both in denouncing the Eurocentrism implicit in the European approach to other cultures, and in appealing to the possibility of a non-Eurocentric Europe as a space for democracy. Derrida's deconstruction of the nation state has been important for a critique of Kemalism,[4] and for rethinking the armed conflict between the Turkish state and the

PKK (Kurdistan Workers' Party) (Direk 2010). Derrida's philosophy has also offered a coming to terms with ethnic and cultural identity claims. His *Monolingualism of the Other* (1998), for instance, has been referenced in relation to the demand for Kurdish language education (Direk 2005). Most recently, Derrida's thinking on religion and its relationship to secularism has received attention. Indeed, Derrida has been a philosophical interlocutor in making sense of the Turkish experience of modernity.

Conversely, when one reflects on the essence of Europe from a Derridean perspective, Europe's experience with Turkey as a Muslim other appears as a significant site for the manifestation of such an essence. Interestingly, the Turkish Prime Minister's Office of Public Diplomacy, headed by Associate Professor İbrahim Kalın (advisor to Prime Minister Recep Tayyip Erdoğan), took up this perspective; in May 2012 it organised a public lecture series entitled 'Europe as an Idea', as part of which Ian Almond and I discussed what it may mean to 'deconstruct Europe'. As this event shows, it is also with reference to Derrida's philosophy that Turkey has sought to express its disappointment with Europe. Recently, Derrida's reflections on religion and his relation to Islam have attracted the attention of Muslim intellectuals.[5] Yet the reception of Derrida's philosophy in Turkey is not my focus here. I shall limit myself to showing that Derrida's philosophy can be of help in conceptually negotiating the relationship between Europe and Turkey. In order to show this, I shall first look at Derrida's philosophical approach to Europe, and then focus on the deconstructive implications of the relationship in question.

At stake in Derrida's philosophical strategies of reading, dating from the 1960s and 1970s, was the deconstruction of metaphysics. These strategies revealed some quasi-transcendental structures beneath the metaphysical hierarchies composed of binary oppositions. The question of what 'deconstruction' may mean in the political context was soon raised, and it is my contention that, in the 1990s, the political orientation in Derrida's thinking becomes clearer. He offers reflections that bring deconstruction to bear on the problems of sovereignty, democracy, identity, the theological dimension of politics, nationalism and cosmopolitanism, with the overall aim of deconstructing politics by pointing to the metaphysical thinking that sustains political concepts and rethinking these concepts in aporetic ways.[6]

It might be useful to recall here some of the most important tenets of Derrida's deconstruction of politics. In 'Force of Law' (1992a) Derrida relates the practice of deconstruction to the idea of justice. He argues for the deconstruction of institutions as a way of revealing their injustices and identifying what needs to be transformed within them. He situates deconstruction between law and justice. Deconstruction must take law into account while simultaneously attending to that which exceeds the law – justice as undeconstructable and unconditional.

This structure of deconstruction as situated between law and the idea of justice has shaped Derrida's reflections on Europe. In 1992, Derrida published *The Other Heading*, a text full of wonder, hesitation and anticipation about this new, unified Europe. But he also made suggestions, proposing an ethico-political idea of Europe. Old Europe, as Paul Valéry imagined it, posited itself as the head, pioneer and leader of human civilisation on earth (Derrida 1992b: 20–1). Europe was the *arche* and *telos* of civilisation as such. Derrida did not want the new Europe to return to this well-known Eurocentrism. He expected Europe to rethink 'identity' in terms of internal difference and as a relationship to the other.

Let me emphasise that Derrida never presented himself as a philosopher of identity, and refused to think of identity as sameness in the sense of self-coincidence. An identity based on internal difference, difference with oneself, is, for Derrida, the ontological condition for respecting difference in social relations. Derrida is not a moral cosmopolitanist who would make geographic demarcations among groups of people, national, ethnic, racial differences among human beings irrelevant from a moral point of view. But respecting a difference should not be to reduce the other to that difference through which he or she is rigidly identified. Self as a movement of *différance* lies at the ground of both the other's historical identification and ethical subjectivity as hospitality. In 'On Cosmopolitanism' *la ville refuge*, in which the politically persecuted is offered refuge and asylum rights, gives us a simile for the fundamental openness that pertains to ethical subjectivity as hospitality (Derrida 2001a). Thus, although Europe can no longer be conceived of as the disseminator of universal truth, it can still be signified as responsible for the universal and for difference. As Rodolphe Gasché notes, 'the idea of Europe as a cosmopolitan idea is first of all a challenge to the European; the universality at stake in cosmopolitanism challenges, first and foremost, its own inventor' (Gasché 2009: 344).

In *The Other Heading*, Derrida also identified some of the risks facing Europe: the return of nationalisms at the heart of Europe; the construction of European transnational identity in nationalistic terms; the degrading of democracy in technocracy; and, worst, sovereign technocratic redrawing of the political dividing line between friend and enemy as that between native European citizens and others, namely immigrants. As Europe suffers more economic problems, immigrants are increasingly seen as responsible for the economic loss or lack, and their public appearance – with different languages, clothing, customs and religions – becomes the subject matter of a discourse of allergic criticism. Europe calls for deconstruction today because the 'good Europe' is no longer easy to believe in. Such a deconstruction must point to what is unjust and unethical in Europe, without aiming to dissolve or demolish Europe itself. Nonetheless, what is worth deconstructing must have, in itself, some hidden potential, some saving power, for the sake of which it is still worth preserving and making a commitment to.

There are multiple ways of deconstructing Europe, which demonstrate that at present Europe risks over-identification; it returns to a myth of the origin, the proper, thus trying to coincide with itself by way of expropriating, rejecting, abjecting and excluding the other. Recently, Ian Almond discussed five such ways.[7] The first deconstruction realienates origins; it shows that things considered emblematic of Europe have non-European origins. It reveals that the origins are elsewhere, thus reinserting the other into the heart of the sameness of Europe. This strategy forgets that the power of the origin abides even when the origin is revealed to be false or illusory, given that the subsequent layers of meaning reiterate it. The second deconstruction consists of the redesignation or reconfiguration of space and culture, with the effect of renaming. For instead of calling Europe, like Valéry, 'the cape of the Asian continent' we could, following Friedrich Nietzsche, call it 'a little peninsula of Asia'.[8] Yet it is not clear that one can effectively undermine the narrative of European identity by mere symbolic manipulation. The third deconstruction consists of making manifest the 'internal othering' at work in Europe. Europeans de-Europeanise themselves by orientalising their European neighbours, as in the Africanisation of Italians, the Turkification of Greeks and so forth. The fourth deconstruction proposes deuniversalisation, or provincialisation. It reveals that some of the ideas and traditions considered European are also found elsewhere, undermining the positing of Europe as the disseminator of universality. The fifth and final deconstruction examines the strategies of commonality: if certain beliefs, alliances and cultural practices are also found elsewhere, then they cannot be attributed specifically to European culture.

From Almond's five ways of deconstructing Europe, it follows that a de-Christianisation of Europe is necessary, which is inseparable from a de-Islamisation of those parts of the world that identify with Islam in exclusionary ways. Almond evokes 'de-Christianisation' when what is at stake is an explanation of the fifth way of deconstruction, which seems to respond to the political discourses on European values that result in the identification of Europe in Christian terms. However, the meanings of 'de-Christianisation of Europe' or 'de-Islamisation' are not clear. If this is neither a call for collective conversion nor a disavowal of faith, can it be understood as a demand for a more secular lifestyle? In order to answer that question, one must focus on the role that secularism and religiosity play in legitimating technocratic policies. The banning of Muslim women from wearing the niqab in public spaces in France, to take one example, can be seen as just a symptom of a complex structural relationship between technocratic government and secularity/religiosity. Now, although this law claims to defend Europe's secular public space, the ethical value language that accompanies it uses and affirms Christianity. The law attempts de-Islamisation but rather than secularising Europe, it makes Christianity the dominant pole of identification. Secularism means that the state is equidistant from all religions, but such interventions in public spaces amount to predisposing it in favour of the dominant religious creed.

The Islamisation of immigrants and the exclusion of Muslim women from the public space are not the only symptoms of the complicity between technocracy and its political theology; others can be seen in some of the obstacles in the way of Turkey's accession to the EU. At present, technocratic decision-making at the heart of the EU is tied up with a political theology. Technocracy implements decisions that are taken in anti-democratic ways, and limits the possibilities of negotiation. The political system itself seems 'theological' if people do not have the right to change it, and if it transcends and forecloses the open space of democracy by predetermining it in technocratic ways. Moreover, it is also possible to ask, from a Schmittian point of view, whether European sovereignty does not make itself manifest by deciding on friends and enemies, and whether religiosity/secularity does not in the present play a role in distinguishing between them. In that respect, the historical modification that the sense of opposition between Islam and Judaeo-Christianity has undergone in western Europe deserves attention. Furthermore, there is surely a complicity between technocratic programmes such as 'interreligious dialogue', 'religion as conversation starter', 'the role of religion in peace-building' and so on and the theological politics of sovereign decisionism. Technocratic politics of religiosity create more rigid religious identifications and oppositions rather than exploring the resources of faith for negotiating social problems.

The relationship between Turkey and the EU provides a guiding thread for a deconstruction of the EU. This deconstruction would examine the disparity between the philosophical idea of Europe, Europe as a project and Europe in its present political experience. Becoming a member of the EU has been a long process, during which Turkey has made great efforts to respect the political, economic and social norms of other candidates, and, certainly, respecting such norms has had a positive effect on social and political life in Turkey.[9] However, Turkey's accession to the EU has not been addressed in public debates and arguments according to conditions that are valid for all member countries. As Riva Kastoryano remarked, 'the nature of the debates and arguments produced by Turkey's accession make it a candidacy in a class of its own' (2006: 275). The EU seems to be following a strategy to maintain its customs union with Turkey (signed on 6 March 1995), a one-sided relationship that grants Europe economic advantages over Turkey but leaves Turkey at a disadvantageous position in international commercial relations. For example Turkey counts as an EU member when it imports from the US and as a third world country when it exports to US. Thus the EU neither likes to refuse nor likes to admit Turkey. The debates have primarily been about cultural and spiritual values.

It is no longer easy to believe in the good Europe because Europe does not conform to its philosophical idea in Kant, Husserl and Derrida. Although the conditions under which Edmund Husserl and Derrida engaged in their reflections were different, the essential issue they discussed – the exemplarity of Europe – remained the same. Europe was under the threat of Nazism when Husserl tried to say that Europe's essence is the phenomenological attitude of going back to the things themselves, in order to clarify the origins of scientific knowledge. Europe meant, for Husserl, being critically in touch with the most primordial experiences. It referred to a certain attitude or practice of philosophy, more than to identification through the appropriation of a historical philosophical heritage. Taking responsibility for the tradition meant investigating its hidden assumptions and challenging them in order to open new possibilities. This is where Husserl located the exemplarity of Europe in relation to other cultures. The essence of Europe did not consist in the manner in which people appeared: their clothing, their lifestyle, the way they dwelt and built cities, the technology they used, the way they wrote, their use of a specific alphabet or their measurements of objective time and space. In contrast to the idea of Europe as perceived by Kemalist modernism, the European *eidos*, according to Husserl, did not have anything to do with contingent features of the European lifestyle. It meant reflectivity and 'the historical teleology of infinite goals of reason' (Husserl 1970: 299).

In early Derrida we find several notions such as dissemination, iterability and trace that enabled him to deconstruct Husserl's historical teleology of reason. However, this deconstruction continued to respect Husserl's conception of the European *eidos* as responsibility for sense. Indeed in *The Other Heading* Derrida redefined the idea of Europe according to two constituent elements: first, responsibility for sense, the inherited body of knowledge, and second, openness to the other. Although these two elements are equally primordial, Derrida fantasised about a Europe with permeable borders. He inquired into these dimensions in the experience of hospitality, in which what is at stake in the subject's reception of the other is identity. This is another way of saying that for Derrida it would be fundamentally wrong – irresponsible – to imagine Europe on the basis of the conservation of an identity, and to designate it with reference to a particular race, historical culture or religion. 'Europe' should be the name of a cosmopolitan, democratic and pluralistic space.

What about secularism? In an interview after 9/11, Derrida defended his continued commitment to Europe in the following way:

> I persist in using this name 'Europe', even if in quotation marks, because, in the long and patient deconstruction required for the transformation to come, the experience of Europe inaugurated at the time of Enlightenment (*Lumière, Aufklärung, Illuminismo*) in the relationship between the political and the theological, or, rather, the religious, although still uneven, unfulfilled, relative and complex, will have left in European political space absolutely original marks with regard to religious doctrine ... Such marks can be found neither in the Arab nor in the Muslim world, nor in the Far East. (Derrida 2003: 116–17)

Although Derrida here notes the secularisation of Europe, he is often read, as in Naas (2008), as making secularism uniquely formative of Europe, as distinct from the Muslim world. The problem here is that Europe has a Muslim population of approximately seventeen million people. Islam in western Europe owes its presence to immigration from the Middle East and Africa throughout the twentieth century, and that immigration was partly caused by the social and economic effects of Western colonialism and the subsequent processes of decolonisation. As the American interpretation of Islam on the grounds of the experience of 9/11 became more prevalent, western Europeans became less comfortable with this Muslim religious presence. However, Islam in eastern

Europe is quite different: there its presence can be traced back to the Ottoman presence in Europe and has created its own historical forms of life. Its social meaning in countries such as Romania, Albania, Bulgaria and Bosnia-Herzegovina is not determined by the interpretation of Islam post-9/11. Muslims in western Europe suffer the constant pressure of Islamophobic discourses that hold immigration responsible not only for economic problems, but also for social problems. This perception of Islam in western Europe often frames public discussion about Turkey's accession to the EU. Even when the proponents of Turkish participation succeed in showing that Turkey's membership may contribute to the EU's growth for economic and geopolitical reasons, it is still difficult to get around what I name 'the argument from cultural and religious diversity'. In fact there is no real argument there but a cultural and religious identification over and against the religious and cultural diversity of immigrant populations.

As it retreats into identification in terms of race and religion and fortifies the racist trends inherent to it, Europe betrays its philosophical idea. If Europe rigidifies its boundaries in the face of the other, it will become an enclosure for some antiquity – the site, or a shelter, for a threatened identity. For example, when the French argue that wearing the niqab undermines the principles of their republic, they expose the extent to which they perceive the other as a threat to their identity (See Göle 2006). In France today, most votes are shaped by manipulative anti-Islamic discourses, which cast doubt upon Europe as a democratic space. The threat to one's existence or identity is the determining affect at the existential ground of all nationalisms. Those who retreat into their identity lack an open relation to the other that could give rise to new universals. Indeed, Europe today is not a Judaeo-Christian space; it is a space that is defined by what it excludes, namely, Islam. The present Europe calls for deconstruction because its real politics are shaped by the logic of abjection. When identification becomes abjection and exclusion, the ethical relation to the other is precluded. This logic determines Europe's politico-theological sovereignty, which at the same time exerts itself as technocracy – decisionism that programmes, calculates and manipulates opinions in a way that eradicates a democratic pluralistic public space.

Gestures that promote xenophobia and Islamophobia contradict with Europe as a philosophical project, involving legal, political and ethical ideals. 'Europe' would mean for a Derridean politics cosmopolitan law, which transcends cultural and religious identities; democratic political life; and an ethics of hospitality that implies unconditional respect (infinite responsibility) for the alterity of the other. Derrida's idea of Europe not only promises equality in secularism, but also implies responsibility for the alterity of the other, and thereby pluralism. I think that including a country with a majority Muslim population would be a first step towards a truly cosmopolitan and pluralist Europe, for it would amount to a reaffirmation of Europe as a secular space where all forms of religious discrimination would be outlawed.

Given this framework, the experience of secularism in present-day Europe is also in need of deconstruction. In what follows, I shall attempt a deconstruction of European secularism by reversing the classical logic of exemplarity – taking not Europe but Turkey as exemplary. As is well known, modern Turkey followed as its model the French *laïcité*, making it one of the founding principles of its constitution and relegating religion to the private sphere. The political Islamic movements that flourished in the second half of the twentieth century challenged *laïcité*, and returned religion to the public sphere. This experience proved that religion could not be isolated from political life. The Turkish case exemplifies how religion and politics intertwine at three levels: first, religion can, and does, contribute to a secular-national identity, even though the official discourse is against religion of any kind; second, despite the official practice of *laïcité*, the state cannot privatise the communitarian aspects of religion; third, relying on the function of religion in the formation of a secular identity, a particular religious interpretation (in the Turkish case, Sunni Islam) can gain primacy not only over other religions, but also over other interpretations of the 'same' religion.

Could there be a higher framework over and above the religions that exist in a society, a framework that transcends all particular religions and assures their right to exist? Secularism had indeed promised such a framework. Yet it did not (at least in the form reinforced by the Kemalist ideology of twentieth-century Turkey) create a space in which all religions could be freely practised. Ideally speaking, a normative legal framework could provide the norms all religions have to comply with, and thus help to resolve religious tensions that are otherwise irresolvable. By looking at Europe today, with a specific focus on France, one may ask whether such a framework really does exist. Officially, *laïcité* justifies the exclusion of Islam from the public sphere; yet it is also possible to read this as discrimination against Muslim Europeans, and further, as reinforcing the primacy of (Catholic) Christianity over other religions (see Laborde 2009: 27).

Historically speaking, secularism has carried within itself an ambiguity. On the one hand, committing itself to building a secular society, it has attempted to erase all religious residues from the public sphere. According to the secular ideal, European identity must transcend all religious faith and be capable of being expressed in terms of aesthetic, political, ethical and cultural ideas. As it makes religious beliefs and practices a private matter, this ideal also bears within itself the promise of a non-hierarchical relation between religions. However, as is clear from recent French juridical practices which ban the niqab (misnamed the burqa) from the public space, the secular ideal has betrayed both of its functions, for it now explicitly warrants priority and privileges to (Catholic) Christianity over Islam. In other words, the French 'secular' higher framework allows a hierarchy of degrees of acceptability for religious practices, which gives Muslim practices of sacrifice – wearing the niqab, circumcision and such – their social sense and value. As a result, they are perceived as regressions to primitive practices that have been long surpassed by civilised societies. In short, the present European secular framework is unjust because it holds a particular religion, Christianity, at the summit of a religious hierarchy and fails to treat all religions equally.

The French state defends *laïcité* because it sees it as an essential component of French (European) identity. And it applies sanctions to Muslims in France because it perceives their conduct – or, at times, their very being – as a threat to this identity. One may argue that this politics of exclusion cannot be seen as a matter of technocratic policy-making. There must be something more fundamental that enables decisions that have such an effect. One may wonder if, without an original 'breach' within 'secularism', a hierarchy of religions – in which Christianity stands over and above the others – could come into being. If there is indeed such a breach, then Islamophobia in Europe can be neither the trace of a past experience that haunts European historical consciousness, nor a consequence of historical tensions among religions. In other words, it is not a resurfacing of the fear that Europeans once felt in the face of the Ottoman invasion of Europe. If Islamophobia derives from the problematic nature of European secularism, then it must be considered as an affect embedded in European political institutions.

The theologico-political nature of secular sovereignty operates through a political religiosity; it proceeds with the decisionism of technocracy to the effect of socially producing this particular affect to ground European Muslims' deprivation of their rights as free citizens. Just like all constitutions, the secular framework, too, stands in need of interpretation. All general, abstractly formulated laws can be perverted or turned into their opposites as they are translated into particular laws through bureaucratic measures and technocratic strategies. Giorgio Agamben showed how Western democracies could create spaces that deprive citizens of civil rights and reduce them to mere members of the human species that do not have the right to have rights (Agamben 2011). The invention of multiple obstacles aimed at making admission of Muslims to European citizenship extremely difficult gives us another actual example of such a space – even if those obstacles have no constitutional or legal basis and are purely cultural impediments.

Why has secularism failed to sustain a plural and democratic order and diversity in daily life? First, as the French and Turkish examples show, the secular framework gave primacy to the religion of the majority. Second, as sociological literature has taught us, secularism had an insufficient conception of religion, for it reduced religion to a matter of individual faith and allowed only for a private religious life. However, religions of the book have always been about community, and not necessarily about individual faith. Third, whether national or transnational, political unities are never merely political and economic projects; they also have strong cultural and philosophical dimensions. In these latter dimensions, religion as such and religious differences play important roles. Today, one of the most important issues facing Europe concerns locating religion and religious differences in a pluralist democratic order and in daily life practices. Both Turkish and European technocracies believe that interreligious dialogue towards peaceful coexistence could cope with these differences. It should be stressed that this is another elitist-technocratic project, aloof from the everyday reality of ordinary people.

Religiosity in Europe calls for a new philosophical reflection on the ideas of liberty, equality, fraternity, enlightenment and religious tolerance. Although the 'universal' republican ideas of liberty, equality and fraternity originally applied only to bourgeois men, they gradually included the proletariat and women. Now, a new step towards universalism must be taken, by embracing the Muslim difference that is externalised as 'the non-European element'.

In concluding, it is worth recapitulating the following point. If the universalist idea of Europe is no longer effective, and debates over religiosity abound, these developments are expressions of a historical truth: soft or hard, a religious core remained in the making of Europe, which is why Europe was never a product of pure secularism. I suggest that the present discourse on religiosity in Europe, appropriated by a bureaucratic and instrumental rationality, makes use of this truth for the wrong reasons: it appeals to religiosity in Europe with an attitude that elevates the self and excludes the other; it rearticulates and recontextualises cultural, economic and political problems in terms of 'religion'. The deconstruction of Europe offered in this chapter paves the way for new philosophical reflection that would offer a larger framework by setting aside bureaucratic and instrumental rationality. It shows that religious identification does not enable Europe to better solve its concrete problems; Europe should affirm religious and cultural pluralism in order to embrace a new cosmopolitan universalism. It is my contention that this is part of what is at stake in Turkey's accession to the EU.

Notes

1. I would like to thank the Research Fund at Galatasaray University for supporting this project.
2. In the Kemalist discourse, however, the desire to correct the people's deficiencies through Western culture is always counterbalanced by a desire to preserve authentic Turkish culture as an antidote to what is considered to be inappropriate, such as extreme modernity, liberality, immorality, and ethnic and class conflict (see Ahiska 2005: 87).
3. The relation of the left in Turkey to Westernisation/Europeanisation is indeed a complex issue. A preliminary account can be found in Çulhaoğlu (2002).
4. Derrida himself made remarks on Kemal Atatürk, whom he referred to as 'K.A.'. He alluded to the violence of Atatürk's revolution, which by passing a law on 1 November 1928 imposed an alphabet employing Latin letters, thereby prohibiting books written in Ottoman script, and mandating that not only all official but also all private correspondence be written using the new alphabet (Malabou and Derrida 2004: 13). This letter has been translated into Turkish and published in a special journal issue devoted to Derrida's philosophy (Derrida and Malabou 2006).
5. Recep Alpyağıl (2007) and Ian Almond (2012) have addressed the philosophical issues that pertain to Sufism in Derrida's terms. Derrida is also evoked in debates around contemporary political Islam in Turkey (see Demirhan 2012).
6. Some of Derrida's works from the 1990s and later focus more explicitly on political issues. A (non-exhaustive) list can include *The Other Heading: Reflections on Today's Europe* (1992a), *Specters of Marx* (1994), *Politics of Friendship* (1997), *On Cosmopolitanism and Forgiveness* (2001b), *The Work of Mourning* (2001c), *Rogues: Two Essays on Reason* (2005) and *The Beast and the Sovereign* (2009; 2011a).
7. Ian Almond, 'Five Ways to Deconstruct Europe', İstanbul Şehir University, 7 May 2012. The lecture is due to be published in 2014 (Almond, forthcoming).
8. I have modified the expression, but similar formulations can be found in Valéry (2000a) and (2000b). Derrida cites 'Notes sur la grandeur et décadence de l'Europe' (Valéry 1960: 931) in *The Other Heading* (Derrida 1992a: 12); see also Naas (1992: lv). The expression 'the little peninsula of Asia' is found in Nietzsche (1996: 365).
9. Turkey's way of coping with the PKK in cities has been to imprison people for, legally speaking, no valid reasons. Judicial power is used as an arm against the pro-Kurdish dissidents. For me, it is clear that Turkey will fail to satisfy Copenhagen criteria on democracy and the non-violation of human rights if the war between the Turkish state and the PKK continues. However, I also think that

Turkey's membership of the EU could provide the legal framework for solving this problem.

References

Agamben, Giorgio [2009] (2011), 'Introductory Note on the Concept of Democracy', in Giorgio Agamben, Alain Badiou, Daniel Bensaid, Wendy Brown, Jean-Luc Nancy, Jacques Rancière, Kristin Ross and Slavoj Žižek, *Democracy in What State?*, New York: Columbia University Press, pp.1–5.
Ahıska, Meltem (2005), *Radyonun Sihirli Kapısı*, Istanbul: Metis.
Almond, Ian [2004] (2012), *İbni Arabî ve Derrida*, Istanbul: Ayrıntı.
Almond, Ian (forthcoming), 'Five Ways to Deconstruct Europe', *Journal of European Studies*.
Alpyağıl, Recep (2007), *Derrida'dan Caputo'ya Dekonstrüksiyon ve Din*, Istanbul: İz.
Bora, Tanıl (2002), 'Milliyetçi-Muhafazakâr ve İslâmcı Düşünüşte Negatif Batı İmgesi', in Uygur Kocabaşoğlu (ed.), *Modernleşme ve Batıcılık*, Istanbul: İletişim, vol. 3, pp. 251–268.
Çulhaoğlu, Metin (2002), 'Modernleşme, Batılılaşma ve Türk Solu', in Uygur Kocabaşoğlu (ed.), *Modernleşme ve Batıcılık*, Istanbul: İletişim, vol. 3, pp. 170–88.
Demirhan, Ahmet (2012), 'İslam(cılık) sınavında demokrasi', *Star Gazetesi, Açık Görüş*, 15 December, http://haber.stargazete.com/sondakika/islamcilik-sinavinda-demokrasi/haber-712298 (last accessed 27 June 2013).
Derrida, Jacques [1978] (1989), *Edmund Husserl's Origin of Geometry: An Introduction*, Lincoln: University of Nebraska Press.
Derrida, Jacques [1989] (1992a), 'Force of Law: The Mystical Foundation of Authority', in Drucilla Cornell, Michel Rosenfeld and David Gray Carlson (eds), *Deconstruction and the Possibility of Justice*, New York: Routledge, pp. 3–67.
Derrida, Jacques [1991] (1992b), *The Other Heading: Reflections on Today's Europe*, Bloomington: Indiana University Press.
Derrida, Jacques [1993] (1994), *Specters of Marx: The State of the Debt, The Work of Mourning, and the New International*, New York: Routledge.
Derrida, Jacques [1994] (1997), *Politics of Friendship*, London: Verso.
Derrida, Jacques [1996] (1998), *Monolingualism of the Other: Or, The Prosthesis of Origin*, Stanford, CA: Stanford University Press.
Derrida, Jacques [1997] (2001a), 'On Cosmopolitanism', in *On Cosmopolitanism and Forgiveness*, London: Routledge, pp. 1–24.
Derrida, Jacques [1997] (2001b), *On Cosmopolitanism and Forgiveness*, London: Routledge.
Derrida, Jacques (2001c), *The Work of Mourning*, Chicago: University of Chicago Press.
Derrida, Jacques (2003), 'Autoimmunity: Real and Symbolic Suicides', in Giovanna Borradori (ed.), *Philosophy in a Time of Terror: Dialogues with Jürgen Habermas and Jacques Derrida*, Chicago: University of Chicago Press, pp. 85–136.
Derrida, Jacques [2003] (2005), *Rogues: Two Essays on Reason*, Stanford, CA: Stanford University Press.
Derrida, Jacques [2008] (2009), *The Beast and the Sovereign, Vol. 1*, Chicago: University of Chicago Press.
Derrida, Jacques [2010] (2011a), *The Beast and the Sovereign, Vol. II*, Chicago: University of Chicago Press.
Derrida, Jacques [1973] (2011b), *Voice and Phenomenon: Introduction to the*

Problem of the Sign in Husserl's Phenomenology, Evanston, IL: Northwestern University Press.

Derrida, Jacques and Catherine Malabou (2006), 'İstanbul Mektubu', *Cogito* 47–8: *Derrida: Yaşamı Yeniden Düşünürken*, 17–36.

Direk, Zeynep (2005) 'Derrida'nın ardından: Ölüm, kültür ve dil', *Toplum ve Bilim* 102, 17–33.

Direk, Zeynep (2006), 'Derrida ve Sorumluluk Olarak Avrupa Fikri', *Cogito* 47–8: *Derrida: Yaşamı Yeniden Düşünürken*, 213–22.

Direk, Zeynep (2010), 'Yasa, Siyaset ve Adalet', in Aykut Çelebi (ed.), *Şiddetin Eleştirisi Üzerine*, Istanbul: Metis, pp. 214–54.

Gasché, Rodolphe (2009), *Europe, or The Infinite Task: A Study of a Philosophical Concept*, Stanford, CA: Stanford University Press.

Göle, Nilüfer (2006), 'Europe's Encounter with Islam: What Future?', *Constellations* 13(2), 248–62.

Husserl, Edmund [1936] (1970), 'The Vienna Lecture: Appendix I – Philosophy and the Crisis of European Humanity', in *The Crisis of the European Sciences and Transcendental Phenomenology: An Introduction to Phenomenological Philosophy*, Evanston, IL: Northwestern University Press.

Kastoryano, Riva (2006), 'Turkey/Europe: Space–Border–Identity', *Constellations* 13(2), 275–87.

Keyder, Çağlar. (1997), 'Whither the Project of Modernity? Turkey in the 1990s', in Sibel Bozdoğan and Reşat Kasaba (eds), *Rethinking Modernity and National Identity*, Seattle: University of Washington Press, pp. 37–51.

Laborde, Cécile (2009), 'Républicanisme critique vs républicanisme conservateur: repenser les "accommodements raisonnables"', *Critique internationale* 44, 19–33.

Malabou, Catherine and Jacques Derrida [1999] (2004), 'Istanbul, 10 May 1997', in *Counterpath: Traveling with Jacques Derrida*, Stanford, CA: Stanford University Press, pp. 3–36.

Mutman, Mahmut (2001), 'İnsanlığın kıyısında: Haklar', *Toplum ve Bilim* 87, 44–64.

Mutman, Mahmut (2002), 'Avrupa Avrupa Duy Sesimizi (S'il vous plaît!)', *Birikim* 159, 41–53.

Naas, Michael (1992), 'Introduction: For Example', in Jacques Derrida, *The Other Heading: Reflections on Today's Europe*, Bloomington: Indiana University Press, pp. vii–lix.

Naas, Michael (2008), 'Derrida's *Laïcité*', in *Derrida from Now On*, New York: Fordham University Press, pp. 62–80.

Nietzsche, Friedrich [1878] (1996), *Human, All Too Human: A Book for Free Spirits*, Cambridge: Cambridge University Press.

Valéry, Paul (1960), 'Notes sur la grandeur et décadence de l'Europe', in *Oeuvres 2*, Paris: Pléiade, pp. 930–4.

Valéry, P. [1919] (2000a), 'La Crise de l'esprit', in Yves Hersant and Fabienne Durand-Bogaert (eds), *Europes: de l'antiquité au XXe siècle*, Paris: Robert Laffont, pp. 405–14.

Valéry, P. [1924] (2000b), 'Note (ou L'Européen)', in Yves Hersant and Fabienne Durand-Bogaert (eds), *Europes: de l'antiquité au XXe siècle*, Paris: Robert Laffont, pp. 414–25.

Further Reading

Çiğdem, Ahmet (2009), 'Avrupa: "Yer" ile "Yasa" Arasında', in *D'nin Halleri: Din, Darbe, Demokrasi*, Istanbul: İletişim, pp. 57–66.

Chapter 10

Christianity, Secularism and the Crisis of Europe

Ian Anthony Morrison

As Derrida suggests in the opening pages of *The Other Heading*, the question of Europe is both 'a question that will always be of current interest' (Derrida 1992: 4–5) and the product of the pressure exerted by a particular imminence. The question of what is Europe and the response to it always refer both to the ever present (the essential Europe) and to the particular or contingent (Europe as it is, that which is 'afoot in Europe') (Derrida 1992: 5), and demand a conciliation of the two. In the two decades since the publication of Derrida's text, the question of Europe has been raised in relation to (among others) the apparent crisis of Europe's engagement with two immanent others, in the form of the presence of Muslim migrants in Europe and the attempts by Turkey to gain membership of the European Union. In response to these others, a dual and seemingly contradictory definition of Europe has emerged, Europe as both secular and Christian. Europe is secular in relation to its Muslim migrants, and Christian in the face of Muslim Turkey. Within this dualistic definition, no contradiction, excess or difference is permitted or acknowledged. Instead, a socio-historical paradigm in which Christianity and the secular form a necessary and symbiotic relationship is evoked.

This chapter will investigate this response to the imminent question of Europe and demonstrate that the dual engagement with the Muslim migrant and the Turkish state exposes the confluence of what are portrayed as competing 'thick' and 'thin' definitions of Europe and European identity. I will suggest that Europe's engagement with these immanent others draws attention to the difference and contradiction at the core of what are presented as unified, ipseic definitions of Europe. Revealing the autoimmune process at work within these definitions of Europe presents an opportunity to re-evaluate the relationship between Europe, Christianity and the secular, and discloses new possibilities for a Europe to come.

Europe as Secular

As Rodolphe Gasché (2007: 2) suggests, the question of Europe – of defining and delimiting what is (and can be) meant by Europe and what is (and can be) constituted in the name of Europe – is perennial, and 'draws its urgency and actuality' from that which is imminent. It is for this reason that Derrida writes that the question of 'today' is intimately linked to the question of Europe. If, as Derrida asserts, the question of Europe is always the product of, or a response to, the 'pressure' exerted by that which is imminent, then crucial to an investigation of the conditions of possibility of this questioning is an investigation of the imminence that provokes a particular historical response.

In recent years the subject of Europe has been raised in response to an engagement with two immanent others: the Muslim migrant and the Turkish state. In this sense, the question of Europe has been raised in response to what are portrayed as extra-, rather than intra-, European phenomena. While the presence of Muslims in Europe, and concern regarding this presence, long predates Derrida's engagement with European identity, in the years since the publication of *The Other Heading* a discourse has emerged in which this presence is depicted as a threat to Europe. Although this discourse contains numerous, divergent positions regarding both the specific reasons for this concern and the solutions offered to contend with it, there is a shared understanding that the presence of Muslims in Europe is an issue requiring urgent attention.

The most extreme, although by no means marginal, articulation of these concerns can be found in the discourse on the rise of 'Eurabia' and the 'Islamisation' of Europe. In the work of authors such as Bruce Bawer (2006), Oriana Fallaci (2006), Walter Laqueur (2007), Melanie Phillips (2006), Mark Steyn (2009), and Bat Ye'or (Giselle Littman) (2005), as well as that of a plethora of bloggers including Fjordman (Peder Are Nøstvold Jensen), Andrew Bostom, the members of the Infidel Bloggers Alliance and the contributors to sites such as Gates of Vienna, Nueva Europa – Nueva Eurabia and Islamización de Europa, Muslim migrants are described as the vanguard of a demographic and cultural conquest of Europe by Islam. Ye'or, perhaps the most (in)famous of voices declaring the rise of Eurabia, describes what she sees as 'Europe's evolution from a Judeo-Christian civilisation, with important post-Enlightenment secular elements, into a post-Judeo-Christian civilisation that is subservient to the ideology of jihad and the Islamic powers that propagate it' (Ye'or 2005: 9). According to Ye'or, the rise of this 'civilization of dhimmitude' is the result of 'jihad by other means', a strategy of playing upon

Europe's material interests, as well as the purportedly Western ideals of tolerance and human rights, in order to further the process of the Islamisation of Europe.

Proponents of the Eurabia thesis also place a great deal of emphasis on demographic factors in their attempts to demonstrate the ongoing Islamisation of Europe. In doing so they regularly point to low European birth rates and the increase of Muslims as a percentage of the European population, owing both to immigration and to the apparently higher birth rate of the Muslim population within Europe, a view exemplified by Fallaci's statement that 'the sons of Allah are multiplying like rats' (Broughton 2003). Similar positions have been advocated by political actors, primarily, although certainly not exclusively, on the far right of the political spectrum, who have called for a cessation of Muslim immigration, if not the deportation of Muslim migrants already residing in Europe. Geert Wilders, the leader of the Netherlands' Freedom Party – which received just under 1.5 million votes in the 2010 general election and entered into a support agreement with the minority government (Mock 2010) – has campaigned on a platform that aims to halt the 'Islamisation of Europe' by banning the Koran, introducing a 'headscarf tax' and prohibiting immigration from those countries declared to be Muslim (BBC 2010).

These reports of an emerging – or for some, an already existing – Eurabia are not simply the ravings of fanatics at the fringes of European politics. Not only have parties espousing such views received considerable support in recent elections and entered into minority government arrangements in several states, these ideas are increasingly being advocated by traditionally mainstream political actors (Zúquete 2008). These views form part of a broader discourse in which the very presence of Muslims in Europe is considered problematic. This concern with Muslims relates primarily to their supposed inability to integrate into European society owing to their apparently intractable religiosity. Primary among the concerns is that of divided loyalties and obligations. As Michael McConnell (2000: 91) suggests, 'the essential problem is that religious believers have an allegiance to an authority outside of the commonwealth'. The loyalty of religious subjects is always suspect as, according to Rousseau (1968: 179), they 'have never known whether they ought to obey the civil ruler or the priest . . . [They have] two rulers, two homelands . . . two contradictory obligations.' Consequently, the citizenship of the religious subject is always 'partial' (Spinner-Halev 2000) or 'ambiguous' (McConnell 2000).

What is of concern in the aforementioned discourse is the ostensible inability of the religious subject, manifest here as the Muslim subject, to overcome such divided loyalties by recognising the necessary distinction between the religious and public spheres, and behaving according to the standards of each. The first concern in this regard is related to the ostensible absence of a separation of civil and religious spheres in Islam. Islam is construed as all-embracing, a system of belief in which everything pertains to religion. Even Charles Taylor, that oft-cited proponent of multiculturalism, argues that Islam poses a particular problem for European secular society, as 'for mainstream Islam, there is no question of separating politics and religion the way we have come to expect in Western liberal society' (Taylor 1994: 95). Secondly, the loyalty of Muslims to the democratic state is seen as compromised by an overriding allegiance to the global *umma* (Laborde 2005: 321). It is asserted, consequently, that Muslims find it difficult if not impossible to bracket their religious identity, values, obligations and loyalties, and adopt the persona of the universal citizen proper to the public sphere.

This concern with the inability of Muslim migrants to integrate into secular European society is particularly evident in the recent institution of citizenship testing and contracts for migrants. Recent Dutch immigration requirements, for instance, oblige applicants to view a two-hour film entitled *Coming to the Netherlands*, whose contents include nudity and homosexuality, in order to demonstrate their willingness and ability to participate in what is considered secular, liberal Dutch society. France, the United Kingdom and several other European states have also recently instituted citizenship tests for new entrants. Migrants to the United Kingdom are now required to take a test in order to, in the words of former Home Secretary David Blunkett, 'protect the rights and duties of all citizens and confront practices and beliefs that hold them back' (Zúquete 2008: 336). France has also instituted several measures ostensibly aimed at ensuring the integration of migrants. Newcomers must demonstrate their ability and commitment to integrate into French society by passing tests that assess their knowledge of French language and history and republican values, and by signing a 'social integration contract' (Zúquete 2008: 336). In these and other similar cases, it is deemed necessary to demonstrate to 'foreigners' that they must be willing to put aside their ostensible religious beliefs and practices in order to be welcomed and integrated into secular European society.

It is within this discourse of divided loyalties that the presence of the religious, and particularly Muslim, subject has emerged as a focus of concern in recent years. Muslims are positioned as unable to comport themselves in the manner necessary to be the secular subjects proper to the European public sphere. Ostensibly unable to overcome the divided loyalties of religion and citizenship, Muslims are constituted as a threat to social cohesion, and to the fabric of the secular democratic state. Confined to what Samuel Huntington refers to as their 'bloody boundaries' (Huntington 1993: 35), these troubling features of Islamic society and the Islamic subject need not be of immediate concern for the governance of European states. However, as writers such as Homi Bhabha (1990) and Seyla Benhabib (2002) have noted, in the era of globalisation and migration the exoticised religious other is no longer necessarily distant. In the 'diaspora space' (Brah 1996: 16) of Europe, the racialised, exoticised, primitivised and stigmatised other exists side by side with the 'self', and becomes the target of various techniques of alterity.

This recent discourse of Islam as a problem for Europe has thus focused primarily on the protection of what is seen to be an already-secularised European society and culture from infiltration by exogenous religious threats. In this way it is consistent with the logic of immunity. According to Derrida, 'the immunitary reaction protects the "indemnity" of the body proper in producing antibodies against foreign antigens' (Derrida 1998a: 73n). While it is in the domain of biology 'that the lexical resources of immunity have developed their authority' (Derrida 1998a: 73n), immune functions are present in all attempts at ipseic definition. As Derrida has demonstrated in his investigations of various oppositional structures – nature and culture, faith and knowledge, the religious and the political, the nation and the foreigner, the European and the non-European, to name only a few – such definitions function through the construction of borders clearly demarcating the unified self from its external other. It is within such a discourse of ipseity that the religious practices of Muslim immigrants are seen as both an impediment to their integration into secular European society and, if unchecked, a threat to that same society. Within this discourse, religion appears, not as an endogenously generated entity that must be cleansed from the social body, but as an external contaminant to an already purified, secularised Europe.

Europe as Christian

Since the early 1990s, the subject of Europe has also been raised in relation to a second immanent other, the Turkish state. Beginning with its formal application for membership of the then European Community in 1987, Turkey has engaged in an ongoing series of contentious negotiations related to its accession to the European Union. The question of potential Turkish membership in the EU has formed the basis of significant debate regarding the definition and boundaries of European identity, and, as Ioannis Grigoriadis (2006: 147) has noted, has 'acted as a proxy for a larger and overdue debate on the future shape of the European Union'.

In academic literature, the debate has often been framed as one between two competing definitions of European identity. According to the first, the 'thin' definition, European identity is marked by a set of economic, institutional and legal principles, including the rule of law, democracy, human rights and secular governance (Barker 2012; Dostál et al. 2011: 197). On the basis of this definition of European identity, adherence to these purportedly universal principles – and thus, the attainment of European identity – is said to be possible for all. European identity is, therefore, defined by adherence to certain principles, and membership of the EU based on a state's ability to demonstrate this adherence. In this sense, the EU appears as the manifestation of a Europe defined by a certain set of principles, adherence to which serves as a marker of Europeanness.

In contrast, the second definition holds European identity to comprise a set of characteristics unique to particular peoples and subjects owing to a common European history and culture. Within this 'thick' definition, European identity is considered the product of unique historical experiences. As such, there is no possibility of Europeanisation for those who have not shared in these experiences. States or peoples cannot become European; they either are or are not. Translated into EU membership, it is only those states that are already European that may join the EU by demonstrating their adherence to the set of economic, political and social criteria consistent with the 'thin' definition of European identity. In other words, the boundaries of any possible future configuration of the EU can contain only those states that are already marked by an essential Europeanness.

The official negotiations concerning Turkey's accession to the EU would seem to correspond to the 'thin' definition' of European identity. According to the agreed-upon protocol of negotiations, if Turkey is to gain membership of the EU, its laws, institutions and practices must become 'aligned' with those of the thirty-five chapters of the *acquis communautaire*, the body of EU law. As such, accession is to be determined on the basis of Turkey's ability to meet and adhere to European standards in areas such as the development of institutions, trade, finance and health regulations, security, immigration, human rights, environmental and consumer protections, and social policy.

However, these negotiations, and the acceptance of Turkey as European, or even potentially European, have always seemed to involve more than simply adherence to a set of principles. As Turkish officials and many critics of the EU accession process have noted, there has been an inconsistency in the standards applied to Turkey and to other states – particularly the former communist states of central and eastern Europe (CEE) – in determining suitability for EU membership (Kalaycıoğlu 2010; Toghill 2011). Others have pointed to the different ways in which the potential accession of Turkey and that of the CEE states have been framed. The potential membership of the CEE states has been portrayed as a 'return to Europe' (Kubicek 2005:67; Sedelmeier 2005), the return of an entity to that to which it essentially belongs. Framed in this manner, there appears to be a distinction between essential Europeanness, which the CEE states are said to possess, and alignment with European values, which they must exhibit or attain in order to join the European Union. A state may be European in the 'thick', but not – or not yet – in the 'thin' sense of the term. As such, regardless of their adherence to 'European principles', the Europeanness of the ECC states remains unquestioned within debates concerning their entrance into the EU.

In contrast, disputes regarding potential Turkish membership have concerned both Turkey's adherence to the *acquis communautaire* and its essential (non-)Europeanness. In recent years, several European heads of state and EU officials have stated unequivocally that Turkey should not be considered for full membership of the EU, regardless of its ability to adopt 'European principles'. This opposition is based on the classification of Turkey as an essentially non-European entity. Turkey has been defined as an 'unsuitable civilisation' by the former West German Chancellor Helmut Schmidt, as 'not a European country' by the former French President Valéry Giscard d'Estaing, and as not belonging in Europe 'simply because it is Asia Minor' by the then French President Nicolas Sarkozy (Hurd 2010: 189). Meanwhile Herman van Rompuy, President of the European Council since 2009, argued in 2004 that 'Turkey is not a part of Europe and will never be part of it' (Laçiner 2009). Turkish membership of the EU has also been unpopular within European public opinion, regardless of Turkey's ability to adhere to the agreed-upon principles of accession. When asked in several polls whether they would be 'in favour or against Turkey becoming a member of the European Union in the future', a decisive majority of EU residents have repeatedly responded negatively (Dostál et al. 2011: 203–4).

Jose Casanova (2004) has argued that primary among the obstacles to Turkish accession to the EU is its identification as Muslim. In contrast to Muslim Turkey, Europe is increasingly defined on the basis of its Christian (or Judaeo-Christian) heritage (Zúquete 2009: 324–9; Hurd 2010; Toghill 2011: 12–15). For example, in 2004 Van Rompuy argued that Christian values formed the core of Europe's identity (Laçiner 2009), while Pope Benedict XVI, in his call for a re-Christianisation of Europe marking the fiftieth anniversary of the Treaty of Rome, similarly declared that Christian values 'make up the soul of the continent', and, as such, that Christianity has 'not only a historic but [also] a foundational role vis-à-vis Europe' (Zúquete 2009: 327). Sarkozy, Chancellor Angela Merkel of Germany and others, such as the former Polish Prime Minister Jarosław Kaczyński, have argued that it is necessary for the EU to officially acknowledge the Christian character of Europe (Beita 2008; Charlemagne 2009; DW 2007). Within each of these statements, the unique essence of European identity is defined by, and seen as the product of, a Christian history and culture.

In contrast, Turkey, despite its avowed and deeply institutionalised secularism, is defined by a history and culture of Islam. The experiences of Christianity and Islam are not seen as simply marking the different historical experiences of Europe and Turkey. Rather, these differing historical and religious experiences are portrayed as having produced essentially different cultures and civilisations. Consequently, they are said to relate not only to the past but also to the present, continuing to define and differentiate that which is European from that which is non-European. The preservation of this definition of Europe requires that this distinction from its Muslim/Turkish other remain intact. Accordingly, the entry of Turkey into the EU would mark the 'end of Europe', would mean that 'the liberation of Vienna in 1683 [was] in vain', and would render the EU 'nothing more than a free trade community', as Giscard d'Estaing, Schmidt and the Dutch politician Frits Bolkestein put it (quoted in Hurd 2010: 189).

This equation of historical experience and essence is perhaps most evident in the divergent responses to the bids by Poland and Turkey to join the EU. During the negotiation process leading to Poland's accession to the EU, the Polish Episcopate, in clear opposition to the official secular ethos of EU governance, 'embraced European integration as a great apostolic assignment' (Casanova 2004: 2). This public call for Poland to serve as the vanguard in a project to 'restore Europe for Christianity' prompted little concern, as secular Europeans were confident in 'their ability to assimilate Catholic Poland on their own terms' (Casanova 2004: 2, 3). Yet the prospect of Turkey's accession to the EU generated significant anxiety, despite the fundamentalist secularism practised by the Kemalist Turkish state. Here, Christian Poland, while potentially at odds with the secular basis of modern European governance, was seen as less of a threat to secularism than a Turkish state that had been militantly secularist for over seventy years. Much of the opposition to Turkish accession to the EU, it seems, was unrelated to the actual practices of the Turkish state, but to the status of Islam – and, therefore, Turkey as an essentially Muslim entity – as 'the other of European secularity' (Casanova 2004: 7).

Europe as Secular and Christian, Universal and Particular

It is this equation of historical experience with essence that allows the bridge to be traversed between seemingly opposing definitions of European identity. On the one hand Europe is defined on the basis of a common set of potentially universalisable principles. On the other, it is defined as a unique essence, rooted in historical and religious particularities. European identity, therefore, is defined as at once universal and exceptional.

While portrayed within the literature as competing visions of Europe and European identity, the dual engagement with the religious migrant and the Turkish state exposes the confluence of these purportedly opposed positions. Muslim migrants appear as a problem for the thin definition because they are said to be unable or unwilling to abide by the principles governing European identity. Yet, as the discourse surrounding Turkey's accession to the EU makes clear, this inability to become European is considered the product of the religious background that unalterably shapes Muslim subjectivity.

The ostensibly universal principles said to define modern European subjectivity appear as the product of unique European historical and cultural factors, in particular Christianity. As Engin Isin (2002: 117) has demonstrated, within Western discourse, citizenship is portrayed as 'a unique occidental invention that oriental cultures lacked'. Europe appears in this orientalist narrative as both exceptional and universal, as it is only as a result of the unique accidents of European history and culture that the citizen, 'as a secular and universal being without tribal loyalties' (Isin 2002: 117), was able to emerge. In the work of Max Weber (1981) and others, the emergence of this uniquely European, yet universal, subject is largely attributed to certain elements of Christian theology. Weber points specifically to the Pentecostal miracle, in which Jesus's disciples were divinely bestowed with multilingual abilities and an evangelical mission, a mission that was furthered by Paul's espousal of the need for 'fellowship with the uncircumcised' (Weber 1981: 322). The Pentecostal miracle articulated a notion of community based in a commonality of faith rather than blood. As such, it served to undermine and permit the transcendence of kinship associations. As a supra-ethnic, transnational religion, espousing a doctrine of brotherhood, Christianity is said to have promoted both the institutional foundation and the sense of ecumenism necessary to form a secular community of citizens.

It is within such orientalist narratives of European exceptionalism that the reconciliation between the supposedly competing conceptions of European identity can be located. It is here that Europe can claim to be at once Christian and secular. Christianity appears as the necessary foundation upon which modern, secular Europe stands. In forging this identity between historical Christian Europe and contemporary secular Europe, this discourse once again engages in a logic of immunity. Instead of acknowledging the apparent contradictions at play in the attempt to define Europe as at once secular and Christian, an attempt is made to efface this difference and maintain a unified, ipseic Europe defined in opposition to its Muslim other.

Of course, a demonstration of the presence of elements of Christian theology in ostensibly modern secular norms is not limited to reactionary conservatism and xenophobia. Critical voices, including Derrida himself, have repeatedly demonstrated the unacknowledged relationship between theological, political and moral norms and concepts. In doing so, Derrida does not, however, attempt to forge an identity between elements that appear to be defined on the basis of a relationship of absence. For instance, he does not try to demonstrate that that which claims to be purely political is truly theological or vice versa. Rather, he consistently argues that identity always requires relationships of otherness and supplementation, and can only be constituted through an ongoing process of identification. As such, the identities of European and non-European, Christian and non-Christian, secular and religious, are 'never given, received or attained' (Derrida 1998b: 28). For Derrida, then, European identity never exists as a thing-in-itself. On the contrary, it is always immersed in a relation of supplementation with the other shore, that which is constituted as non-European.

Moreover, as Derrida (1992: 9–10) asserts, 'there is no culture or cultural identity without this difference to itself'. It is this difference that the ipseic definitions of Europe discussed above attempt to efface. According to the logic of immunity at play in the oppositional structure of the relation between the secular and the religious, the definition of Europe as at once secular and Christian appears contradictory. The definition of Europe must be protected from this contradiction either through an exteriorisation of one of the elements or by creating an identity or continuity between things that appear to be contradictory. The only difference that these definitions permit or acknowledge is that of the exterior. Europe, whether defined as secular, Christian or concurrently secular and Christian is defined in relation to its external Muslim other. It is this external difference that appears as the threat to Europe. As such, the crisis of Europe that is proclaimed in recent discourse concerns (among others) the ability to protect Europe against contamination by this external source.

However, as Derrida asserts, a unified, ipseic Europe, like all ipseity, cannot be realised. The question of Europe cannot be resolved by buttressing its immunity against external antigens, or resolving apparent internal contradictions. Unlike immune processes, which seek to protect the host body by protecting it from that which is foreign to it, 'the process of auto-immunization ... consists for a living organism ... of protecting itself against its self-protection by destroying its own immune system' (Derrida 1998a: 73n). The concept of autoimmunity reveals that each identity contains a force that promotes its self-destruction. It is this 'internal-external, non-dialectizable antinomy' (Derrida 2005: 35) that works against, and makes impossible, any ipseity. Thus, the logic of autoimmunity upsets the oppositional structure of interiority and exteriority. Rather than exteriorise or resolve the difference at play in the definition of Europe as concurrently secular and Christian, universal and particular, it acknowledges the undecidability at the heart of this seemingly contradictory identity.

In closing itself off on the basis of European exceptionalism, Europe 'shirks the responsibility that comes with having an identity and a heritage' (Cauchi 2009: 8). Through this closure, Europe becomes a nonidentity. The task that Derrida sets for Europe, therefore, is to maintain an opening to otherness. Europe must be Europe-to-come, defined not by its secularism, Christianity or an identification of the secular and Christian, but by an openness to a 'secular to come' (Cauchi 2009), 'a radical secularity without secularism' (Naas 2007: 38).

It is in relation to Derrida's conception of autoimmunity that we can understand his assertion that the question of Europe is at once perpetual and always the product of a particular imminence. Deconstruction is at work within all constructions of a unified, ipseic Europe. As such, the integrity of any unified conception of Europe is always under threat from the autoimmune processes that work to undermine the dualistic structures upon which it rests. As a unified, ipseic Europe can never be realised, Europe will always be subject to questioning. Yet, as this chapter has demonstrated, it is in response to a particular imminence that the work of these deconstructions is disclosed. It was in response to the dual engagement with the Muslim migrant and the attempts by Turkey to gain membership of the EU that the seemingly contradictory definition of Europe as both secular and Christian emerged in recent years. This imminence provided the opportunity to engage with and disclose the autoimmune process at work within this definition of Europe. As such, it has presented an opportunity to reopen the question of the relationship between Europe, Christianity and the secular.

References

Barker, J. P. (2012), 'Turkish Religious Identity and the Question of European Union Membership', paper presented at Institute for Cultural Diplomacy: Ankara Conference on Peacebuilding and Conflict Resolution, 17–19 April.

Bawer, Bruce (2006), *While Europe Slept: How Radical Islam is Destroying the West from Within*, New York: Broadway.

BBC (2010), 'Surge for Dutch anti-Islam Freedom Party', BBC News website, 10 June, http://www.bbc.co.uk/news/10271153 (last accessed 28 June 2013).

Beita, Peter B. (2008), 'French President's religious mixing riles critics', Christian Today website, 23 January, http://www.christiantoday.com/article/french.presidents.religious.mixing.riles.critics/16423.htm (last accessed 28 June 2013).

Benhabib, Seyla (2002), '"Nous" et les "Autres" (We and the Others): Is Universalism Ethnocentric?', in *The Claims of Culture: Equality and Diversity in a Global Era*, Princeton: Princeton University Press, pp. 24–48.

Bhabha, Homi (1990), 'The Third Space', in Jonathan Rutherford (ed.), *Identity: Community, Culture, Difference*, London: Lawrence & Wishart, pp. 207–21.

Brah, Avtar (1996), *Cartographies of Diaspora: Contesting Identities*, London: Routledge.

Broughton, Philip Delves (2003), '"Rats" slur writer is facing Muslim race case', Telegraph website, 6 September, http://www.telegraph.co.uk/news/worldnews/europe/france/1440773/Rats-slur-writer-is-facing-Muslim-race-case.html (last accessed 28 June 2013).

Casanova, José (2004), 'Religion, European secular identities, and European integration', Eurozine website, 29 July, http://www.eurozine.com/pdf/2004-07-29-casanova-en.pdf (last accessed 28 June 2013).

Cauchi, Mark (2009), 'The Secular to Come: Interrogating the Derridean "Secular"', *Journal for Cultural and Religious Theory* 10(1), 1–25.

Charlemagne (2009), 'Europe should be Christian, says Cameron's new ally', *The Economist*, 1 June, http://www.economist.com/blogs/charlemagne/2009/06/europe_should_be_christian_say, (last accessed 28 June 2013).

Derrida, Jacques [1991] (1992), *The Other Heading: Reflections on Today's Europe*, Bloomington: Indiana University Press.

Derrida, Jacques [1995] (1998a), 'Faith and Knowledge', in Jacques Derrida and Gianni Vattimo (eds), *Religion*, Stanford, CA: Stanford University Press, pp. 1–78.

Derrida, Jacques [1996] (1998b), *Monolingualism of the Other: Or, The Prosthesis of Origin*, Stanford, CA: Stanford University Press.

Derrida, Jacques [2003] (2005), *Rogues: Two Essays on Reason*, Stanford, CA: Stanford University Press.

Dostál, Petr, Emel Akçalı and Marco Antonsich (2011), 'Turkey's Bid for European Union Membership: Between "Thick" and "Thin" Conceptions of Europe', *Eurasian Geography and Economics* 52(2), 196–216.

DW (2007), 'Merkel wants EU charter to make reference to Christianity', DW website, 21 January, http://dw.de/p/9jbe (last accessed 28 June 2013).

Fallaci, Oriana [2004] (2006), *The Force of Reason*, New York: Rizzoli International.

Gasché, Rodolphe (2007), 'This Little Thing that Is Europe', *CR: The New Centennial Review* 7(2), 1–19.

Grigoriadis, Ioannis N. (2006), 'Turkey's Accession to the European Union: Debating the Most Difficult Enlargement Ever', *SAIS Review* 26(1), 147–60.

Huntington, Samuel P. (1993), 'The Clash of Civilizations?', *Foreign Affairs* 72(3), 22–49.

Hurd, Elizabeth Shakman (2010), 'What Is Driving the European Debate about Turkey?', *Insight Turkey* 12(1), 185–203.

Isin, Engin F. (2002), 'Citizenship after Orientalism', in Engin F. Isin and Bryan S. Turner (eds.), *Handbook of Citizenship Studies*, London: Sage, pp. 117–28.

Kalaycıoğlu, Ersin (2010), 'The Political Criteria: Fair or Strict Conditionality?', presentation at European Studies Centre, St Anthony's College, Oxford, www.sant.ox.ac.uk/esc/esc-lectures/Ersin.doc (last accessed 28 June 2013).

Kubicek, Paul (2005), 'Turkish Accession to the European Union: Challenges and Opportunities', *World Affairs* 168(2), 67–78.

Laborde, Cécile (2005), 'Secular Philosophy and Muslim Headscarves in Schools', *Journal of Political Philosophy* 13(3), 305–29.

Laçiner, Sedat (2009). 'Turkey's EU Membership: EU's Identity Crisis', Journal of Turkish Weekly website, 22 December, http://www.turkishweekly.net/columnist/3251/turkey-39-s-eu-membership-eu-39-s-identity-crisis.html (last accessed 8 July 2013).

Laqueur, Walter (2007), *The Last Days of Europe: Epitaph for an Old Continent*, New York: Thomas Dunne.

McConnell, Michael W. (2000), 'Believers as Equal Citizens', in Nancy L. Rosenblum (ed.), *Obligations of Citizenship and Demands of Faith: Religious Accommodation in Pluralist Democracies*, Princeton, NJ: Princeton University Press, pp. 90–110.

Mock, Vanessa (2010), 'Wilders makes shock gains in Dutch elections', *The Independent*, 11 June, http://www.independent.co.uk/news/world/europe/wilders-makes-shock-gains-in-dutch-elections-1997293.html (last accessed 28 June 2013).

Naas, Michael (2007), 'Derrida's Laïcité', *CR: The New Centennial Review* 7(2), 21–42.

Phillips, Melanie (2006), *Londonistan*, New York: Encounter.

Sedelmeier, Ulrich (2005), *Constructing the Path to Eastern Enlargement: The Uneven Policy Impact of EU Identity*, Manchester: Manchester University Press.

Spinner-Halev, Jeff (2000), *Surviving Diversity: Religion and Democratic Citizenship*, Baltimore: Johns Hopkins University Press.

Steyn, Mark (2009), *Lights Out: Islam, Free Speech and the Twilight of the West*, Montreal: Stockade.

Toghill, James (2011), 'Are the Official Economic and Political Obstacles to Turkey's EU Accession Merely a "Fig Leaf" Covering Real Unofficial Cultural and Religious Reservations?', *POLIS Journal* 6, http://www.polis.leeds.ac.uk/assets/files/students/student-journal/ug-winter-11/james-toghill.pdf (last accessed 28 June 2013).

Weber, Max [1923] (1981), 'Citizenship', in *General Economic History*, London: Transaction, pp. 315–37.
Ye'or, Bat (2005), *Eurabia: The Euro-Arab Axis*, Madison, NJ: Fairleigh Dickinson University Press.
Zúquete, José Pedro (2008). 'The European Extreme-right and Islam: New Directions?', *Journal of Political Ideologies* 13(3), 321–44.

Index

abjection, 142
Adorno, Theodor 12
aestheticising of politics, 22
Agamben, Giorgio, 145
Al-Andalus, 123
alterity, 15, 17, 32, 54–5, 66, 76, 86, 100, 105, 125, 130, 134–5, 143, 153
anti-Semitism, 51, 121–3, 130
anxiety, 12, 16, 99, 156
aporia, 5–6, 23–5, 32, 80, 83–8
   aporetics, 32
   of exemplarity, 24
   of law, 87–8
   of time, 80, 87–8
Arendt, Hannah, 87, 121–2
Aristotle, 15
asylum, 95–6, 102–3, 137
Atlantic, 65, 67, 69–71, 74–6
Auden, W. H., 71–2
Auseinendersetzung, 49, 58
austerity, 1–2, 25, 50, 61
Australia, 17, 104
autoimmune
   character, 55
   condition, 54
   process, 149, 159–60
autoimmunity, 8, 50, 54–5, 159
autonomy 84–5, 92

Balibar, Étienne, 7, 109, 111, 117–18
barbarism, 44, 131
becoming, 6, 56, 134
   different to itself, 58
   European, 7, 128, 130–1
   of Europe, 3

being, 40, 52, 90, 99, 113, 115, 121, 144
   European, 4, 12, 56, 112
   non-identical to itself, 50
   political, 49
   Roman, 56
   self-same, 52
   universal, 157
Benjamin, Walter, 22, 24
Bennington, Geoffrey, 45–6, 47n
Bible, 30, 36
border, 67, 73, 92, 97, 102, 123, 141, 153
   control, 97, 105
   European, 12, 17, 66, 76, 103, 117
   mechanisms, 101
   national, 26
   practices, 95–6, 103
   sovereign, 97, 99
Brague, Rémi, 6–7, 49–50, 56–8
Britain, 8n, 18, 27n, 62–3, 65, 72–3, 97; *see also* United Kingdom *and* UK
Burke, Edmund, 84–5

Calarco, Matthew, 51–2
Canada, 104
cap, 9, 16–17, 27n, 68
cape, 17
cape, 16–17, 20, 23–3, 26, 37, 65, 68, 138
   'the other', 17, 22, 26
capital, 17–22, 25, 27n, 63, 69
   city, 18; *see also La capitale*
   financial, 18–9; *see also Le capital*
capitalism, 18, 20, 22, 67–8
Cassano, Franco, 66–70, 76, 77n
Chambers, Iain, 66, 68

China, 16, 92, 104, 117
Christianity, 25, 36, 100, 124, 139,
    143–4, 149, 156–60
  medieval, 45
citizenship, 101, 105, 116, 118, 145,
    151–3, 157
civilisation, 44, 58, 63, 113, 124–5,
    129, 137, 156
  European, 41–2, 56
  Judeo-Christian, 150
clarity, 35, 39, 45
  conceptual, 46
  lack of, 5, 35, 40
closure, 7, 96, 103–4, 159
cognitivism, 43
commutarian territorialism, 104
communitarianism, 7
colonialism, 21, 58, 141
colonisation, 40, 51
  decolonisation, 141
constitution, 6, 16, 81–2, 84–7, 90, 92,
    143
  European, 6, 81, 88, 91
  French, 84
  of *Dasein*, 47n
  of Europe, 8
  of European identity, 57
  of European self, 8
Constitutional Treaty, 81
constitutionalism, 80, 83, 92
continent, 17, 34, 41, 47n, 64, 100,
    111, 156
  Asian, 138
  Asiatic, 37
  of Europe, 18
  of Laurentia, 74
  old, 65, 68
  solipsism of, 67
cosmopolitan, 41, 95, 103–4, 141
  anti-, 103
  belonging, 95
  citizenship, 101
  community, 101
  democratic left, 134
  desire, 41–2
  duties, 103
  ethics, 99, 105; *see also* ethics of
    cosmopolitanism
  Europe, 143
  justice, 96
  law, 142
  legacy, 105
  rights, 7, 95, 102

solidarity, 7, 96
universalism, 7, 146
cosmopolitanism, 7, 99, 121, 134,
    136–7
  ethics of, 99; *see also* cosmopolitan
    ethics
countersignature, 6, 84, 90; *see also*
    signature
crisis, 1–5, 9, 49–50, 103, 108, 112,
    149
  current, 9, 108
  debt, 1, 61
  Eurozone, 1
  financial, 2
  Nietzschean affirmation of, 5
  of being, 5
  of Europe, 50, 108–9, 116–17,
    159
  of identity, 2–3
  of today, 51
  potentiality of, 5
  today's, 2, 4, 7
culture, 7, 11, 18–20, 39, 51–2, 55, 58,
    113, 118, 125–6, 138, 140–1
  Christian, 127, 156
  difference to itself, 6, 52,
    158
  eccentric, 57
  European, 23, 33, 53, 56–8, 98,
    127–8, 138, 153–4, 157
  foreign, 103
  Hebrew, 128
  Jewish, 124–5
  Kampf, 30
  Mediterranean, 67, 123
  non-European, 34
  of the other, 3, 52
  of totalitarianism, 101
  of unity, 54
  Oriental, 157
  regional, 43, 46
  Turkish, 146n
  universalisable, 41–2
  Western, 135, 146

Dasein, 36, 40, 47n
debt, 1, 3–4, 7, 25–6, 61
  crisis, 1, 61
Declaration of Independence, 83, 86,
    88
deconstruction, 5, 7, 38–9, 85, 129,
    137–43, 146, 159–60
Deleuze, Gilles, 67, 73–5, 77n

democracy, 4, 7, 56, 80, 83–5, 95, 98, 105, 116, 118, 130, 134–7, 139, 146n, 154
  democracy to come, 5, 8, 134
Denmark, 71, 100
Derrida, Jacques
  'Faith and Knowledge', 83
  'Force of Law', 87
  Gift of Death, 83
  influence on Turkey, 135–6
  Of Grammatology, 36
  Of Spirit, 37
  On Cosmopolitanism and Forgiveness, 51
  on autoimmunity, 55, 153, 159
  on 'cape', 16–17
  on capital, 18–20
  on cosmopolitanism, 42, 99
  on cultural identity, 11, 13, 32
  on debt, 4
  on Eurocentrism, 56
  on European Constitution, 81
  on exemplarity, 13, 22, 63, 120, 128–9
  on hospitality, 97, 99, 137
  on identity, 44–6, 51–3, 55–6, 85–6
  on law, 83, 87–8
  on Mediterranean, 65–7, 122
  on non-European, 109–10, 113–14, 116
  on origins of Europe, 54, 113, 125
  on responsibility, 4, 31, 51–2, 112, 134, 141, 143
  Rogues, 83
  The Other Heading, 9, 37–8, 40, 46, 50, 76, 85–6, 91, 122, 129, 137, 141, 149
  Voice and Phenomenon, 134
difference, 6, 10, 46, 67, 96, 98, 114, 120, 149
  originary, 73
  with itself, 3, 11, 52, 86, 137, 158
différance, 137
discrimination, 101, 143

economic technology of governance, 50–1
enlightenment, 56, 85–6, 98–9, 105, 109, 121, 129–30, 134, 141, 145, 150
ethos, 67, 69, 104, 156
  of hospitality, 102

EU, 6, 66, 81–2, 95, 102–3, 134–5, 139–40, 142, 154–7; see also European Union
Eurabia, 150–1
Eurocentrism, 43, 49, 56, 83, 92, 129–30, 135, 137
Europe
  and Brague, 56–8
  and Gasché, 31–5, 39, 111
  and responsibility, 4, 6, 31–2, 38, 40, 45, 50–1, 56, 83, 91, 112, 117, 134, 14–41, 143, 159
  and Said, 108–10
  and Turkey, 135–6, 140, 142, 154–6
  and Valéry, 19–20, 23, 26, 37, 65, 68
  aporetic condition of, 7
  aporia of, 23–4, 104
  as a 'continent', 17–18
  as a philosopheme, 39, 43, 45
  as a philosophical concept, 35, 40, 134, 140, 142
  as a political entity, 50–1, 70
  as an ethic-political idea, 134
  as chance and danger, 112, 120
  as Christian, 8, 98–9, 139, 144
  as cultural region, 42–3
  as eccentric culture, 57
  as 'exemplary', 13, 22, 24, 46, 58, 100, 120, 122, 128, 140
  as foreign to itself, 6, 56–8
  as geographical and political entity, 43
  as heading, 41, 86, 96
  as ipseity, 104, 149, 158–9
  as irruption of the other, 128
  as non-identity, 3, 11, 54, 91, 113, 120, 125, 131; see also non-coincidence with itself
  as philosophy, 113
  as regional culture, 43
  as Roman, 6, 71
  as Romanity, 49–50, 56–7
  as secular and Christian, 157–60
  as spirit, 53, 75
  as 'vanishing mediator', 7, 117
  autoimmunity of, 50, 55
  de-Christianisation of, 138–9
  deconstruction of, 134, 136, 138, 142
  Derrida's problem of, 108
  essence of, 3, 57, 140
  example of, 44–5
  for citizens, 103
  heritage of, 54, 97

Europe (*cont.*)
  idea of, 38, 45–6, 111, 120–1
  Islamisation of, 150–1
  legacy of, 5, 125, 131
  multicultural, 100–1
  non-coincidence with itself, 63, 68;
    see also as non-identity
  of hope, 42, 54, 56, 58
  of rights, 99, 102, 105
  philosophical and geopolitical senses
    of, 38
  project of, 82, 142
  promise of, 80, 91, 122
  secularisation of, 139, 143, 153
  singularity of, 14–15, 21–3
  sovereign identity of, 54, 104
  thick definition of, 149, 154–5
  thin definition of, 149, 154–5
  to-come, 50, 55, 58, 120, 149
  'today', 14–15, 36, 38, 46, 61, 130
  'under siege', 96, 103
  utopian understandings of, 95
European
  belonging, 95, 98, 103–5
  citizenship, 145
  commons, 98
  constitutionalism, 83, 91
  cultural identity, 10–11, 13–14, 32,
    61, 108
  culture 7, 23, 33, 52, 56–8, 98, 127,
    138, 154, 157
  eidos, 140–41
  example, 42–3
  exceptionalism, 69, 158–9
  exemplarity, 100
  heritage, 80, 83, 98, 125
  hope, 42
  hospitality, 99
  humanism, 41, 44, 109
  hybrid, 65, 86, 118
  identity, 3–4, 7, 50, 53, 56–8, 63, 66,
    71, 76, 80, 81, 85–8, 98–9, 104–5,
    124, 138, 144, 149–50, 154, 156–8
  integration, 82, 156
  legacy, 25
  memory, 31, 130
  multiculturalism, 101
  policy, 7, 51, 104
  public opinion, 155
  public sphere, 153
  responsibility, 4–5, 21, 38, 40, 51
  secularism, 143–4
  self, 8, 131

sovereignty, 139
spirit, 53, 65, 122
subjectivity, 42, 157
technocracy, 145
tradition, 17, 19, 22, 44, 96
transnational identity, 137
unity, 2
European Commission, 2, 95–6
European Parliament, 2, 96
European Union, 9, 18, 50, 62, 66, 71,
  80–1, 99, 102, 117, 149, 153–5;
  see also EU
Europeanisation, 58, 134–5, 154
eurozone, 1, 18, 61
  crisis 1
event, 23–4, 36, 38, 75, 88
exclusion, 53, 55, 88, 101, 103–5, 130,
  139, 143–4
exemplarity, 13, 21–2, 24, 83, 100, 128,
  140, 143; see also exemplary
exemplary, 13, 22, 24, 43–4, 46, 58, 63,
  75, 92, 120, 122, 128–9, 143; see
  also exemplarity

foreign, 111, 121, 130, 159
  anti-, 101
  cultures, 103
  policy, 90
foreigner, 42, 55, 57, 100, 152–3
Foucault, Michel, 52–3, 109
freedom, 6, 56, 67–9, 77n, 80, 83–5, 90,
  99, 102–3, 126
Freud, Sigmund, 109–10, 113
  Moses and Monotheism, 110
future
  citizens, 82, 91
  constitution, 81
  Europeans, 92
  generations, 80–2, 88–91
  incalculable, 86
  openness to, 5, 15, 55, 76
  others, 90
  people, 6, 81–5, 88–9, 91–2
  self, 90
  uncertain, 16
  unforeseeable, 5, 55

Gasché, Rodolphe, 31–5, 37–41, 43,
  45–6, 53–4, 108, 110–12, 125,
  137, 150
Germany, 19, 25, 61, 69, 99–100, 117,
  122, 156
  East, 12

Gilroy, Paul, 71
Graeco-Christian
   heritage, 33, 36, 39, 41
   identity, 32
Greece, 4, 31–2, 50–1, 67–70, 77n, 113, 125
guilt, 4, 22, 46

Habermas, Jürgen, 41, 81–2, 92
heading, 16, 23, 27n, 41, 45, 58–9, 86, 91, 96, 108, 129
Hegel, G. W. F., 10, 68–9, 71
   Phenomenology of Spirit, 10
Heidegger, Martin, 10, 27n, 31, 36–7, 40, 47n, 58, 69, 77n, 114
   Being and Time, 10, 36
   Dasein, 36, 40, 47n
Herzfeld, Michael, 68
Herzl, Theodor, 122, 124–7, 129
heterogeneity, 5, 22, 26, 75
historicism, 34, 113
Hölderlin, Friedrich, 14, 37, 58
Hollande, François, 16
hospitality, 7, 56, 97, 99, 102–4, 116, 130, 134, 137, 141–2
humanism, 40–1, 44, 109
human rights, 96, 99–102, 104–5, 129–30, 134–5, 146n, 151, 154
Husserl, Edmund, 5, 31, 35, 37, 53, 108, 110, 125, 129–30, 140–1
hybridity, 32, 123

identity, 12, 17, 25, 31, 35, 38, 49–55, 57, 84–6, 91–2, 98, 136–7, 141–2, 158–9
   -building, 82
   crisis of, 2–3
   Europe's, 30–1, 35–7, 39, 44–6, 58, 98, 104, 113, 125, 156
   Group, 97
   ipseic, 8
   Jewish, 110
   political, 134
   religious, 152
   secular, 143
   secular-national, 143
   self-same, 5, 50, 52–5
   sovereign, 54–5
   traditional logic of, 59
   Turkish, 134
immanent other, 149–50, 153
immigrant, 51, 57, 99–100, 102, 124, 138–9, 142, 153

immigration, 51, 97, 99–100, 103, 141–2, 151, 154; *see also* emigration *and* migration
immunity, 159
   logic of, 153, 158
inclusion, 83, 90–1, 95, 98, 101, 114
individual, 5, 12–13, 21, 24–6, 49, 52
   as self-identical subject, 4
   faith, 145
   freedom, 69, 77n, 102
   rights, 85
individualism, 12
individuality, 5
integration, 2, 82, 85, 99–101, 103, 124, 145–53
intergenerational justice, 80, 83
ipseic
   definitions of Europe, 149, 153, 158
   Europe, 158–9
   identity, 8
ipseity, 6, 153, 159
   absence of, 5
   Europe as, 104
   non-, 104
Ireland, 8n, 50, 71–2
Islam, 32–3, 44, 136, 138–9, 141–4, 150, 152–3, 156–7
Islamic, 66, 113, 135, 143, 150, 153
Islamisation, 139, 150–1
   de-Islamisation, 138–9
Islamophobia, 51, 142, 144
Italy, 4, 27n, 50, 67–8, 77n

Jefferson, Thomas, 84–7, 90, 92
Jews, 7, 110, 115, 120–4, 126–31
Judaeo-Christian
   civilisation, 123
   heritage, 156
   space, 142
   tradition, 109
Judaism, 32–3, 44, 125, 127
justice, 80, 83, 87, 89, 96, 103, 135–7

Kant, Immanuel, 36, 41, 47n, 97, 102, 134, 140

La capitale 17; *see also* capital
Laïcité, 143–4
law, 22, 41, 80, 83–5, 87–91, 96–7, 102, 118, 137, 154
   aporia of, 87–8

law (cont.)
  constitutional, 80, 84
  cosmopolitan, 142
  -making, 86–7
Le capital, 17; see also capital
legitimacy, 84, 88–90, 103
Leitkultur, 99–100
Levinas, Emmanuel, 5, 30, 36, 39, 43–4, 108
liberty, 84, 116, 145
Limpieza de sangre, 123
Lisbon Treaty; see Treaty of Lisbon

Maastricht Treaty, 50
Maccabees, 126–7, 131; see also Maccabean type
Maccabean type, 127
Marx, Karl, 20–1, 27n, 88
  Capital, 20
Mediterranean, 6, 12, 65–71, 73–7, 122–5, 131
Merkel, Angela, 101, 156
Milchman, Alan, 49
minority, 7
  rights, 101, 135
modernity, 40, 63, 66, 68–9, 85, 128, 135–6, 146n
  European, 24, 27n, 41
multiculturalism, 101, 152
multiplicity, 54, 66–7
Muslim
  Europeans, 143
  immigrants, 153
  migrants, 8, 149–52, 157, 160
  minority, 7
  other, 7, 134, 136, 158–9

Naas, Michael, 13, 55, 122, 128–9, 141
nationalism, 41, 51, 56, 71, 75, 96, 105, 121–2, 136–7, 142
Netherlands, 81, 151
Nietzsche, Friedrich, 4–5, 10, 32, 52, 67, 114, 138
non-European, 7, 34–5, 41, 51, 54, 57–8, 69, 82, 109–10, 112–13, 116–18, 125, 130–1, 138, 145, 153, 155–6, 158
non-identity, 3, 11, 54, 120, 125

occidentalism, 115
openness, 5, 7, 23, 28n, 33, 45, 51–5, 58, 75–6, 95–6, 104, 109, 111–13, 115–17, 137, 141, 159

fundamental, 111, 137
lack of, 7, 51
radical, 52, 58, 113
orient, 122, 124, 131, 132n
oriental, 124, 126, 131
  culture, 157
  Jew, 128
  other, 7, 123
  within Europe, 7, 120
orientalism, 108, 113, 115, 124; see also occidentalism
orientalist, 51, 121, 123, 157–8
origins of Europe, 6, 11, 30, 37, 58–9, 111
  alterity at, 54
  difference at, 3
  differential unity at, 54
  Greek, 31
  multiplicity at, 53–4, 116
  multitude at, 54
  not identical to itself, 113
  outside itself, 57, 111, 138
  plurality at, 66
Orkney, 64–5, 72, 74, 77n
Ostjuden, 121, 126, 130
otherness, 53–4, 100, 120–1, 158–9

particularity, 23, 42–3
Paine, Thomas, 84–5
Palestine, 124, 126, 130–1
Pascal, Blaise, 53, 87
Passerini, Louisa, 42
philosophy, 30, 33–4, 36, 38–9, 45, 47, 67, 113, 120, 125, 134, 140
  Derrida's, 135–6, 146
  Greek, 53–4
Plato, 16
  Platonic, 32, 43
pluralism, 7, 143, 146
Poland, 97, 156–7
postcolonial, 66
  autocracy, 21
  certainties, 35, 45
  criticism, 34
  orthodoxy, 35
  theory, 39–41
  thinking, 40
  thought, 111
postcolonialism, 109
potentiality, 5, 123
presentism, 85–7
private sphere, 143; see also public sphere

Index

public sphere, 129, 143–4, 152–3; *see also* private sphere

racism, 51, 55, 96, 130; *see also* xenophobia
rationality, 33, 44, 83
  instrumental, 145–6
Redfield, Marc, 129–30
Reformation, 5, 24, 68
  Counter-, 5, 24
refugee, 102
  ecological, 102, 104
religion, 18, 24–5, 27n, 83, 124, 136, 138–9, 142–6, 152–3, 158
religiosity, 139, 144–5, 151
religious
  diversity, 100, 142
  other, 153
  otherness, 100, 145
  pluralism, 7, 146
  subject, 151–2
  tolerance, 145
responsibility, 4, 6, 22, 31–3, 38, 40, 43, 45–6, 50–1, 56, 81–3, 91, 109, 112, 117–18, 134–5, 140–1, 143, 159
rights, 82–3, 85, 87, 95–7, 102, 116, 118, 135, 137, 144, 152; *see also* human rights
  civil, 105, 145
  cosmopolitan, 7, 95
  enjoyment of, 82
  of others, 7, 96
  Palestinian, 130
  right to have, 145
  universal, 97
Romanity, 49–50, 56–7
Rosenberg, Alan, 49
Ruppin, Arthur, 122, 125, 127, 129

Said, Edward, 108–10, 112–13, 115–18, 130, 132
Saxa Vord, 62–3, 72–4
Second World War, 11, 18, 21, 25, 68, 98
secularism, 7, 136, 139, 141, 143–5, 156–7, 159
self-determination, 85, 96
self-identical, 15, 114
  origins, 6, 73
  subject, 4
self-identification, 55, 86, 90–1
  of Europe, 3

self-identity, 5, 14, 24, 55, 85
Shetland, 64–5, 72–4, 77n
signature, 88, 90; *see also* countersignature
singular, 3–5, 21–3
  alterity, 15
  and individual, 13, 24–5
  and universal, 92n
  being, 20, 24, 26, 52
  entity, 12, 49
  existence, 5
  heterogeneity of, 26
  hope of, 121
  source, 113
  unity, 3
singularity, 3, 5, 13–15, 21–4, 26, 27n, 51, 87, 120, 124, 129
solidarity, 96, 99, 102–05
sovereignty, 7, 71–2, 77n, 96, 134–6, 139, 142, 144
Soviet Union, 9, 50, 62, 73
spirit, 12–13, 19–20, 22, 31, 37, 53, 63, 65, 68, 75–6, 103, 105, 122, 124, 127, 131
subject, 53, 74, 120, 141
  colonial, 126
  in difference with itself, 85–6
  legal, 82, 84
  Muslim, 152
  non-coincidence with itself, 87–8
  religious, 151–2
  self-identical, 4, 52
  universal, 157
subjectivity, 104
  ethical, 137
  European, 42, 157
  Muslim, 157
  political, 86

Taylor, Charles, 152
technocratic
  governance, 7, 134
  government, 50, 139
  politics, 139, 144–5
technocracy, 137, 139, 142, 144
territoriality, 67, 69, 71
theological, 26, 42, 139, 141, 158
  economy, 26
  politics, 7, 134, 136
  power, 17
  sovereignty, 142
tolerance, 95, 99, 103, 151
totalitarianism, 96, 101

Treaty of Lisbon, 25, 28n, 81, 88, 92n
Treaty of Rome, 156
Turkey, 7–8, 117, 134–6, 139–40, 142–3, 146, 147n, 149, 153–7, 160

United Kingdom, 63, 77n, 152; *see also* Britain *and* UK
United States, 18–9, 21, 26, 61–2, 78, 129; *see also* USA *and* US
unity, 10, 14, 23–4, 53, 80, 92, 98, 111–12, 130
  cultural, 18
  differential, 54
  European, 2–3
  spiritual, 53
universality, 19, 21, 33, 35, 40–1, 43, 125, 129, 137–8
UK, 18, 27n; *see also* United Kingdom *and* Britain
Unst, 62–3, 72–4
US, 81, 84, 88, 92, 140; *see also* United States *and* USA

USA, 104; *see also* United States *and* US

Valéry, Paul, 5, 10, 13–14, 16, 19–21, 23, 26, 37–8, 40, 46, 65, 68, 75–6, 111, 122, 137–8

West, 12, 34, 63, 68, 71, 73, 76, 123, 126, 155
Western, 10, 25, 62, 65, 67–9, 72, 101, 104, 123, 131, 139, 141–2, 145–6, 151–2, 157
Westernisation, 135
wholly other, 108, 114–15, 120

xenophobia, 51, 55, 96, 100, 117, 130, 142, 158

Yiddish, 126
  erasure of, 125–6

Zionism, 7, 121–31
Zionist, 121–7, 131